LESSONS LEARNED FOR MY SONS

Wisdom for Everyday Living and Inspiring Others

By David Watson

Terry,

Enjoy the book. I hope it makes its way to the Parcier bookshelf!. Take care.

David

feb 2024

i

First paperback edition December 2023

Editor: Catherine Nikkel
Book Cover & Interior Designer: Julia Baxter
Publishing Consultant: Makini Smith

ISBN: 979-8-9891828-0-0 *Hardcover*
ISBN: 979-8-9891828-1-7 *Paperback*
ISBN: 979-8-9891828-2-4 *E-book*

TABLE OF CONTENTS

INTRODUCTION

"the action of introducing something"

When I was growing up, almost every playground had a teeter-totter. Two people sat across from each on the teeter-totter, and one thrust themselves up while the other went down. There was the force field of gravity, and then the acceleration and weight of each kid made it fun. What thrilled me was when all aspects were in harmony, and my friend and I were in balance. Neither of us was touching the ground, yet we teetered in the air, balancing in a way that seemed like magic.

When I first met David Watson, we were both in the acceleration stage of our careers and personal lives.

On the teeter-totter, we were both pushing off the ground. I led a small team of sales professionals at PTC (more on PTC in the story called **Company**) and had just given birth to my first child. David had his first son and was interviewing at PTC after working at a few tech companies. Looking back, I don't know if I would characterize our lives and behaviors as "in harmony." David came across as having an overabundance of self-confidence and know-how. PTC was a tough place to find stable footing, and I wanted to build a team with staying power. It was important to me to have a group of individuals with different perspectives and personalities. I felt the diversity made us a better team because we would challenge each other differently. After interviewing David, I realized he had experience in the tech start-up world, where he learned the intensity of meeting financial objectives. He was smart and had strong financial analysis capabilities. All in all, he would bring a unique set of skills to the team, so he was in.

Dave and I worked together over the following five years in acceleration mode. We drove hard and were at the top of our game. But it took a toll. Gravity hit us hard a few times, and the teeter-totter suddenly dropped. Neither of us had our eye on balance, even though we told ourselves we did. There was so much stress from being on the go at my house my oldest daughter started pulling out her eyelashes and eyebrows to deal with her anxiety. Dave burned some relationships internal to PTC by exuding his self-confidence in a way that was disrespectful to his co-workers. Neither one of us knew how to find our equilibrium.

Fast forward six years, and in 2013, David and I started working together again. At Pariveda Solutions, we spent 7 ½ years building a consulting organization in Seattle. Dave and I have gone through life changes, maturing through life's lessons and intentionally developing into better human beings. I brought David to Pariveda because I wanted to work with someone who challenged me, provided me with candid feedback, and supported my growth. David was my ideal teeter-totter partner, the one I needed to provide that thrill of balance: both feet off the ground, suspended in the air, supporting each other in harmony. I trust over the years, I have provided Dave the same satisfaction of equilibrium he has provided to me.

With the lessons you learn from this book, I hope it helps you find your balance and harmony when you need it. It is a gift Dave has provided to me, which I cherish. Now, it is a gift to all of you.

Margaret Scovern
V.P., Pariveda Solutions

BACKDROP

"provide a background or setting for."

Lessons Learned for my Sons. The idea for an entire book about lessons learned germinated from the simple desire of a father to share his high and low points with his boys.

At the time, I was a Vice President (VP) with Pariveda Solutions. Pariveda is a technology and management consulting firm emphasizing mentoring, coaching, and learning/development. As a VP, one of my responsibilities was mentoring 3-4 Principals (one level below VP). I'll further delve into that experience with you through several stories I'll share in this book like **Company** and **Work**.

Another responsibility of a VP was to be active in our marketing efforts — which included blogging, posting on LinkedIn, writing articles for our website, etc. As I considered what I might write about that would be valuable to others, I realized that many of my VP colleagues had *much* more experience with complex technology solutions, long-lasting implementation programs, and delving into enterprise architecture discussions.

What would I write about that might interest others?

"Lessons Learned for my Sons". That was the title of the first full article I wrote on LinkedIn on August 22, 2017.

What came to me was that my "best" audience would be my two sons — Ryan and Cole — versus trying to explain technology to some unknown "audience" on LinkedIn. Too often, I'd share a story with my boys and get a response like this with their eyes rolled up, "Dad, we don't need to talk about the interview process for another 6–7 years… why are you telling us about this now?".

My first few articles were about what experiences I've had at work or home that would be valuable to share with my boys — even if they didn't "need" them right now. Since I was sharing them in the public domain, I quickly realized that many of these lessons applied to everyone. I was going to call the book *Lessons Learned for...Everyone* because you can insert sons, daughters, friends, work colleagues, direct reports, leadership, executives, moms, dads, etc. to replace the word *Everyone*. But I love the title as it appears on the cover!

Over time, I shifted away from 4–5 page articles that might take half a day or more to consider, write, edit, and share. The idea of shorter posts seemed easier — both for me to create and share and, more importantly, for the reader to enjoy and benefit from. The idea of shorter posts led me to the concept of stories in this book that are limited to just a few pages at most, making them easy to digest for you, the reader.

Someone I'd like to give credit to is Brené Brown. Not only have I devoured all of her books, but I also benefited greatly from her online programs. I'll share my lessons learned about vulnerability and more later in the book. The purpose for bringing up Brené Brown is that one of her books, *Atlas of the Heart*, gave me an initial idea about how to share my lessons learned with everyone.

Additionally, I subscribe to Merriam Webster's "Word of the Day". My idea of introducing each story in this book with a word and its definition is more of a prompt for me to share a story and the associated lessons learned with that word. Some stories will simply be a story with a lesson learned. Other stories include a framework to leverage, a process to follow, or bulleted comments - mini lessons if you will.

My goal was not only to make the stories easily digestible and accessible but also to enable the reader to flip to any story, read it within a few minutes, and absorb the simple lessons learned from that story. While I hope that all 110 stories (not including these stories that precede Chapter 1) have value for every reader, I realize that some stories will resonate nicely, and others might seem like, "Why did he share that?". However, the crucial part for me is that you garner some lessons learned that you can apply to your daily lives — or even share some lessons learned in the service of helping others.

Why 110 stories?

My goal was to publish this book while I was still 55. I thought sharing at least two stories for every trip I've made around Planet Earth would be the correct number — instead of a round number like 100 or any other frequently used Top Ten-like number.

Now, how to organize the stories in this book?

The easiest way for me to categorize the stories was based on my journey:

When did I learn these lessons? Before college? During college? My first job? My first leadership role? During my personal life? Using a chronological sequence made more sense to make it easier for me to *write* the book.
But I wanted to focus on YOU, the reader of the book.

I'm currently the "Relationship Activator & Optimist" at ThinqShift. Our mission at ThinqShift is "Crafting Fabulous Leaders to succeed and reinvent the world." As we engage with our clients, much of our time is spent helping individuals, teams, and entire organizations shift their mindsets, behaviors, and cultures against the backdrop of their business and personal challenges.

How can I take that same approach with a book?

Here's what makes sense as the easiest possible way for the reader to absorb any single story, an entire chapter of stories, or, if you are enjoying yourself, the whole book.

CHAPTER GUIDE

	LOW	MEDIUM	HIGH
FIND A PRO	CHAPTER 7 Been There, Done or Seen That	CHAPTER 8 Match.com Be Selective About Your "Pro"	CHAPTER 9 Get As Much Help As You Can
WITH A FRIEND	CHAPTER 4 Bounce Casual Ideas Off of Each Other	CHAPTER 5 Dial A Friend if You're In Need or In Trouble	CHAPTER 6 Lifelong Friend Who's In Trouble With You!
ON YOUR OWN	CHAPTER 1 Practice When You Can	CHAPTER 2 Work Intentionally to Get Better	CHAPTER 3 Work So Hard That You Can Teach Others

How to Build a Habit

Level of Difficulty

Each chapter has 10–15 stories, sorted by themed chapters as shown in the table.

This framework is based upon my experiences during thousands of hours of coaching and mentoring across hundreds of individuals, teams, and organizations.

The "Y" axis (vertical) is based upon my assessment of the most effective way to build a new habit with the lessons learned.

On Your Own
You can figure this one out individually.

With a Friend
Getting some help — from a friend, work colleague, family member, etc. — would be the most effective method.

Find a Pro
Consider working or collaborating with someone more formally — a coach, therapist, or mentor. My goal wasn't to create a "self-help" book but rather a book where you can help yourself, help others or collaborate with others to help each other — depending upon how the story impacts you.

The "X" axis (left to right) is based on how difficult I feel it might be for an individual to build a new habit. Low, Medium, or High difficulty. The backdrop here is also essential; it's the underlying method of creating a habit.

Unconsciously Incompetent
This is the earliest stage of habit formation. At this point, you are entirely *unaware* (unconscious) of your habit, so you can't even work to improve it (incompetent).

Consciously Incompetent
Think about awareness. You still need to improve with this habit (Incompetent), but at least you are *aware* (consciously) it is something you are working on.

Consciously Competent

At this point, you are not only aware of (consciously) what you are working on but also getting pretty good with this habit (competent) with *practice*.

Unconsciously Competent

Now, you are so good that it becomes a *habit* (competent) that you no longer need to think about it (unconsciously), and it happens naturally.

The rewiring of the neurons in your brain takes a while to build a new habit. Everyone will go through these four stages at different speeds and with varying amounts of effort needed. My assessment of Low, Medium, and High difficulty is based upon my experiences, both personally and as a coach/mentor, of rewiring the brain for a new habit or behavior.

Full disclosure, my "alignment" of the stories across the nine chapters in this book is my perspective. You, the reader, might discover something I've labeled "Worked so hard you can teach others how" might be "Been there, Done or Seen that" because you built that habit with your coach. I understand. Again, my bigger picture goal was to make it *easy* for you to read one story in any sequence at any time — like the classic "choose your own adventure" books I read growing up. This is more of a reference book across 110 individual lessons learned than some novel or "must read it all" business book.

The last concept I want to share is about money. I plan to donate 100% of any profits from this book to charity — which, as appropriate, you can read about in a few pages in the little story called **Charity**.

LESSON LEARNED

In summary, as I write each story and finalize this book, I still focus on sharing as many of my work/life lessons learned as if I'm sharing them directly with Ryan and/or Cole. My transformation during the process was the realization that many others might benefit from these lessons. And this is a great way to share lessons learned with others in a digestible way. Think about your own backdrop for how you might leverage these lessons learned to help yourself build new habits, support and serve others, and simply enjoy a few hours with some stories that might resonate with you in some way or even by activating your own memories of stories from your life and those lessons learned.

CHAPTER

"a main division of a book, typically with a number or title."

How would you write or share the chapters of your own life? Here's my methodology.

Chapter 1: Practice When You Can

Lessons Learned in this chapter should be pretty straightforward. These are some lessons you can work on without help from other folks. And the progressions through the habit-building process should be reasonably quick.

Chapter 2: Work Intentionally To Get Better

These lessons require some additional and focused effort. You may need to break the work down a bit into smaller components. It would be best if you created some intentionality with them as well. You should be aware as you shift from incompetence to competence.

Chapter 3: Worked So Hard You Can Teach Others How

Again, these are lessons that you can build on your own. Certainly, there are excellent sources of inspiration and education — books, online videos, podcasts, etc. — but a lot of hard work is involved with moving through these lessons on your own.

Chapter 4: Bounce Casual Ideas off Each Other

This chapter is about having a "reporting" buddy.

You'll still be doing a lot of work individually, but it is nice to share what is working or what isn't with someone else in a friendly way.

Chapter 5: Dial-a-Friend if You Are in Need or Trouble

This next lesson is a much more formal version of working on a habit — when you have a genuine accountability buddy. Instead of a casual update, as in the previous chapter, this is about having someone you'd call and check in with formally. They will hold you accountable to your goals and encourage you to improve if you need to be on track. In most situations, you've given them the power to criticize you if you aren't reaching your goals. In fact, that's what you want when you call them.

Chapter 6: Lifelong Friend Who Is in Trouble With You!

My thinking about this title goes like this. Say you had a rough night and, for whatever reason, got thrown in jail. A good friend or colleague from Chapter 5 is the person you would call to come bail you out. A great, lifelong friend sits beside you in jail and says, "That was fun!". Now, this is the friend you need for this chapter!

Okay, I'm not suggesting you need to go to jail with a friend. But the idea is that these lessons learned are challenging to do alone. And best accomplished with a friend who is working on the same lesson learned or is deeply invested in you as a person and sincerely wants to help you grow/ develop further in your mutual lifetimes.

Chapter 7: Been There, Done or Seen That

Think about the lessons learned from this chapter in terms of experiential learning. Having someone professional, whether a coach or a formal mentor, is helpful to help you through the habit-building process. Often, this is something the other person has either experienced themselves or coached someone else through — and they can share those patterns of success as well as the lessons learned from their failures or observing the failures of others.

Chapter 8: Match.Com: Be Selective About Your Pro

These lessons learned require someone more experienced to help you. Not just any coach, mentor, or professional can assist you. Be choosy. The ultimate goal is to connect with someone who can support you based on a very specific situation aligned with the right knowledge to share at the right time.

Chapter 9: Get as Much Help as You Can

These are the lessons that take years to learn and master. You might work with multiple pros across your growth and habit development process. You'll need to connect with the pro on every level — head, heart, gut, and soul. There might even be a progression, one pro helps you through the first stage, and you shift to a second pro to take it to the next level.

LESSON LEARNED

My goal is to help you understand which stories might interest you in a specific chapter versus needing to read them in sequence.

My first perspective of arranging the chapters was based on my chronological experiences. Then I realized that everyone would leverage these lessons in their own way. Therefore, the lessons I've aligned by chapter may differ from how you need to learn them. For example, you may need to call a friend where I tried doing something on my own. Or you could accomplish something by yourself where I needed to hire a pro.

As it turns out, the chapters are set up as a "choose your own adventure" perspective — and the stories can be read in any order as 110 different short, stand-alone stories. In any case, the organization of the chapters and stories within gives you a more profound and effective way of consuming some or all of this book. Pick a chapter to read. Or delve into a specific story. You could even open the book to a random page and start reading a new story. Find a path forward to build the lessons learned most beneficial to you or others with whom you might be sharing these lessons with the objective of serving others.

AUTOBIOGRAPHY

"an account of a person's life written by that person"

How would YOU write your autobiography? This is a long process... nothing feels "auto" about it!

I'm still determining how many total stories are needed to write a comprehensive autobiography. However, this book will have 110 stories that comprise a significant portion of the "account of my life," and I hope that future books will add more stories to provide a fuller picture of my life.

This story is a mini-autobiography summarized by the seven original chapters I created to organize the many stories in my head. That truly felt like an autobiography as the seven chapters were entirely chronological — which is very different from the final results of 110 stories across nine chapters as I shared above in the **Backdrop** section.

What follows below are my original several chapters in "autobiographical form."

Before I Went to College

I was born in Cincinnati, OH — where my parents grew up. We lived in Cincinnati until I was in kindergarten and then moved to Michigan. We were in Michigan until I was in fourth grade, and we moved to Illinois. More specifically, Sleepy Hollow, IL.

My grandma moved from Ohio to Michigan to Illinois with us and always lived 10–15 minutes away. At the time, I didn't think about the fact she was my only relative outside of my parents and brother. We had a lot of great times with my grandma.

What do I remember along my journey from elementary school to middle school to high school?

Sports were my passion. Academics was something I was good at. Friendships were easy to develop. And to remember to have fun along the way.

My strong academics allowed me to be accepted at both University of Illinois (U of I) and Northwestern (see the story called **Choice**); I decided to venture down to Central Illinois for four years at U of I.

During my Years in College

My four years at U of I were a blast. Outside of my mom and dad's amazing financial (academic only) support, I predominantly learned how to be independent, earn my own spending money and live on my own — or with great roommates! And road trips were a blast — whether for Illinois football or basketball games away from home, Spring Break trips with college friends, or awesome summer adventures.

Taking classes, learning complex topics, and studying for quizzes and exams were significantly different at U of I than in high school. And I'll share some of those lessons learned later in the book.

Most of my close friendships developed through my fraternity — though I also met many other friends through high school connections, engineering classes, sorority dances, and more.

And even though I had worked at Italian U-Boat and mowed yards for cash, my college years were my first exposure to "real work" across several summer internships.

After graduation, I took a few weeks off and headed back home. Only to leave a few weeks later for Central Illinois — again.

In my First "Real" Job

Peoria, IL. That is where my first job took me to work at IBM (see the story called **Strength**). As my career progressed, I shifted between roles where I was an individual contributor, a manager (team leader), and an executive (leader of leaders). For my categorization purposes during the early phases of my book, any job where I was an individual contributor would have fallen in this category.

When I Was Part of a Team

Being part of a team includes roles in my career where I worked on teams who collaborated closely, and even acted as a team leader in some instances. You can follow my career quest via LinkedIn, so I won't bore you here with the details!

When I Was Asked To Lead a Team

This is where the word "Management" gets involved. For these roles, several people directly reported to me. In addition to helping them achieve their goals from a business perspective, I was also responsible for their internal career development and externally facing engagements. And in several instances, these roles led to high-level roles where I was managing teams of teams.

When I Was the Boss

This is most of my tenure as a VP with Pariveda and my current role with ThinqShift.

When I Was Away From Work

This might have been called "Personal Life," but I liked the heading as is. Even though they applied to my work, many stories happened in my personal life after work, on weekends, and over the summer.

That's my autobiography chronologically as I first envisioned writing this book. But I realized that organization was best for ME and not for YOU, the reader. As I shared in the definition of **Chapter** above, I reconfigured the book to consider YOUR perspective instead of my own.

LESSON LEARNED

Though I have a few friends who have wanted to be a pilot, teacher, or nurse since age ten (and still are!), the twists and turns in my life brought me to this point. I'm grateful for the lessons I learned from others and hope to share as many or more with you.

COMPANY

"a commercial business"

What career stops would you include with your resume or LinkedIn summary?

Many of my stories reference one of my employers or customers I worked closely with over the years. The purpose of this quick story is to give you some brief background about the companies I've worked with since many played an essential platform for my own lessons learned. The story called Autobiography was more about flow…this story is more about my specific stops along the way.

In reverse order of my career journey

ThinqShift: This is where I'm fortunate to be today and hopefully remain for the balance of my career journey. We are all about providing Leadership

Services to our clients, crafting fabulous leaders as they succeed in their business roles, and, more importantly, seeking to make a difference in the world. My time here is about facilitating, teaching, advising, coaching, counseling, leading, consulting, guiding, and more.

Today is your Day! Leadership Services: I started this Limited Liability Company (LLC) because almost everyone at ThinqShift is a 1099, or contract, employee. Today! is the legal entity I needed to form to focus 100% of my effort on ThinqShift.

Emerald Technology Group (GetGreen): Not an employer at all, but I'm an investor and advisor in this little startup focused on helping individuals understand how to build sustainability habits.

And I'm still actively involved in these three, and a few other, adventures currently - which I'll discuss further in the next story called **Work**.

Moving to ThinqShift and Today! was the second *huge* career shift in my life.

Pariveda: Technology and Management Consulting organization. I was a Vice President with many accountabilities — delivery, execution, leadership, mentorship, sales, business development, coaching, enterprise architecting, etc. It was a great experience for over eight years.

CRAFT: Part of my journey inside Pariveda included running a small software company *inside* of Pariveda. CRAFT was a fun little ride as well.

Joining Pariveda was my first *huge* career shift. Before Pariveda, I was involved in mostly software and technology companies.

Oracle: One of the largest software companies in the world. I spent several years at Oracle selling to notable companies like Amazon.com and Nintendo, to name a few.

Vistagy: A small software company — ironically focused on composite design software for the aerospace and automotive industries. Who would have thought my Ceramic Engineering degree would benefit me in the future? I didn't.

PTC: Another $1B+ software company. My biggest customer was Boeing.

eCash Technologies: A startup software company. I was the first employee and played about a dozen roles until I eventually moved into sales/business development.

InterTrans Logistics/i2 Technologies: InterTrans Logistics was a small software company selling to the logistics industry. i2 Technologies was a larger supply chain company that acquired us.

COMSI: An IBM Distribution firm. This meant I was a full-time IBM employee who worked 100% on a commission since COMSI employed me.

IBM: The largest computer company in the world at the time. It was my first job out of college.

Before these highlighted companies, I worked with small companies part-time in high school and college — some were internships, and others were simply summer jobs to earn spending money for the school year.

LESSON LEARNED

A company is a great proving and learning ground for who you want to become. Remember that a company is more than just a business — it is a collection of people, technology, processes, clients, partners, and more. YOU make the company... don't let the company make you.

WORK

"activity involving mental or physical effort done in order to achieve a purpose or result."

I like the word Work here instead of Job.

My role at ThinqShift is the only "Work" I'm doing right now where I'm getting paid (in the definition of a Job). Everything else I'm doing is focused on a different result than financial.

ThinqShift

Our mission at ThinqShift is to "Craft Fabulous Leaders to Succeed and Reinvent the World." We deliver this to our clients through Leadership Services — broken down in the following manner:

ReWire®: One-on-one coaching and advisory service. This is "executive coaching" to some people, but we often leverage some of our ShiftUp! Academy content.

ShiftUp! Academy: Our one-to-many training and development service. This is where our Intellectual Property (IP) resides. Some people might call this "leadership training."

Orchestrate: Our consulting and advisory services. It is more facilitation and usually includes lighter training, development, and coaching.

Our clients engage us most frequently when there are significant transformations in someone's career quest, changes to the organization's evolution, or variations in the overall market maturity. Therefore, we focus on the shifts needed in individuals' behaviors, mindsets, and thinking preferences to adapt to these rapidly changing situations.

Our goal is to serve others, and you can find me at david.watson@thinqshift.com, on our website at thinqshift.com/david, or on LinkedIn at linkedin.com/in/david-watson-4875/.

Emerald Technology Group (GetGreen)

GetGreen is a mobile application that "lets your organization lower emissions, remove existing carbon, and engage your employees on the journey. Sustainability programs succeed when your team supports them." Download the free app at getgreen.eco.

I'm both an investor and Executive Advisor for GetGreen. Teaching everyone sustainability habits aligns directly with my personal goal of supporting myself and others to avoid putting 3.2 million tons of carbon into the atmosphere before my last turn on Planet Earth. Please read more about this in the **Environment** story.

You can find me at watty@getgreen.eco or on the website at getgreen.eco/about.

ATDps — Association for Talent Development Puget Sound

ATD is "a local association committed to talent development professionals in the Puget Sound area. We are here for our members and the broader talent development community in the Puget Sound."

My role with ATDPS is that of Director of Programs. Like other board members and volunteers, I'm giving my time and passion to ATD in support of serving others in the learning and development space.

You can find me at programs@atdpugetsound.org. Or on the website atdpugetsound.org/BOD.

University of Washington Honors Program Advisory Board

I'm grateful to my friend Tina for getting me involved with the Honors Advisory Board. Another volunteer position. Serving the needs of others who strive to serve the needs of others themselves? Sign me up!

Here's the mission for UW Honors Program: "The University Honors Program engages a diverse population of students through a rigorous interdisciplinary curriculum that promotes expansive, innovative thinking and conscious global citizenship. We ask students to take intellectual risks; seek an understanding of the interdependence of all branches of knowledge; engage with the complexities of difference and diversity; take leadership roles in navigating global change; and value a life of continuous learning and personal growth."

LESSON LEARNED

There are many aspects of Work. It can be more of a job but also a volunteer position where you have an opportunity to give back in the form of time, money, passion, experience, and more. And while you are definitely focused on accomplishing some "purpose or result," if you are doing it for the right reasons, it won't feel like work. Do everything you can to shift a Job (for money) to Work (for passion and love). And enjoy the **People** you meet through Work for sure!

PEOPLE

"human beings in general or considered collectively."

Note: Maybe I should have called this chapter "Mammals" because I'll add a couple of dogs to this list. I treat them like real people, I'm just sayin'.

This chapter briefly describes some of the key people in my life who were part of my journey and helped me with these lessons. In most cases, the individuals listed below were involved in more than one of my stories and lessons learned, so I wanted to give some background here first. Then, for the many other people who have played a role in my life, I'll share my connection with them in the specific lessons learned.

Ryan

My oldest son. He went to the University of Colorado and graduated with a degree in Environmental Design. His focus going forward will be more on creativity, product design and building. He's very hands-on and is a fantastic artist as well. As a firstborn son myself, it was incredible to learn so many new lessons from Ryan directly that were so different from my lessons learned growing up. I get goosebumps when I recall the first time I held him in my arms in the delivery room.

Cole

He is currently at the University of Washington studying Marine Biology. I connected with Cole in so many different ways that I initially connected with Ryan. As a second son, Cole taught me an entirely different set of lessons — far beyond those I experienced as a firstborn observing my younger brother growing up. I always smile and get goosebumps yet again when I think about the first time I held Cole.

Michael, Jack, and Katie

Speaking of my younger brother, Michael and I were the only two sons (and kids) in my family growing up. His two children are the same ages as Ryan and Cole. In fact, Jack is just five days older than Ryan and graduated from my alma mater — the University of Illinois. My niece Katie is at the University of Michigan and is just two months older than her cousin Cole. Michael still lives in the Chicago area and does a great job connecting in person with our mom. Being in Seattle, I haven't spent as much time as I might have liked with Michael, Jack, and Katie, but our times together are filled with joy, laughter, and fun.

Mom

What can I say about my mom? She was a Math Teacher and instilled a "study hard" behavior in me early. When my dad passed away, I connected with my mom on a much deeper level than I ever had. She lives in the Chicago suburbs and does as well as she can without my dad. Some days I still feel like a little kid when I'm speaking with my mom and other days, I need to take care of her. We have an amazing relationship today.

Dad

I'll speak about my dad often in this book because I don't have the chance to share these lessons learned with him now. He passed away just before the pandemic in early 2020. I'll speak to it across various chapters in the book, but I wish I could have shared many of these lessons learned and told him how grateful I was for him being part of them. Tears come quickly for me when I think about my dad; at least now, they are almost always tears of joy.

Grandma

Only a few lessons learned relate to my grandma. She was important to me as I didn't know my other three grandparents. And since my parents were only children, I didn't have aunts, uncles, or cousins. So my grandma was the only family I had outside of Mom, Dad, and Michael. Unfortunately, she passed away in 1993, and I'm grateful for the lessons learned she shared with me.

Natalie

We were friends through middle and high school and then went to the University of Illinois. Only some people are fans of the Greek system, but Natalie and I both joined the Greek system during our first year at U of I and shared many great experiences. As it turned out, her sorority and my fraternity often interacted — parties, dances, football games, tailgating before games, etc. In addition, we ended up playing tennis against each other often. As a result, we became much closer in college than in high school. Natalie was my first experience with losing someone. She passed away in 1990, and I remember being one of her pallbearers. I'm not sure I've ever felt such a weight on my heart.

Nick

Another connection through U of I, Nick and I were fraternity brothers. We were roommates and part of a small group of 6–8 fraternity brothers who all hung out together — in the frat house, at parties, at bars, playing sports, screwing around on campus in general, etc. In fact, my first few years of work post-college were in Peoria, IL — Nick's hometown. We spent even more time together for a few years after college. So when Nick passed away in 2014, it hit me like a ton of bricks. While we didn't hang out often after I left Peoria (I lived in Seattle, and he lived in Chicago), we connected on a different level post-college as we both nearly died (through other circumstances). "Beating death" was our connection and I was deeply saddened when his cancer returned and he couldn't beat it yet again. Unlike a heavy weight on my heart, Nick's passing felt more like someone taking my heart out of my chest.

Vips

Founder and CEO of ThinqShift. We connected through a previous employer and worked together during his earliest days of ThinqShift. He is a friend, mentor, trusted advisor and more, and I'm grateful that when I called him to seek advice on my next career step, he offered me an opportunity to join him at ThinqShift. As a result, many lessons learned that I plan to share will include Vips and ThinqShift. I'm honored and grateful that Vips asked me to be a part of his journey to serve Fabulous Leaders through the balance of his time on earth.

April

My storytelling coach. I thought I was a pretty good storyteller before working with April. She's been instrumental in my journey to shift from LinkedIn posts and articles to writing a book. And while she gets full credit for being a storytelling coach, she's really my book-writing coach and a huge inspiration. Thanks!

Don

My professional coach. We met years ago during a leadership training event I attended. I asked for ongoing coaching, and I'm fortunate that I was aligned with Don. He's been a great coach, guide, advisor, consultant, and more to me. And I still work with him — albeit less often than I used to.

Claudette

My therapist. She's been with me through many challenges and helped me along the way. I'm flattered when she reminds me how much I've changed over the years, and I have to compliment her back because she was so important along the way.

Melanie

My ex-wife. We had an incredible journey together over three decades. While we are now divorced, I'm grateful for everything she did — for me, our sons, and everything. A divorce is a sad situation, and I have grieved about it for years. I'll always love Melanie and hope she finds much happiness in the following chapters of her life. As you'll see in the book, she's involved in many of my lessons learned — both directly and indirectly.

Many Other People

There are many other people involved in my lessons learned. But if they are only part of one or two stories, I'll quickly provide their background in the first story. And there will be many others I won't explicitly name, but they were also part of my stories.

Suki

My cute little female chocolate lab. She's over two years old and has been my great companion. In some ways, getting Suki started out as a "pandemic response" to being alone. But pandemic or not — I was going to get another dog eventually. The opportunity to adopt the niece of another friend's dog was an excellent opportunity and when Suki cuddled up to me when I visited, the deal was done. She was coming home with me. I knew it in my head and heart and gut — she gave me warm feelings all over and not just in my arms. As you'll read, dogs are a big part of my life. My other labs over the years were Mwenzi & Maisha (both passed away — our dogs "pre-kids") and Amani & Upendo (both living with Melanie now).

LESSON LEARNED

Throughout your lifetime, please attempt to make this list as LONG as you can. Subjectively, I'm biased about relationships because it is my number one value. (Yup - please read **Values**). People are social creatures that build and maintain and grow as many (or as few if they are *super* deep) relationships as possible during their lifetime. More isn't always better for many situations — but more is definitely better in this case!

ACKNOWLEDGMENT

"an author's or publisher's statement of indebtedness to others, typically one printed at the beginning of a book."

The definition states everything except for the specific "others" I wish to say "Thank You" to.

To April Adams Pertuis, who has been through the entire journey with me the whole way. She was there when we started to work together to improve my storytelling. After a few sessions, she asked me what my goal was. Surprisingly, I said, "To write a book." And we were off to the races.

To Catherine Nikkel, who made this book 10x better through her editing expertise.

To many friends in Seattle — Patty, Tina, Steve, Mark, and others — who "gently" asked about the progress I was making and were super supportive when the answer to their kind inquiries was "No progress." And to the many other friends outside of Seattle who offered similar encouragement.

To my mom, who read a few of the stories and is involved in many others. She continually told me how proud she was of me for writing the book.

To Ryan and Cole, who inspired the original theme of "Lessons Learned" and are a central part of many of my stories and subsequent lessons learned.

To Rich Litvin, who starts the "Who" portion of his website with "I help extraordinary people achieve impossible goals." I hope I can become one of the "extraordinary people" Rich is working with, and I hope this goal becomes an "impossible goal" that I achieve. Also, for the record, one of the questions Rich likes to ask is, "What is the book you want to write?".

To Suki, who sat tirelessly beneath my desk for many of the stories written here. When I was stuck in my thoughts, she was more than happy to take me for a walk to clear my head!

To Tracy, a close friend from high school, who frequently encouraged me along the way — especially when I'd get stuck on something or not be as motivated as I should have been.

To Vips, the founder of ThinqShift and who is also writing a book. We shared a few of our own lessons learned as we are both going through this process. Many of my stories incorporate some of the excellent offerings across ThinqShift's Leadership Services.

To many amazing authors like Brené Brown, Simon Sinek, Adam Grant, Daniel Pink, Dr. Seuss, and others who wrote incredible books of their own. I've synthesized bits and pieces of your wisdom into many of my stories throughout this book.

Lastly, double thanks to Tina for being the first to read and greatly improve this book.

LESSON LEARNED

Always say "Thanks" to those who help you along the way.

CHARITY

"an organization set up to provide help and raise money for those in need."

The often shared phrase that fits here is, "It's better to give than to receive."

My first goal for this book was to write it for Ryan and Cole. The idea started with me as a father sharing "Lessons Learned for My Sons." It evolved to sharing lessons learned for everyone to serve the needs of others.

In that spirit, I'd like to share any profits from this book to serve the needs of others too. Or, more specifically, to serve the needs of two charities that align closely with the interests/passions of Ryan and Cole.

Cole was interested in Marine Biology forever. He's getting his degree in Marine Biology and wants to make his impact in the oceans. As such, I'm donating half of the profits from this book to the Ocean Conservancy. I've donated to the Ocean Conservancy for decades, and I hope you'll consider doing the same.

The Mission Statement of the Ocean Conservancy:

"Ocean Conservancy is working with you to protect the ocean from today's greatest global challenges. Together, we create evidence-based solutions for a healthy ocean and the wildlife and communities that depend on it.".

Ryan is great with his mind and hands and graduated with a degree in Environmental Design. Architecture might be in his future, but he focuses on product design (and art). Before he went to school, he traveled to Guatemala with a program called Global Visionaries. Afterwards, he spoke about how impactful it was for him to observe how other cultures lived and how he could help them (and others). As such, I'm donating half of the profits from this book to Global Visionaries.

The Mission Statement of Global Visionaries:

"Through experiential activities, workshops, community service in Seattle (optional), and a cultural immersion to Guatemala, GV prepares Seattle-area high school students to define and address environmental and social justice issues in their communities while developing as leaders and becoming more aware of their global citizenship."

You can donate your time, money, or passion to many charities — locally, nationally, and globally.

LESSON LEARNED

Giving time, money, or passion to others in need is a tremendously generous gift. And while the focus is on others, I promise that what you get in return is even more transformative for you. Please consider whatever contribution you can make to some charity that means a lot to you.

FUTURE

"the time or a period of time following the moment of speaking or writing; time regarded as still to come."

I prefer to live in the present versus dwelling in the past, but the future is enthralling too!

When I first started writing this book, thinking about a second book didn't seem like a possible future endeavor in any way. However, after going through this process, I'm excited about writing another book and several other possibilities that may or may not come to fruition.

Here's what I'm thinking about in terms of "Lessons Learned" in the future!

Lessons Learned...for Everyone — #2

My intention for book number one was to select 110 stories — two for each of my years on this planet. I already have another 100+ stories written via posts on LinkedIn or other ideas floating around in my head.

For book number one, I'd usually start with a specific word and think about what it means to me and when I first "learned" about it, then I'd write the story.

For book number two, I will start with the stories and lessons learned and discover a word that represents the story and lesson.

Lessons Learned.... From Many Others

I want to inspire many others — friends, family, work colleagues, people who enjoyed the first two Lessons Learned books, etc. to share their OWN lessons learned with me. I aim to use the same formula — bundled with a theme — short stories that anyone can read individually and leverage the lesson learned.

Lessons Learned... About Personal Growth

Though I weave many personal growth stories into Lessons Learned #1, there are many other personal growth stories worth sharing with everyone. In my day-to-day coaching, I'm fully aware of NOT crossing the line between coaching/mentoring and what should be covered with professional therapists. But based upon several dozen stories rattling around in my head, there is probably a gray area where sharing more deeply personal growth stories in the context of lessons learned would be tremendously valuable to others. Examples might include more sensitive topics like religion, politics, sex, or alcohol — and my experiences and lessons learned across those more personal topics.

The future is mostly about Lessons Learned #1, but considering the above possibilities motivates me to complete Lessons Learned #2 as quickly as possible.

LESSON LEARNED

When thinking about the future, remember to learn from the past and relish the present - simultaneously.

CHAPTER 1

Practice when you can

Building a daily habit of taking my dog Suki for a walk is an excellent example. Of course, we take several walks daily, but I also don't beat myself up if we miss one if the weather is terrible or Suki seems tired and content in her bed. I literally practice with her multiple times each day.

FOREBODING

"fearful apprehension; a feeling that something bad will happen."

Scary movie or haunted house, anyone?

Walking (or running) through a haunted house — knowing someone is about to jump out from around a corner and scare the crap out of you. That's what I think about when I think of foreboding.

Many of my stories about growing up revolve around my activities in sports. Baseball was definitely my favorite sport growing up — probably because I was very good. I was almost always on the All-Star team — even though I was typically a year or two younger than most other kids in my league.

One weekend, my dad took me, my brother, and our neighbor to a Chicago White Sox baseball game. We all wore our uniforms because there was an opportunity to get down on the field and hit a few pitches from a Major League baseball player. I'm still unsure how I was selected, but I assume it was because my dad was offered one spot and chose me since I was the oldest.

In any case, I got ushered to the field and stood in line with other kids waiting for our opportunity to hit baseballs in front of thousands of fans. Foreboding? Yes.

I might never make contact with a pitch. I might fall down running the bases. I might let the bat slip out of my sweaty, nervous hands. I might totally embarrass myself. Plus, that dude on the mound was a *Major League Baseball player.* And twice as tall as me as well!

Here are some thoughts I share with others as I observe them experiencing foreboding.

Be Grateful for What Led Up to This Point
- Consider the hard work or other investments of time, energy, etc., that created your past joyful experiences
- Stop for a moment to congratulate yourself and others for the efforts that evolved into this current opportunity — foreboding or not
- Take your time thinking about the future
- Reflect upon what worked and what didn't… and celebrate yourself

Foreboding what might happen, that young baseball player should have recalled the many All-Star games he played and the many other games he played where he had many hits.

Enjoy the Moment

Just be present with this emotion. Feel whatever you are currently feeling. Take a moment to truly register that feeling everywhere — head, heart, stomach and those tingling sensations in your fingers and toes. And if the good news or great moment is shared with someone else, recognize that you can also enjoy this time with others.

For example, somehow, I discovered some excitement in being on a major league baseball field and having an opportunity to hit against a *real* pitcher.

Please Don't Assume a Negative Future Event

Most of us know the meaning of the word assume — especially when you break it down into three parts. Just *don't* do it. Why consider only the negative potential of the future? Keep a positive mental attitude from now on and if you find yourself leaning into the "what if something bad could happen" phase, work to shift your focus to how you might be able to prevent that pending negative event from even occurring versus assuming it is inevitable. Certainly, up at the plate, I was thinking about striking out. But I also remembered how many home runs or solid base hits I've had before stepping into that batter's box.

Sadly, the media leads us to believe there is a lot of negativity around the world. And bad news travels 4–5 times faster than positive news. But I promise you that if you look for good news, you'll find *tons* of it out there. Take a minute to truly absorb and experience the joyous feelings associated with positive news and remarkable events. Then when you have your own experiences, you'll remember to be grateful for the past, to be vulnerable enough to fully enjoy the current moment, and to look forward with positivity versus encountering any sense of foreboding.

One of Charlie Brown's quotes is, "*I think I'm afraid to be happy because whenever I get too happy, something bad always happens.*"

So I was happy to be able to hit some baseballs that day. And I did make solid contact a few times. So it was a great experience.

TEAM

"a group of players forming one side in a competitive game or sport."

That's the definition of the noun… here's the definition of Team as a verb: *"come together to achieve a common goal."*

I played on many different sports teams and I engaged with some amazing folks across teams at work and nonprofits. But it took me to become a coach for the first time to understand what a team was all about.

When it was time to engage my son in sports, we had to "build" our own team. I agreed to coach with another dad in my neighborhood jointly. We were both athletes, played on team sports forever growing up, and still had teams we were involved in. No problem being a coach and leading the team. What could go wrong?

Initially, I volunteered to be a coach for self-centered reasons. I would have to get my son to and from practice every day and attend every game. What a great excuse to never miss one of my son's practices or games! Though I certainly missed a few here and there, being the coach afforded me the opportunity to spend as much time as possible with Cole or Ryan.

That last assumption was wrong.

While I spent time with one of my sons in the car to and from practice, I quickly realized that not everyone on the team had the same skills as my boys. I'm bragging about my kids right now. We spent a lot of time together at home before being on this team. They were more skilled than most of the players because we practiced a lot and repeated many of the same drills I used to support the team.

That meant I needed to spend time with the other kids helping them to improve — or help them learn how to play from scratch.

Lesson #1 of a Team
Understanding the Team's Individual Skills Before Knowing How To Proceed.

Once we closed the skills gap, we had to figure out how to get everyone working together. Most boys wanted to play in the dirt or throw the ball at each other. Getting kids to play catch with each other or run the bases with awareness of each other was another challenge.

Lesson #2
All About the Harmonization of the Team.

And like everything in life, there are rules. I don't have a baseball rule book with me right now, but I know there are hundreds, if not thousands, of rules to follow. We needed to teach the kids which rules were most essential and why.

Lesson #3
Establish the Guidelines by Which the Team
Needs To Operate.

We also had goals. As a recreational sport, the main idea was to have fun. But each boy's competitive spirit kicked in, so winning also became a goal. Most importantly, though, the goal was to establish a *common* goal that everyone would work towards.

Lesson #4
Clarify to Everyone Why They Are Working Together as a Team and How It Benefits Everyone.

Though I know that leadership manifests itself at almost any age, I was still surprised to see some initial leadership traits evolve with some team players. My son and a few others were also interested in helping their friends get better. So there were mini hierarchies formed — and it was a good thing. The coaches were the de facto "leaders" at the team's top, but the individuals who wanted to help others became leaders themselves.

Lesson #5

The Formal Hierarchy of a Coach-Player Is Obvious, but the Most Important Hierarchies Are Self-Directed Within a Team Framework.

It was great to see individual and team improvements throughout the season. We celebrated the little victories (catching a fly ball for the first time) and worked on areas where we could improve (striking out or dropping the ball). Many times, a smaller group of players celebrated success or identified something everyone could do better.

Lesson #6

Celebrate Your Victories, Enjoy Growth Opportunities for Individuals and the Team, and Cherish the Memories of Working Together.

Many of my stories talk about happiness and joy and just having fun. That's a general lesson I'll apply across the board.

Lesson #7 of any Team — Have Fun!

Without any question!

LESSON LEARNED

Humans are social creatures — whether you are introverted or extroverted. Being on a team of any kind is an excellent learning experience across many perspectives. The seven lessons learned shared in this story can be applied to any team.

So join one if you haven't been on a team before, and have a blast! The relationships you build and form can last a lifetime.

SMILE

"form one's features into a pleased, kind, or amused expression, typically with the corners of the mouth turned up and the front teeth exposed."

Seriously… think about smiling. It's tough NOT to smile. Come on, you know you want to smile right now!

The smile in the painting of the *Mona Lisa* is known as the most famous smile in the world. While the various forms of smiley emojis are making every attempt to pass her up, this smile is the standard bearer.

I saw the *Mona Lisa* in person while in college when I spent a week in France one summer. That was an incredible experience — to see this fantastic work by Leonardo da Vinci. However, learning more about da Vinci and everything he put into that famous painting made me appreciate the painting and her smile that much more.

But a smile is also much simpler than all the amazing effort da Vinci put into his work.

No Money
Smiles don't cost anything…they are totally free.

Add the Eyes
Some of your best smiles include someone's eyes. If you look at someone's eyes closely enough, you can tell their EYES are actually smiling at you too.

Infectious
You know how one person yawning causes others to yawn? Smiles are the same way. Smile around anyone, even a stranger, and you'll usually get a smile back.

Painless
I have no idea how many muscles it takes to smile, but I never feel as if smiling is a difficult (physical) thing to do. And whether this is a fact or my own belief, it takes more muscles and effort to create a frown than a smile!

Self-Inflicted

Think about smiling right now and you'll likely smile. It's a gift you can give to yourself just as easily as you give to others.

No Words Are Needed

Whether on the streets in your hometown or on travels worldwide, a smile is an excellent method of communicating with others without speaking.

Other Body Parts

When I try to make a frown, I feel my whole face scrunched up. But when I smile, I feel relaxed in many other body parts — besides my cheeks!

Dopamine

You can generate your own dopamine rush with your own smile or by observing others smile versus waiting for a certain number of "Likes" on social media or crossing something off on your weekly "To Do" list.

DO IT FOR OTHERS!

My most rewarding thought about smiles is how infectious they genuinely are. Rarely will you discover that a smile from you isn't returned by others.

Show your teeth or don't. Just smile and enjoy the rewards.

LESSON LEARNED

Just try NOT to smile. It makes me smile when I try to frown on purpose. Give it up — smile and enjoy the many rewards. No reason NOT to smile. DO IT NOW (please)! Talk about something that is super easy to practice any time and build your own "smile habit." And as you intentionally smile more often, you'll get many more smiles back in return.

ACCOMPANY

"go somewhere with (someone) as a companion or escort."

But where to go?

First time in Europe. An American in Paris who can't speak French. No Google Maps or cell phones. No car or Uber or Lyft. Hmmm…. It was the first time in my life I truly needed to have someone accompany me.

As a young child, it is obvious that you need your parents or other adults to accompany you to places. Over time, you discover the balance of going on adventures alone or as a group with your friends. We all learn about accompanying each other.

Even in high school and college, it was fun to drive to downtown Chicago with my high school friends or go on road trips to other colleges or fun locations with different groups. My adventures outside the United States included family trips to Canada and Mexico.

And while I'm grateful to my family and friends for "going along for the ride" on many adventures in my lifetime to date, it wasn't until my first summer after I started college that I experienced the need to have someone accompany me somewhere.

My dad had been doing business with an excellent company in Spain. The company's owner had a daughter a year older than me who wished to travel to the U.S. So, Dad and the owner came up with the idea of doing our own exchange program. For me, it meant an opportunity to live with a family in Spain for more than half of a summer. What a blast!

The family took me everywhere — the Pyrenees, the running of the Bulls in Pamplona, great cities along the coast like San Sebastian, and many other local trips in Spain and France. The company's owner had an upcoming work trip to Paris for the week. Guess who got to accompany him? More importantly, one of his key employees was also coming along — mainly to accompany ME.

We had a whole week to explore and enjoy all Paris had to offer. I'm sure I was naive enough to think I could walk the streets of Paris by myself and figure it out. However, there was no way my adopted father, for the summer, would let me be alone. So he had one of his employees accompany me for that entire week.

We had a great time traveling and exploring together.

We both came up with fun ideas the other didn't even consider.

We helped each other with some minor challenges — language, for one. Neither of us spoke French and not everyone in France is a big fan of Americans. So I pretended to be from Canada.

We challenged each other with what we wanted to do and see — and the best way to get there — using the metro, walking, trains, cabs, and more.
We even created a few opportunities for each of us to have some alone time while still being together — like exploring different parts of the Louvre for a few hours here and there.   Being alone gave me a sense of independence and freedom in another country while simultaneously helping me to appreciate the benefits of being at the Louvre with someone else.

On the surface, the value of accompanying each other starts out as $1 + 1 = 2$. But when we consider the additional values accompanying one another, the value feels more like $1 + 1 = 3$ ... or maybe even $1 + 1 = 4$ or 5!

Since those days, I have valued tremendously the word accompany. Whether I'm the leader or follower, or it is a mutual journey, there are many benefits to doing stuff together.

LESSON LEARNED

Accompany often refers to physical travel. But it can also be applied to other experiences like spending time with someone in person, speaking with someone else on the phone, or engaging with someone online. To some degree, we all enjoy time by ourselves. So I encourage you to dig into the experience of accompanying others and letting yourself be accompanied by someone else. The rewards are totally worth it. Even palpable.

ADMIRATION

"something regarded as impressive or worthy of respect"

What feels out of reach for you personally but you can appreciate how someone else reached that goal?

A few years ago, I was at a conference in Las Vegas when one of my colleagues called me with an "important" observation. Like me, he was a huge baseball fan. He noticed Pete Rose in a sports memorabilia shop signing books, baseballs, bats, and more. Fortunately, the timing was such that I could close out my meetings and hustle over to meet him. For the record, I wanted to hustle over to meet him because Pete Rose was also known as "Mr. Hustle" during his playing days.

The back story is that Pete Rose was the first person I truly admired. I was born in Cincinnati, Ohio. My parents were big Cincinnati Reds fans, so, of course, that was my *first* favorite baseball team and one of the stars of the team was Pete Rose.

Not only was he an incredible baseball player, but he also attended the same high school my parents attended. How cool was that? I could dive into my parent's old yearbooks and see photos of Pete Rose on the same pages as my mom and dad. In addition to being an all-state baseball player, he was also all-state in basketball and football. Since I enjoyed playing all sports — you can easily guess why he was the first person I admired in sports!

The Cincinnati Reds won a couple of World Series championships in 1975 and 1976 — further instilling the *coolness* of Pete Rose in my head and someone I admired.

Decades later, I've learned to admire more than just people. I've since developed into admiring places, art, culture, nature, situations, and more. There are many nuances to admiring someone or something — someone's abilities or character, or career accomplishments. The best is that your admiration for someone or something can inspire you to more significant innovation — basically building upon their own lessons learned and forming your own improved lessons learned.

While I was watching the 2022 PGA Championship, I found myself experiencing a great sense of admiration for what Justin Thomas accomplished (overcoming one of the largest deficits ever to win his second major golf championship) across a few different perspectives. Unlike my simplistic admiration of Pete Rose, my admiration for Justin Thomas went much deeper.

Don't Give Up

One of my favorite quotes comes from Jim Valvano, the former head coach for North Carolina State's basketball team, who passed away from cancer just a few months after sharing his advice to "Don't give up... don't EVER give up". I greatly admire anyone with the perseverance to look at extremely difficult circumstances as a challenge to overcome versus an excuse to stop trying. Justin never gave up as he overcame a huge deficit.

Abilities

I'll use air quotes to define myself as a "golfer." I enjoy golf. But I'll never have the skills or abilities that Justin Thomas has on the golf course. However, watching the clutch shots he made at key instances on the final day of four rounds of golf inspires me to improve my own game. I have the confidence that I can get better, but let's be clear, don't expect to win a PGA Championship — ever.

Accomplishments

Sometimes, setting impossible goals is the best way to motivate yourself to accomplish great things. I often look at the accomplishments of others and use their great successes as a motivational tool for overcoming my own challenges. If you haven't seen it, check out *Hidden Figures* and experience what three amazing women had to overcome to accomplish incredible success at NASA (and life). Whether *Hidden Figures* or Justin Thomas in golf, you quickly learn to admire how much hard work and effort goes into what you might only see as the end result.

Character

Character is usually described as the key attributes that define someone. Character is how you act/behave when no one else is looking. I often learn from people with high moral values and use their behaviors to encourage me to build upon my values, passions, and character. For example, I've seen some things Justin Thomas does away from the golf course, like his foundation to help children in need. I admire his approach to life as much as his approach to competitive golf.

Followership

Some people I admire are people you just want to spend time with. They tend to have some essence about them and I'd love to spend time with them to glean anything that they are willing to impart. Maybe I can play a round of golf with Justin someday?

Back to Las Vegas... I spent too much money on a book about Pete Rose's life to simply spend ten minutes with him for a few photos and a fun conversation. He didn't remember my parents at all but did recall great memories from Western Hills High School. I shared how much I admired him as a kid and how his hustle, effort, and hard work inspired me to be the best I could be in baseball, basketball, and golf. And how I applied the same hard work to my career growth and development as well.

Pete signed the book to my mom and dad, and I gave it to them as a fun little Christmas present that year. Sadly, it was one of the last Christmas presents I ever gave my dad as he passed away the following spring. We shared some fun stories about Pete Rose during that time and how much I admired Pete Rose. AND I shared how much I admired my dad too!

LESSON LEARNED

Take a few minutes each day to discover something or someone you admire and feel how that person, place, or thing inspires you to greater heights in the future. That *something* might be a unique natural wonder or a simple admiration for a small gesture from someone during a regular day. The feeling you get from simply offering your respect to something or someone else is an excellent gift for yourself.

The key is to embrace the joy you feel and leverage that joy in your life's journey.

AMAZEMENT

"a feeling of great surprise or wonder."

I wish I could have a sense of amazement daily.

As my boys were into their teenage years, several families talked about travel and fun places to visit before our children were not as interested in going on the proverbial "family vacation" any longer. Being at the Gulf of Mexico or at Priest Lake in Idaho no longer seemed interesting to teenagers on their path to becoming young adults, even with water skiing involved.

We discussed what would be fun for everyone across three families and a group of teenage boys. Europe had a lot of great options, but one of them bubbled to the top quickly — Italy. Several others had been there and offered up great options to explore. So we quickly planned the trip with three main stopping points in Rome, Florence, and Venice.

As if major cities like Rome and Florence didn't offer up enough incredible experiences on their own, we also took many cool side trips. Pisa and the Leaning Tower. Pompeii and the incredible ruins after the Vesuvius eruption. Cinque Terre and the amazing views from each of the cities and from the water. Tuscany and exceptional wines. All were incredible.

But Venice is what stood out to me. The first few days were incredible — especially for a group of young teenagers. While the sights were something to behold, the boys loved that no cars were anywhere. Transportation was walking or biking or boating through the canals. As parents, we loved the safety factors of no cars anywhere.

The boys could run around anywhere, and we let them. They were thrilled to get away from the parents, and the parents had fun chasing them down. Running over bridges, across open plazas, and winding around numerous churches and century-old buildings was pretty inspiring.

Then I saw it. Just a small sign. In front of a church. But it was no longer a church. It was a museum about Leonardo da Vinci. Being a massive fan of da Vinci, I had to take a quick peek inside — even though we had already seen 2–3 different da Vinci museums.

Amazing!

I thought I understood what being in amazement was like, but then I was transformed into someone walking through the many da Vinci books I have at home. As if I was walking along the pages and seeing 3-D versions of DaVinci's most significant works. I lost track of everyone else on the trip because I was stunned by what I saw.

To some people, I'm sure there were just a bunch of interesting contraptions. I've read several books about da Vinci and watched several shows. But seeing all of this in the flesh unfolding in front of your eyes is incredible!

There were 20–25 life-sized replicas of da Vinci's inventions. Unbelievable to see, at full size, what I had only read about or seen pictures of in books and other museums. And several of the inventions offered the opportunity to actually interact with them. So, yes — I had the chance to PLAY with replicas of something Leonardo da Vinci actually invented.

We weren't planning to visit this museum and didn't even know about it. We found it by wandering around Venice and letting the boys do whatever they wanted.

Indeed, I've seen a lot of amazing things in my life. This experience stuck out for me because of the many different circumstances coming together — an unexpected discovery, something I was already passionate about, an opportunity to learn in a hands-on manner, seeing something that not only excited me but also interested my sons and the ability to visualize what these incredible ideas looked like in real life and more.

Just amazing.

LESSON LEARNED

Experiences can be incredible and awe-inspiring, and even life-changing. And you can plan for many of these experiences. It would help to truly feel amazed if you were open to something unexpected. Make every attempt to bring joy and wonder into your life… then be aware of the fun surprises that lead to amazing experiences.

CONSTANCY

"the quality of being faithful and dependable." and *"the quality of being enduring and unchanging."*

How many sit-ups can you do right now? My stomach muscles hurt just thinking about sit-ups.

When I think about doing core exercises, my first thoughts go back to high school and having to do a certain number of sit-ups in gym class. My stomach is getting tight right now just thinking about those sit-ups.

One of my recent New Year's Resolutions was strengthening my core. My personal trainer identified specific exercises that would help me over time. And we started *very* low — a single five-minute workout qualified as my core exercise for the day.

Before I started my core exercises in January, I strongly desired to be 100% constant with my workouts. I couldn't miss one. I'd never change how I did them. I'd be entirely dependable and get them done in the mornings, no matter what.

I'd beat myself for a long time when I missed a few days. I'd be frustrated for hours and not let it go. And there were even a few occasions when I said, "Well, I already missed one day this week; what's the big deal about missing a second day?". It totally bothered me to see the app I was using to track my core exercises with open spaces across the many days I missed out. I was starting to be demotivated.

Then I asked myself, "Why?".

Why was I so focused on doing core exercises and not missing a single day? What was so important about being in a state of constancy versus the longer-term benefits? Improving my core was about becoming healthier and getting my body in better shape. Why beat myself up over missing 15 days in one year when I probably did *fewer than* 15 days of core exercises for all of the previous year?

Instead of getting frustrated when I'd miss a day of core exercises, I let the feeling pass quickly and think about one year from today. I envision myself stating that I completed 350+ days of my "daily" core exercises instead of solely being focused on constancy. Then, when I take my dog Suki for walks, I can literally feel how much stronger my core is and how those exercises have helped over time.

Take the four keywords from the definitions above and consider constancy in this sequence:

1. I'm being ***faithful*** to myself for even doing the core exercises.

2. Though I'll miss a day here and there, I'm still **dependable** in my attempt at constancy with my core exercises.
3. The work I'm putting in is **enduring**, as I've been at this for years.
4. And though my specific routine changes, my dedication to core exercises is **unchanging**.

LESSON LEARNED

Why? And to What? Constancy is admirable, but perfectionism is bleeding into the definitions. We have years and even decades to hang out on this planet. Don't lose too much focus on a bad day here and there with anything you are trying to establish some consistency within your life. Use the four keywords at the end of this story as a quick lens to understand the value of constancy with whatever you attempt to do more frequently.

TRAVEL

"go from one place to another, typically over a distance of some length."

Think about it briefly — what was your *best* travel story ever? I'll leave it to you to define "best."

A little under three hundred miles from where I lived in Michigan to where I was born in Cincinnati, Ohio — as far as I can remember, that's my first experience with travel. After I moved yet again to Sleepy Hollow, Illinois, my travels now included trips back to Ohio and Michigan as well as trips north to check out Wisconsin and the Upper Peninsula of Michigan. I became an *avid* reader during those road trips.

My first flight was with my dad between Illinois and Michigan. Over time, we flew to California and Mexico to visit our timeshare in Cancun. We drove to Canada and expanded our driving trips to many other states in the US. The understanding that we could fly almost anywhere created an aperture for me to view travel as a never-ending possibility.

When I think about how travel has impacted my life, the most life-changing event in my travel life was going to Spain. During my college years, I spent most of one summer in Spain — more specifically in Guernica, a town in the province of Biscay, in the Basque Autonomous Community in Spain.

Within a drive of just a few hours were so many incredible adventures — Paris, France; the famous cave paintings in Lascaux, France; the running of the bulls in Pamplona, Spain; climbing and hiking in the Pyrenees Mountains in Spain; beach time along the coast of the Atlantic Ocean in the Bay of Biscay and; my most memorable spot — eating fresh calamari as the fishermen delivered it to us in San Sebastian — on the northern coast of Spain. Of course, learning how to surf and drinking cold beers in San Sebastian helped form a positive impression as well. The opportunity to have such a variety of experiences in a concentrated area only fueled my desire to discover other areas around the world.

All of that amazing travel aside...the most impactful part of travel for me is immersing myself in the town's culture. Guernica is part of the Basque country. Therefore, most people speak Basque first, Spanish second, and English a distant third. Not only did I need to get fluent in Spanish quickly (about one week), but I also had to learn passable Basque to communicate with the elders in the town and the children who had not started school yet. I literally had to learn more about the culture by experiencing it rather than simply reading or hearing about it.

Beyond language, l learned new sleep schedules, the value of naps, helping others in a little town, looking out for the interests of the younger and older generation, etc. Living in the town helped immerse me in all elements of culture. The impact was beyond what I could ever imagine. I had no choice other than to adapt to my new environment immediately.

More than anything, travel made me aware that there are many excellent and outstanding people worldwide. Of course, we all have different cultures, values, religions, and beliefs, but we can all be good people and stewards of the earth and treat each other respectfully.

I've always bought into the "depth" argument with travel versus "breadth." We rarely took a vacation where we'd try to get to eight cities in ten days or visit five countries in less than two weeks — though that also has its merits. Being a tourist can be exciting and educational. But you miss a lot if you don't attempt to deeply immerse yourself in learning more about the city or country you are visiting for extended periods. Enjoy your experience. Appreciate what you have compared to others.

While I'm talking about immersing ourselves in another culture, we took one trip to Kenya, where we lived with the Maasai for an entire week.

My sons *loved* this trip and had a blast walking among the giraffes, elephants, and almost every mammal one could discover across Kenya during their morning walks with the Maasai warriors — who were well-armed with spears in case they did see a lion. We visited about four other locations across Kenya with the Maasai warriors as excellent guides. I quickly learned to trust the local experts.

Growing up in the Midwest suburbs, I was relatively well insulated from learning about other cultures outside of school, church, or my neighborhood. So travel helped me greatly appreciate everything I had in the United States and to also appreciate the many important things to others and their cultures. Books and videos are great sources to learn more, but nothing beats being there in the moment with the individuals who live there.

LESSON LEARNED

First, travel no matter how short the time or limited the distance. Give everyone else you meet a hundred percent the benefit of the doubt regarding the stories they share or the information they impart.

Whatever you hear about others is usually not fully informed — learn it directly from others you meet during your travels. Please make your own decisions about good people and how they interact with you.

Lastly, be sure to take in *everything* — not just the interesting tourist stuff, but also the people, smaller places, and things. Experiences matter, and the lessons learned are nearly limitless. I'm certain you will build out your own list of lessons learned based on the unique travel experiences you will fulfill in your lifetime.

SURPRISE

"an unexpected or astonishing event, fact, or thing."

My curiosity is always piqued when someone uses phrases like "I can't tell you because it's a *surprise!*". What about you?

Several middle and high school friends had surprise parties for their birthdays or other events. It was fun to crouch behind a sofa or hide behind a door and then yell "*Surprise!*" when the "victim" would unknowingly enter a surprise party.

Before Melanie and I moved to Seattle from Chicago, I collaborated with her friends and family to create *two* surprise going-away parties on back-to-back days. I thought I had fun jumping out and yelling, "*Surprise!*" when attending a surprise party pulled together by someone else. Working on the creativity, planning, and execution behind a surprise party was even more fun than simply yelling "surprise" for someone else.

So many questions to ask.

Does the person expect anything? How will you get them to the location? Who should be invited, and where will everyone else be hiding on the day of the party?

I loved every minute of the planning and execution process.

I collaborated and devised many ideas with her friends and identified the "best" one. Planning on everything from how to get her to the party location to who she'd want to be there. The execution was my favorite part — especially the little white lies ("We are just meeting your friend here before we head somewhere else").

Fun stuff. The best is when the person being surprised, one, honestly had no idea and, two, either laughed or cried or both in response to everyone jumping out.

Surprises can be something other than a party or an event. It could be as simple as a surprise twist ending to a book (see David Ellis' books for sure!), or a movie (M. Night Shyamalan movies, anyone?), or something bigger in life, like when you find out the gender of your unborn baby. As the definition states, surprises can also be a fact or an object.

While some surprises are associated with sad events (for example, a close friend passing away suddenly), most surprises bring me joy, huge smiles, and warmth all over.

Here are a few of my favorite surprises in life:

My Sons

I'm grateful my ex-wife and I agreed to a planned surprise nine months in advance. Neither one of us wanted to know the sex of our child in advance of being born. So we were *totally* blessed by an amazing surprise — twice!

Look for opportunities to *create* surprises for yourself — especially ones that are happy no matter what! Unfortunately, our sons weren't around for those surprise going-away parties I planned for their mother. Still, I'm sure they would have had fun helping me plan and execute if they were around.

My First Job

Getting an offer letter for my first job with IBM was a huge surprise. It seemed as if I was *trying* not to get hired. I didn't know what IBM stood for, and I told the interviewer I switched from computer science to engineering because "I didn't like working with computers." But for some reason, I was surprised with a great offer letter to start with the largest computer company in the world (at that time). Don't consistently lower your expectations — just temper them to stay somewhat realistic.

My Broad Life Experiences

My favorite surprises in life are the little things. Bumping into friends when I wasn't expecting to see them. Turning on music to catch a favorite song I haven't heard in a long time. Getting an email or text from a friend I last heard from a long while ago. You can create surprises daily if you are truly enjoying the present moment.

Looking for surprises in your life is a fun way to enjoy it. And giving the "gift" of surprises to others is even better. Think about the smiles, joys, laughter, and more that you can create by surprising someone. Try it — you'll be *surprised* about how it makes *you* feel.

ADDITIONAL

"added, extra, or supplementary to what is already present or available."

How did you get around before you could drive a car?

It was all about riding my bike everywhere and under most conditions.
Growing up in the Midwest, the rain, heat, humidity, or other terrible
conditions rarely slowed my bike riding down. Of course, a few feet of snow
and/or ice would be a problem. I even tried to ride my bike through the
snow many times. Hitting your brakes on the ice and crashing into a big pile
of snow can be fun… at least when you are young and pliable!

During my sabbatical in 2019, I rode my bike often in the summer. Also, for
my friends who are avid bikers, please note that I'm nowhere near calling
myself a true cyclist *yet*… I'll keep riding my bike for now for fun.

As I was riding to an appointment one day, I was thinking about the reasons
why I enjoyed my time on the bike that amazing summer on sabbatical. I
didn't want to focus on just one part of riding my bike (as a means of
transportation) but expanded upon many additional reasons as well.

Exercise

I love the addition of a new way for me to work out. Stationary bikes and
ellipticals get boring over time.

Fun

There hasn't been a ride where I didn't smile at least once. I'm sure seeing
other people was also part of that.

Competitive

All with myself as I improve my skills on a bike.

Journey

On paths where I've never been, I'm VERY focused on the journey through new areas of Seattle versus simply reaching the final destination.

People

Observing people is a blast. Riding a bike put me on many sidewalks and bike paths I'd never traversed previously. It led me to observe people having picnics, kids cruising on their little bikes, and dogs playing in the grass along the bike paths.

Visualize

Need to keep your head up and eyes open — *always!* Some people don't walk on the right side of the path, and cars don't always stop at bike/pedestrian crossings.

Listen

Eyes are great, but the ears are almost as important. Hearing another cyclist going much faster and passing on my left gave me the cues to shift right and out of their way. And don't get me started on car drivers not paying attention to cyclists.

Experiment

There are many different ways to take the journey to find that destination. I went on different paths — up big hills, around bodies of water in another direction, and with varying speeds on my bike.

Outside

How can you not be outside in the summer? Keeping the car at home and being outside on my bike was the way to go all summer.

Observe

There is so much to observe during my journeys. I saw Lake Washington from a different perspective, noticed the Olympic Mountains from new angles, and cruised around several islands since Washington State ferries are relatively bike-friendly to allow me to reach those islands.

Many people refer to a "win-win" scenario where both parties achieve what they want. I'm a big fan of the "win-win-win-win..." scenarios where I can see many ways people can benefit. That's my definition of additional — considering something you already have or experienced and exploring more deeply how much *more* you can garner from it.

LESSON LEARNED

You can look at ANY activity, event, person, nature, or whatever and list a dozen side benefits of doing that activity. Imagine not only experiencing the initial joy with whatever you are doing but then getting 2, or 10, or 25, additional benefits at the same time! Start with the basic rule of improv comedy: "Yes, and...", then figure out how many more "and"s you can experience based upon your starting point.

NETWORK

"a group or system of interconnected people or things."

But what if you have ZERO connections to the group or system as it relates to people?

My ex-wife had an excellent opportunity to work in Seattle while living in downtown Chicago. We talked about the pros and cons. We debated my job opportunities in Seattle if I left my well-paying Chicago job — especially since her postdoctoral role would pay very little.

We decided that we'd pick up and move to Seattle.

Hmmm... let's come back to that ZERO connection concept. We were only a few years removed from college and had not built extensive personal or work networks. She had several new connections in Seattle for her new job, but I didn't know a single person there.

LinkedIn is based upon first, second, third, and more degree connections to build your network. LinkedIn didn't exist in 1995 when we went through this moving process. So I just told as many of my friends in Chicago as possible and slowly discovered that several of my friends had a network that reached Seattle. I had to network via phone calls and emails to reach first and second-degree connections versus simply searching through LinkedIn.

I learned about "networking" in my early days with IBM and how to network with my college buddies and with friends in Chicago, but networking would play a pivotal role in my life during my move and acclimation to Seattle. I needed to go through some serious growth in my "networking muscles" over the first few years of being here.

One friend connected me with someone who ended up being my first official tour guide of Seattle — taking me out for some fun (water skiing, downhill skiing, golf, hiking) and some productive effort looking at various neighborhoods. I met several folks in his network and felt totally comfortable hanging around Seattle after only just meeting these folks for the first time.

Once we moved, I found other ways to network in Seattle. One of my buddies from our flag football team connected me with a friend of his in Seattle who connected me with his softball team and a new group of softball players. As a result, I quickly joined the team and started the early building blocks of my own network.

I even made it hard on myself by taking a remote job where I'd travel a bunch and not have an office to go into locally. Networking via work would be impossible in Seattle... so I continued to search for other venues to network.

I started playing basketball up the street and met a dude who became one of my best friends in the world. We connected, and he invited me to join his network of "weekend warrior" basketball players who would play two hours of pickup weekly.

The move to Seattle and the need/desire to meet new people significantly shifted my networking skills, knowledge, and experience. I still consider how to more effectively network, but that transition in Seattle was the most pronounced shift in my life.

Today, I don't take any networking for granted. A network might be as small as two people or as big as thousands or millions. I'm never surprised when connecting with people and learning about their networks. And I always look forward to helping others establish and/or connect with their own networks. I'm never shocked when I hear about the intertwined networks of others.   I feel acknowledged when someone says, "You should meet this person," and they are already in one of my many networks.

LESSON LEARNED

Networks are everywhere. You just need to look and ask. Knowing who is in or out of a specific network is nearly impossible in a massive group with thousands of potential connections. So just ask about making a connection within a network. And, more importantly, actively offer to connect others to your own network. Some of my best friends in the world emanated from networking — I hope you discover the same over time if you haven't already.

INVOLVEMENT

"the fact or condition of being involved with or participating in something."

Don't you hate to miss out on things?

We had been in Seattle for about six years and decided our house was too small for two growing sons and two black female Labrador Retrievers. Plus, we were starting to focus on what was necessary for our boys regarding the specific schools they would attend as they journeyed from elementary to middle to high school.

Fortunately, we discovered a great house in a lovely neighborhood just a few blocks from the park and the elementary school. Ryan started immediately at the elementary school, and Cole would begin three years later. We would spend the next eight years between the two boys at that elementary school. Not to mention a much longer time in the neighborhood overall.

After a few weeks, I learned the playground at the elementary school was dilapidated, out of date, and even unsafe for the children at the school. There was an effort to build a new playground — but it would take a lot of work. Fortunately, someone had already pulled together a small group of concerned parents. I quickly volunteered to help and get involved with this group.

Up to this point, I have participated in many different projects at work and across my personal life. But I don't recall truly being physically *and* emotionally involved in something until around this time.

Over several years, we held various fundraisers, dealt with many different individuals and organizations to get help, and met with our group dozens of times to stay on the same page and break out the individual work streams across the group. There were many moving parts, and I was deeply involved in the project.

We raised enough money to build an awesome playground from which thousands of kids benefitted over the years. And while I'm proud to see the final product in place, I'm most reflective on what it meant to be involved.

Multi-Purpose

My initial purpose for getting involved was self-serving — to create a playground my kids and their friends could leverage. As I got more deeply engaged in the process overall, my purpose transformed into focusing on the kids of today and in the future who would benefit from getting this playground together. My involvement addressed more than one purpose.

Holistic

Being involved with the playground committee expanded beyond helping the elementary school. Kids from the neighborhood who weren't at the school could also leverage the playground and, surprisingly, many older kids in middle and high school used the basketball courts and other parts of the playground on the weekends. I'd even walk by and see some adults revisiting their inner child on the playground.

Unintended Benefits

Being involved with this committee also led me to connect with new friends across the community more broadly. Involvement also created a sense of awareness for others in the community who weren't directly involved with the playground — and I also connected with other folks who are now good friends.

Giving Back

Involvement often leads to giving back. Participating in something that is beyond what you are currently doing can be beneficial to many others as well.

Self-Improvement

I also learned a lot from others by getting involved with them. My ability to collaborate with others improved. Eventually, my co-chair left, and I needed to lead the committee — which is very different from managing a team that reports to you directly.

Most things you might get involved with are time-based. You can jump in, experiment with something new and leave if you are interested in something other than whatever you are involved with. But I'd encourage everyone to get involved in something that aligns with your interests, passions, or personal objectives. Your involvement will likely lead to many unexpected benefits.

LESSON LEARNED

Do the work upfront to determine what might interest or benefit you. Get involved. You'll be surprised how many other benefits come from getting involved in something — big or small. Completing the project can be rewarding by itself, but sharing the satisfaction among others can significantly magnify your involvement.

Chapter 2

Work Intentionally to Get Better

When I started my stretch exercises last year, I forced myself to track whether or not I did them daily. Then, I'd look back weekly and monthly to track how often I did them. About a year later, doing my daily stretches is a habit that I want to start the day with. And I never would have learned how valuable stretching would be for me without being very intentional about tracking and holding myself accountable for the hard work.

MEDITATION

"the process of thinking deeply or focusing one's mind for a period of time, in silence or with the aid of chanting, for religious or spiritual purposes or as a method of relaxation."

What do you think of when you hear about Buddhism? Meditation is what comes to me… or the Himalayas… but back to meditation.

In the last year, I've finally started to embrace the idea of meditation. I've had a few starts in the past decades — but mostly stops. I'd get frustrated by how often I'd lose focus. Hmmm — meditation should be beneficial — ha!

My transformation/conversion was pretty basic. I read a story about a man who traveled to Tibet to live with some of the most experience and well-known monks in the world. He figured that some of these well-practiced monks, who had been practicing meditation for decades, would be in deep meditation for hours, if not more than a day. When he asked one monk — "what's the longest that you've been able to fully meditate and have a completely clear head?" he was shocked when the monk replied, "Seven seconds."

Most of my mindset had been, "Why can't I keep my head clear?" and I would constantly focus on the distractions over and over. But after hearing the story about keeping clear for just seven seconds, I began to embrace what many meditation experts talk about — it's about something other than keeping a clear mind all the time. It's more about acceptance that some thought will *always* enter your mind and interrupt you. Your job in meditation is to acknowledge that something filled your mind and to let it go just as quickly.

An interesting aspect of my early days at ThinqShift (see the story **Career** before Chapter 1) is learning about the importance of the cognitive steps we must take to shift our mindsets and behaviors. For me, it was about finding a consistent time to meditate. I came upon an app that helped me keep track of my sessions and offer suggestions for new ones. My current challenge is my desire to explore and enhance the value of meditation in my life. Here is what I'm becoming much more aware of as I build my meditation practice (which takes a *lot* of practice):

Body/Senses

Closing my eyes. Softening parts of my body. Being aware of my posture. Who knew how hard it is to breathe so consistently? Concentrating on just one part of my body at a time takes much more focus than I initially thought. Breathing is a great place to start since our bodies like to do it naturally. The focus on specific body parts or senses was the foundation of this meditation space.

Mind

Wow — this one is tough. Calm down my mind. My biggest lesson learned with meditation is an acceptance that I can't always calm my mind. It is helpful to understand that it is totally fine that my brain goes to about a dozen different thoughts per minute, and I need to accept those thoughts and get back to calm my mind. Initially, I thought calming my mind was about *preventing* thoughts from entering my head. Once I understood the acceptance perspective, it was much easier to say "Hello" to those thoughts and "ask them" nicely to leave. The role my mind plays is important in creating a learning environment for meditation.

Time

Carving out 10–15 minutes daily is the first shift. The second is the time itself. One day a ten-minute meditation feels like one minute. On other days, I felt I had been meditating for 4–5 minutes, and only 45 seconds had passed. Time has never been so noticeable. For those of you reluctant to start, I'm up to 10–15 minutes daily right now — though I started with just five minutes or less per day (and missed many days as well!).

Space

Originally, I used to find a place to sit down and concentrate and meditate. Many people need to discover a quiet location to relax and meditate. Ironically, I discovered walking meditation was best for me. Having my eyes wide open and walking, usually with my dog Suki, was more difficult initially because of the many visual distractions and mental obstacles. But walking and meditating have actually improved my ability to concentrate and focus because there are so many potential interruptions during a 30–45 minute walk that force me to concentrate even more deeply on my meditation.

Today, it is noticeable when I haven't had a chance to meditate for 10–15 minutes in the morning. I'm usually not as focused or relaxed. It was awesome to discover how quickly this became an excellent habit for me after letting those habit-forming steps kick in and become natural. I can focus on specific parts of my body, be more aware of time, have focused breathing, and have more awareness of the space around me.

LESSON LEARNED

One general lesson — anyone can put in the work to build a new habit. My first meditation sessions were all about five minutes to start. My goal was to be intentional — one meditation session daily, no matter how short.   My overall lesson is to create the optimal environment for a new habit to form — mediation in this case.   It required me to be reflective of my body, my mind, the time it would take, and the space in which I would most likely meditate.   Once I understood the optimal environment, building my meditation habit was like riding a bike downhill.

MEMORY

"the power or process of reproducing or recalling what has been learned and retained, especially through associative mechanisms"

Where are my keys? How often have you forgotten where you left your keys or other important objects?

Before we had cell phones and hundreds of numbers stored at our fingertips, we had to write down or, gasp, *memorize* phone numbers to call our friends. As silly as it sounds, using my memory to remember my friends' phone numbers is one of my earliest memories of actively using my memory. We used to spell words with our phone numbers to provide another "cheat code." *Hat Draw* would translate into my home phone number at the time, 428-3729 (if you were curious).

Through middle and high school, there were many times when I needed to memorize the definition or spelling of a word, a specific formula in science or math, or, the worst possible thing to forget ever, your locker combination! So we devised little tricks to remember something or studied endlessly to remember that one physics equation you will never use again (except for the year-end final).

Classwork. This was the first time I consciously tried leveraging my memory for a specific purpose. If I was fortunate, coming into that dreaded Friday quiz, I could only memorize the 20 words for my weekly vocabulary test and remember most of them minutes later. I used other tricks like creating an acronym to memorize a list or an image to remember a formula.

Shifting forward another decade or so, I started to understand the power of memory more proactively. Working at IBM, I had to ingest a ton of technical information that was entirely new to me. I had to memorize computer system numbers, their capabilities, and how they helped our many customers.

It is said that Albert Einstein didn't actually remember his own phone number because he could look it up at any time, and, more importantly, he didn't want to "take up" that space for other brain processing. I know for sure I'm not at that level, but I do make a determination whether or not to memorize specific thoughts in a structure and intentional manner.

Full disclosure — Today, I probably only know three–four phone numbers as storing them on my phone and *not* remembering them allows me to use my memory for more valuable use cases. Thanks, Albert!

In the bigger picture, there are a variety of techniques to turn short-term memories into much longer-term memories — including discerning which memories you genuinely want to retain versus information you can find elsewhere. Here are a few that work for me:

Write It Down or Type It

When I'm in a meeting, I'll take the time to write down some notes from the discussion. Then, I'll type them up — effectively "reading" them again in my head as I type them. When I file my notes away, I usually memorize the key takeaways.

Say It "out Loud" (in Your Head) a Few Times

It takes 10–15 seconds to repeat something you'd like to memorize. Repeating "banana, banana, banana, banana, banana" helps me to buy a bunch of bananas at the grocery store.

Find an Association

I'll do this when I'm in bed at night and want to remember something. I might find something next to my bed, like the magazine I'm reading, and throw it into the middle of the room. When I get up in the morning, and ask myself, "Why is that magazine on the floor?" I think backward, remember throwing the magazine on the floor, and inevitably, remember what I need to recall.

Take It to Bed With You

One of the functions of sleep is to clear out the "stuff" your brain doesn't need and create a long-term memory of what you want to remember. Once the lights are off and you start to fall asleep, think about the key things you want to remember, and your brain should do most of the work after that.

Create a System

When I first had to memorize all the different computers across IBM, they had a system. PS/2 was a personal computer (one digit after the PS). AS/400 was a mid-range computer (three digits), and the ES/9000 was the mainframe and largest computer (four digits). The system helped my long-term memory kick in — and even thirty years later, I still remember them!

Big Picture

Another version of finding an association. But instead of an object, I'll recall the big picture. In the example above, memorizing a lot of technical information about IBM's computers was super helpful in the sales process with new clients. The purpose, or big picture, was establishing myself as an expert and trusted advisor to secure a new business relationship.

Building Blocks

Sometimes it helps to memorize parts of something bigger. With so many different types of computers, I only focused on learning about one system at a time. Eventually, I understood the entire lineup of computers, but one piece of hardware at a time.

We all forget things over time. But memorizing something and recalling it exactly when you need it most is fun. So, got it — that's where I left those keys!

LESSON LEARNED

First, consider what you are memorizing and whether or not it is worth the "space" in your brain. Having an end goal in mind is helpful as you memorize something useful. Creating a specific intention with the information or story you are memorizing will help prioritize what you memorize and make it more likely that you will actually memorize whatever you hope to recall. Develop your own techniques, and feel free to mix in some of the ones I shared above to improve your own memory.

INTENTIONALITY

"the fact of being deliberate or purposive."

Who would you spend time with if you discovered you were dying in three months? Tough question. I had to answer that question while lying in a hospital bed nearly two decades ago, but it resulted in a significant shift in my life.

The quick story — I had stroke-like symptoms and went in and out of the hospital three times over two weeks. Finally, during my third visit, the doctors still couldn't figure out what was wrong with me and casually suggested that I should get my affairs in order. *Just in case* my body didn't recover from whatever the virus was in my body.

They conducted every test, ranging from a simple question-and-answer protocol to a complex set of MRIs and cat scans. There was nothing they could find, and none of the known viruses they scanned me for were apparent. Finally, after my second spinal tap (yes — a large needle was inserted in my spine), the doctors determined it was a viral infection in my brain and spine. But the excellent news was that my white blood cell count was incredibly high, and it was likely that I'd recover. And (obviously) I did.

Up to that point in my life, I wanted to be liked by everyone. I was always open to reaching out to people without them having to contact me first. I enjoyed spending time with them — whether about meeting new people or rekindling old relationships.

My focus was generally flexing my relationship muscles without any intentionality. I wanted to belong to everyone!

Given what I had just gone through medically, I decided to focus significantly on my intentionality as it related to all of the relationships in my life and, more importantly, the *quality* of those relationships.

But how was I going to make this shift? Who was I going to focus on? What friendships would I let go of — or at least spend less time investing in?

When thinking about my will and dying, my first thought was to consider who I wanted to be at my funeral. It sounds morbid — but it was my reality. Unless I'm not up to speed, everyone will eventually pass away. But I did shift away from focusing on my eventual death into more of a "who would I spend time with if I only had three months to live?".

With that question in place, my next step was to figure out where to prioritize my time and investment in deeper relationships. There are many factors to consider, and we could have very different perspectives on what's important.

Some examples of questions I asked in my head about each person on my list at that time:

- How long have I known them?
- What initiated the relationship?
- Would I drive three hours to see them if they were "close"?
- Would I get on a flight to hang out with them?
- If significant others are involved, will the significant others get along? And me with my friends' significant other? And my friend with mine?
- Am I doing a week-long vacation with them?
- Are we on each other's annual Xmas card list?
- When was the last time I saw them in person? Or via Zoom, given the pandemic.
- Do they really want me in their life?

Once I understood the importance of engaging more meaningfully with these friends, I pondered how often and when do we connect? The answer was different for each friend. I learned when it made sense to connect with others more and less frequently. I intended to understand not only the timing, but also the method — in-person versus phone calls versus texts versus emails, etc.

Lastly, I shifted my thinking from the brain to feeling in the heart and belly. Was I enriched after spending time with this person? And was I able to enrich that person in some way?

Intentionality. I was deliberate about selecting the people I wanted to spend more quality time with. And clear about the short-term and long-term purpose of spending time with them.

Not long after this focus on my depth of friendships and intentionality, one of my friends paid a *huge* compliment to me, saying that he felt as if he knew me better now in the past year than he had over the previous 20+ years of being friends. That was an amazing perspective and others have since shared similar experiences about our relationships.

Intentionality works. The questions I shared above helped me to be more selective, deliberate, and purposeful about the relationships in my life. And I keep refreshing my list of questions as life changes. You can be intentional about anything simply by creating your list of qualifying questions and establishing what's most important for you.

LESSON LEARNED

Identify what it is that you'd like to be more intentional about. Like a muscle, it needs attention and exercise. Be super intentional about your purpose and process. You have limited time on earth to dig in deeply across certain aspects of your life — relationships, giving back, helping others through their own challenges, self-growth, stronger family connections, increased knowledge, enhanced or new skills, and more. Being intentional will ensure you understand what is important to you and maximize whatever you'd like to improve in your life.

EXASPERATION

"a feeling of intense irritation or annoyance."

Chairman of the Board — a *huge* title and *important* responsibility. The first time I became the Chairman of the Board, I was greatly under-qualified. And the entire board blew up. More on that in a minute.

An extremely generous family across the street from me hosted a college student from another country. They loved his passion for wanting to help people from his home country. The original mission statement for the nonprofit he started was to provide innovative, sustainable healthcare to underserved, rural communities in Kenya.

Over the years, I attended several fundraising events and felt very committed to the cause. Then, because of my effectiveness in helping them with some fundraising, I was asked to join the board. It was the first time I had formally joined a Board of Directors — pretty fun stuff for a young adult in my early thirties.

The board members were great individuals, focused on helping the founder support the mission. As I've dug into the nonprofit world, one of the questions people ask before giving money is, *"How much of this $$$ will go to the end beneficiary?"*.

In our case, we were well over 90% since the organization relied heavily on volunteers, donations, and grants, and we had very little infrastructure (at the time).

The founder's vision for what he wanted the nonprofit to become was inspiring, and every volunteer, donor, and board member was inspired to help him make it happen. He even received national recognition when Dr. Sanjay Gupta, *CNN*'s Chief Medical Correspondent, named him one of the *CNN* Heroes of the Year.

Where it got exasperating was the disconnect between the founder's vision and what was genuinely possible, given our limited financial resources and a small group of volunteers in the United States. We all wanted to support the enormous vision but knew we weren't there yet.

For example, the founder was ready for us to invest in five brand new ambulances to reach the rural parts of his home country. But our funding

62

profile was such that we barely had enough to consider one used ambulance at that time.

As a board member, I observed several other "conflicts" in real time that demonstrated the disconnect between the board and the founder. I was not the only person getting frustrated and exasperated with the founder.

We all knew something needed to change.

After two–three exhausting board meetings over the course of the next few months, we decided to bring in a facilitator to help us better understand how we can work more effectively together going forward. By then, the founder had already asked the board's current Chairman to move on. We all agreed we needed a new Chairman of the Board to help bridge the gap between vision and what's possible based on our funding profile.

Much to my surprise, a few days after the meeting, the founder called me personally and asked me to become the Chairman of the Board. Of course, I was honored and immediately said "Yes" and "Thank You ."

However, when I got off the phone, my heart sank into my stomach, and I realized I was in over my head (known in the business world as "Imposter Syndrome"). But I knew the other board members well and knew they would be totally supportive. And I was hopeful this change would enable us to close the gap between the founder's visions and our financial realities.

As the Chairman of the Board, I had many one-on-one conversations with the founder. He was open to new ideas — mostly my suggestions in response to the "crazy" or "nearly impossible" visions he'd suggest — that helped move us toward his vision.

But just not as quickly as he wanted.

It was monotonous to explain the same math over and over. Though our fundraising was at an all-time high, the founder continued to expand his vision exponentially beyond what the budget would allow. Wearisome indeed.

All of these conflicts eventually came to a head when I, as the Chairman of the Board, pushed back hard on several specific requests the founder made

— including funding his travel, room & board, and more multiple times per year to his home country.

The board all felt as if the founder was more concerned with his status in his home country versus the original mission of the nonprofit. I had those hard "No" conversations with the founder several times.

The final result? The founder "fired" me and changed the entire board — including the family who initially supported him in starting the nonprofit. Seeing this go awry was disheartening because we all loved his big-picture vision. However, we were all so exhausted with the need for more alignment between our $$$ on hand and what we should do with it. In a way, it was a huge relief for all of us.

As I reflect on the situation years later, I'm grateful for the opportunity to have served as Chairman of the Board — despite the situation becoming exasperating. I learned how to work closely with others and lead via influence. I leveraged my relationships and passions to increase the level of fundraising continually. I discovered new ways to work through challenging discussions and crucial conversations in a non-emotional and professional manner.

LESSON LEARNED

Figure out how to deal with something exasperating — *"intensely irritating and frustrating"* — by focusing on something else. It might be your values. It might be the people you are trying to serve. It might be the other people you are working with in that situation. Then, at the end of the day, consider the positive aspects of what's happening with that situation or person, balanced against whatever is exasperating you, and decide the value of moving forward — or moving on. I'm grateful for the lessons learned I walked away with — even though I had to deal with a lot of exasperation to learn them.

APPRECIATIVE

"feeling or showing gratitude or pleasure."

If you could do something three or four times as often as you do, what would it be?

I could never have guessed how much I appreciated that Pariveda created a culture of having VPs work with their executive leadership coaches. During my first year at Pariveda, I had an opportunity to engage with my own leadership coach — Don. It was the first time in my life I had my own coach who had 100% accountability to help me grow and develop as an individual without any bias towards focusing me primarily on my performance of specific business goals or targets.

I'm still with him today after over nine years of working together! I appreciate you, Don!

My transformation from sales/business development focus into technology/management included many bumps in the road. At ThinqShift, we call these transformative areas "*circles of suck*". It's natural to struggle when you shift from one set of career objectives/accountabilities into something else as your career progresses.

This shift falls into the fundamental category of "what worked for you to get to this point won't work for you going forward." And Don was there to help me through the process.

The first step of my transformation to a VP at Pariveda was attending a leadership program with several peers. It was helpful to meet with several leadership coaches and work with one of them in much more of a one-on-one situation during this program and I was one of the first VPs who wasn't leading one of our offices to attend — I also appreciated that.

Upon my return from the leadership program, we were each given the opportunity to engage further with the coach we had done much of our day-to-day work. I was so appreciative that my company provided us with this opportunity. I immediately said "*Yes*" and started to schedule my one-on-one meeting with Don.

I'm still working with Don today. Less often than I used to. But I'm still so appreciative of Pariveda enabling me to get connected to (and pay for) Don.

How might I demonstrate my appreciation?

Tell the Initiator

When someone does something for you or gives you something, saying "*Thanks*" to that person is pretty basic. I told about five or six others across

Pariveda how much I appreciate their culture of appreciation. And I've even shared with a few more recently that I'm still working with Don one-on-one on my own.

Say "Thanks" to the Delivery

This isn't always possible, but take advantage of saying "*thanks*" to the person delivering whatever it is that you appreciate most. For example, I'm pretty sure every one-on-one session with Don, I'll tell him "Thanks" for being my coach.

Pass It on

Think about whom else you could give the same advice or suggestions my coach gave me. Often, I'll share stories with others about how much I appreciate how my coach helped me through challenging situations. Many companies expect their leadership to provide internal coaching and mentorship. What I learned from working with Don is that an outside perspective is even more valuable. And having an internal coach/mentor *and* an external coach is exceptionally beneficial. I pass that advice on frequently.

Enjoy It Deeply

Make sure you genuinely dig the pleasure, joy, or happiness this experience or event brings you. I took advantage of this gift of coaching by continuing it for a long time while doing it as frequently as possible and I always applied the lessons learned as a point of growth. Frankly, if you don't enjoy it deeply, you shouldn't be doing it anyway.

And even though I'm delivering Leadership Services today to my clients, I still appreciate the work Don does with me to help me grow my career forward every time we interact.

LESSON LEARNED

To acknowledge others who bring you pleasure and gratitude. The people-to-people aspect of appreciation is the most essential part of all of this. And look at all aspects of what you appreciate — the people connecting you, the people delivering it, the people supporting you externally, etc. It is important to be very deliberate about sharing your appreciation for others for whatever reason they deserve.

DISCOVERY

"the action or process of discovering or being discovered."

Discovering — *"find (something or someone) unexpectedly or in the course of a search."*

How much fun is it to find something you weren't expecting?

I used to devour books growing up — Stephen King, Edgar Allen Poe, Agatha Christie, and Robert Ludlum were among my favorite authors. We traveled by car a lot, and I used that time to read. I read a lot when I was home, maybe because whatever was on television at the time wasn't great and we didn't have smartphones with unlimited access to a ton of information so I'd discover a new author and try to read everything they had written.

Sometimes, I'd read a book I enjoyed a second or third time, primarily for my own pleasure. Then, as I got older, I started mixing in "purpose-driven" books. How to do something. Learn more about this topic. Eventually, that translated into reading "business books" to learn something new.

But I never read them to discover something specifically. Until I decided to dive deep through my nearly complete set of Dr. Seuss books that I had read repeatedly to both of my sons when they were little. I didn't think much about the content or seek any insights then. Instead, I aimed to entertain my sons during the day or lull them to sleep in the evenings.

Then I decided to explore the content of the Dr. Seuss books and use them as a basis for business lessons learned. I discovered the value of building a journal to capture lessons learned. Not only did I create a specific reference to valuable content, but I also tended to quickly and deeply absorb the content and underlying messaging.

Purposeful and deliberate discovery. Great stuff. Exploring a new perspective on discovery through various quotes, I read many times for fun. Consider how *you* might discover something new and wonderful on your own — whether in books or any other medium.

The following quotes come from one of my favorite Dr. Seuss books — *Oh, the Places You'll Go*. I'll share below what I discovered after reading these passages over again and contemplating them more purposefully.

"Only you can control your future."

This quote applies to where my boys are now in their own lives. Of course, parents, educators, friends, family, social media, and many other groups can influence one's future. But it's great for my boys to understand they are 100% in control of their future. So am I. And so are YOU.

"Sometimes you will never know the value of something until it becomes a memory."

My boys have realized the value of forming amazing memories from our entertaining adventures over the years, whether it's a positive experience they might take for granted at the time. or a negative situation that they'll learn from. The boys both have a good sense of what defines the value of great memories through the years.

"To the world, you may be one person; but to one person, you may be the world."

Melanie and I have been fortunate to take the boys on trips around the United States and other places in the world. Both boys have seen how much it means to help others in need. They understand how important their contributions are to various nonprofits, in terms of time and money, over the years.

"If you never did, you should. These things are fun, and fun is good."

Whenever something new or different was presented to the boys, our family always talked about experimentation. So the boys were rewarded for always trying something new — tasting fresh cuisine, meeting different people, or traveling to various countries worldwide. Most of the time, as reluctant as they might have been, they ended up having fun. Unless it was a bad-tasting vegetable. But I digress.

"You have brains in your head. You have feet in your shoes. You can steer yourself in any direction you choose. You're on your own. And you know what you know. And YOU are the one who'll decide where to go..."

Enough said.

"Don't cry because it's over; smile because it happened."

Hmmm...I wish I had had this one in my mind before dropping off my oldest son in Colorado when he left home for the first time. Then, at least, I understood that I was crying for my *own* sadness. But, instead, I was thrilled, happy, excited, and smiling when I thought about HIS experience of being on his own in Boulder. And I'm smiling a lot now.

"I like nonsense, it wakes up the brain cells. Fantasy is a necessary ingredient in living."

I tend not to take things too seriously when I don't have to. Injecting silliness and fun and entertainment and laughter at all stages of life is a great ingredient for life. The boys definitely have a very lighthearted nature about them. And this applies to any aspect of your life — work, home, school, etc.

Be silly. Smile. Have fun. Play.

"Today you are You, that is truer than true. There is no one alive who is Youer than You." ... AND ...

"Why fit in when you were born to stand out?"

These two quotes are related. So many people today work hard to conform. There's so much pressure to follow the standards and accept everyone else's beliefs in high school and college. Both of my sons understand they have the freedom to always be themselves. They can stand out by speaking their mind and being their own YOU.

"Today was good. Today was fun. Tomorrow is another one."

What a great quote to end with.

Enjoy the day.
Live in the moment.
Cherish every second.

CONNECTION

"a relationship in which a person, thing, or idea is linked or associated with something else"

2 = 1. 3 = 3. 4 = 6. 5 = 10. 6 = 15. 7 = 21. 8 = 28. 9 = 36. 10 = 45.

$(N \times (N-1))/2$ = Connections. Huh?

I'm giving you the formula for how many Connections you can make where N = Number of People involved. So, for example, two people can only establish one unique connection between themselves but seven people can make twenty-one unique connections.   Most people think about a connection in the context of one-to-one only. But in larger groups, there is an ever-expanding number of potential connections across the group.

One of my friends called our annual journey from Seattle back to Chicago "FOW," where FOW = Friends of Watty (my nickname). It is one of my favorite weekends of the year because I get to be the connector of so many people from all aspects of my life.

Some of my desire to connect with people came from my high school or college days or living in downtown Chicago — those were some of my first experiences learning how to communicate in many different ways. But my desire to connect with others came to fruition when I moved to Seattle. Several of my new Seattle friends were interested in golfing in the Midwest and hitting a few Cubs games at Wrigley Field.

I think my first trip back to Chicago started with three other friends — just a simple foursome in the first year (of over 20 "FOW" weekends since then) and became two foursomes in the second year and then added some of my local high school and college friends to make three foursomes as well as many more than twelve of us in the bleachers at Wrigley Field.

But the power of making connections didn't hit me until friends from different aspects of my life asked about each other or even reached out to each other without me being involved. Incredible!!!

One year, friends joined us from high school, college, three jobs, and several other areas of my life in Seattle. At the same game, the math that weekend was $22 = 231$. Yes — that's 231 possible connections among 22 different people.

Math is crazy, eh?

Now that I understand the value, fun, and power of making connections beyond just my FOW weekend trips back to Chicago, I'm much more intentional about creating opportunities for others to connect. I know some people will attempt to make the "right" connection and be very selective about who they are connecting with. Frankly, I prefer to go the opposite way and *always* offer to make connections between folks because I can't predict the value a connection between two people might result in.

LESSON LEARNED

It can be pleasantly surprising how easy it is to bring together so many people from different backgrounds. Even if you consider it difficult — try it with no expectations. More importantly, you will discover that it's amazing to explore the power of connections through so many different perspectives — having fun, getting referrals, learning more about others, exploring new ideas or points of view, and even learning more about the connections of your new connections! Of course, connecting might not be natural for everyone — especially if you focus only on the outcome.

But I'd strongly encourage you to start with just two people to make one connection and expand it from there — three people to make three connections and then four people to make six connections, and then see the equation above! Be deliberate about helping others make connections; you will also connect with most of those individuals.

INSECURITY

"uncertainty or anxiety about oneself; lack of confidence."

Confidence is one of my values and strengths; how can I be insecure about something?

The foundations of this book were based on my posts and articles written on LinkedIn over the years. So even though I don't consider myself a writer, I can force myself to be a "writer" for these weekly posts and articles. But unlike the many individuals who effectively use YouTube or TikTok to share their own messages with the public, I would *never* consider recording a video about this stuff.

From a personal perspective, I never had an issue with recording a video of something I was doing, but it was almost always in the context of having fun somewhere and sharing it with my friends. Most of those videos were posted to share where I was, who I was with, or what I was doing with friends I'd most likely known for years.

Finally, two different coaches I was working with encouraged me, in their own and very unique ways, to try one video and post it on LinkedIn. So, because I committed to them both, I would at least try it once. I recorded a story for my book about Lessons Learned that week and posted it on LinkedIn and then I recorded a second, and a third and many more since then.

What did I need to overcome internally? I'll use something we leverage at ThinqShift called the three powers to outline various aspects of insecurity:

Content-Specific Insecurity

This is all about being insecure about a specific domain or resource in your life. For example, many individuals are financially insecure. In many cases, we often compare our financial situation to others and feel insecure as a result. I'm pretty sure I'm not going to be a billionaire, so I don't spend time thinking about what content power I'd like to have that they have access to. I accept my financial situation and control what I have the ability to change. I'm not a filmmaker or even a host of my own TikTok or YouTube channels. Besides pushing the record button on my iPhone, I avoided adding much of the other content-specific experience in recording videos (music backgrounds, pauses, words on the screen, links to other sites, etc.) to leverage those to build out my videos on LinkedIn.

72

Where do you have little or no context experience? How can you experiment? Recently, I wanted to experiment with ChatGPT but had zero experience. I decided to carve out time to play around with ChatGPT and decided it was definitely a tool I'd play around with much more often.

Think about an area in your life where you have zero or little content experience and just try it! I figured I didn't know the "right" questions to pose to ChatGPT, but I wanted to experiment more and more after I asked the first, and likely "wrong," question. Just get started.

Positional Insecurity

This version of insecurity is about feeling a lack of support or trust in your relationships — in the workplace, at home, or anywhere else. It can happen with a work colleague, in a romantic relationship, or between friends. Others can feel as if they are in a position of authority over you.

My "easy" advice here is to discuss with the other person and eliminate any perceived positional barriers. Figure out what's needed to rebuild love, trust, protection, value, or whatever else you might miss.

For example, I might see my clients or work colleagues in a position of power over me. When recording my videos, I pretend to speak to one of my friends directly, where zero positional insecurity exists since they might post their video just like I have done.

Think about where some version of a hierarchy exists for you and discover a small area of that relationship where you can exude your own strengths without feeling impacted by someone else's positional power.

Personal Insecurity

We are personally insecure when we are overly critical of our weaknesses or performance. Personal power is the strongest of the powers and means others want to follow you. Once you have created your own self-security with something, it will be easy to avoid personal insecurity.

My trepidation about doing a LinkedIn video falls squarely in this category. So I'm following my advice and "just doing it" without judging myself. Okay — maybe I'll make fun of myself afterward, but I'm accepting my flaws and moving forward.

As I think more about this topic, so much about insecurity is in our heads. In many cases, you might discover that just sharing your insecurities with others is a *huge* step in the right direction to shift to being self-secure. After sharing my worries, concerns, and anxieties with them, I'm grateful for others' help, support, and encouragement.

The next time I feel insecure about something, I will revisit my process of moving into recording videos and what I did to overcome that insecurity. Do I really need deep content expertise to get something done? Why is it important for someone "higher up" than me to approve of what I'm doing? Will people still follow me even if I'm doing it poorly — or not as well as my expectations desire?

What is something that you do well enough that others ask you for help with? What *else* do you do well that others might not know? Maybe you feel insecure about sharing your knowledge because you are not the expert, but you are really good at it. Consider sharing your expertise with others even if you aren't an expert. They will benefit by learning your story — because they will consider *you* an expert in that topic even if you don't look at yourself that way.

If you have a lot of trepidation about sharing something, try using a phrase like "You probably know this already, but I wanted to share this just in case you weren't aware." It is like saying you are insecure without using the words. And in most cases, the other person will acknowledge your offer to share.

Lastly, remember overcoming insecurity takes time, practice, and being messy.

CHILDLIKE

"(of an adult) having good qualities associated with a child."

Who wants to "stop acting like a child"? Not me...

18.

That's the age most countries recognize the shift of a child to becoming an adult. Often, the term is "young adult." How can you make the actual shift of becoming an adult while still retaining some of the best qualities of being a child?? What can you leverage as an adult from your childhood? Or what can you still enjoy as an adult that you enjoyed as a child?

Unfortunately, there is no one correct answer.

The transformation only happened when I was about 24 years old. I had been working at IBM for a few years but struggled. I felt as if I needed to be 100% "on" during the work day. I understood that having fun and enjoying yourself was for after work only — not *during* work. That wasn't IBM's formal statement in any way, but it's how I felt.

At times, the idea of "having fun at work" translated simply into childlike behaviors that would *not* be considered good qualities. For example, returning late from lunch, needing more sleep the night before a big meeting, and enjoying time with new friends from other IBM offices across the U.S. instead of studying for required exams during IBM training classes in Atlanta.

Though I had some fun times at IBM, it felt like I was either "all in on IBM" or "all in on having fun."

Once I left IBM, I moved to Chicago. I joined a company called COMSI — which was an IBM Business Partner. My manager partnered me with a more senior person at COMSI, Joe Post.

In this new role, I learned from Joe how to be very positively childlike. He showed me how to "gently" infuse some of the great qualities of my childlike personality into my day-to-day work. As a result, I was able to have fun while being professional with my colleagues, our business partners, existing customers, and potential new prospects.

Our boss loved a good story and often laughed in the office loudly enough for everyone to hear. I feel as if he thought laughing reduces stress and makes us more productive. Joe taught me how to have fun with our boss and get him to laugh out loud. Joe definitely liked to have fun — and encouraged me to take out our clients for fun as well. It helped me better understand how to mix fun and childlike behavior into my work.

More recently, Vips recommended that I read a book about Arsene Wegner — the coach of the Arsenal soccer club. My favorite quote from the book is, "*Retain your childlike soul and never lose sight of your dreams.*" His quote referenced a group of world-class athletes on an excellent soccer team in the best professional soccer league in the world. The coach wanted his players to be at their best professionally while still having fun in a childlike manner.

Looking back now, I'll share some thoughts about being childlike:

Experiment
Experiment with an audience of one other person. You can ask questions or demonstrate one of your childlike characteristics in the context of being a good adult. Gain the consensus of one other person that those great characteristics are positive. Joe was the person I experimented with earliest in work and the most often. For example, we took one of our clients out for an amazing dinner filled with laughter and great life stories. And NONE of the stories were about work.

Childlike

While I'd love to jump back into my world of being a ten-year-old and having a great time everywhere I go, I considered how to weave just one small childlike behavior into my daily routine at a time before going on to the next one. Instead of going all out into "full fun mode", I'd try something smaller as a mini-experiment to channel my inner child. To start, it was something simple, like sharing a funny story of something that happened to me over the weekend. It made my client laugh big time.

Observe

Observe what works for other adults in similar situations. Many people find the right balance of being a responsible adult while still having fun as if they were a child. Understand how others attend to this balance and use it for your development.

For example, Joe was a great mentor; in this case, he often exhibited childlike behaviors while extremely successful in business. He shared a story of playing a practical joke on one of his customers and how much he appreciated Joe's willingness to break away from the world of "formal business behavior."

I learned both are possible.

Fun

And remember the fun you had as a kid or the joy you see kids having *now*. Over the years, I've been pleasantly surprised to meet children who act more like adults than other adults. I'm spending time in that same situation.

Retaining your childlike qualities can also emanate from children exhibiting adult-like behaviors. I often daydream about fun times growing up and smile when I remember a story or event. And then ask myself — "How could I pull that off at work right now?". My brother and I used to race around my house and time ourselves in competition with each other on weekends. I've done that a few times with work colleagues on the way to grabbing coffee — "last one in line buys!".

If it makes you or someone else smile or laugh, it's probably OK as well. The world can sometimes seem so serious that retaining your childlike behavior is an excellent way to lighten that feeling. Look for feedback from others and lean into what works for you.

LESSON LEARNED

Whether you embrace the fun, curiosity, interest, intensity, or whatever from childhood, retain that childlike focus as an adult where everything can be about wonder and awe — and ENJOY IT! Just remember to apply it situationally but deliberately. There are still times when you need to be an adult, for example, I wouldn't exhibit childlike behaviors in a courtroom or at a memorial service, but at work, home, or other situations that seem slightly less serious, infusing childlike playfulness is usually disarming and good for everyone involved.

AMBITIOUS

"having or showing a strong desire and determination to succeed."

A dark blue, first-place ribbon.

I'm pretty sure that was my first reward for being successful or winning at something, and I've been relatively ambitious in my life ever since (but not for the ribbon)!

For most of my life, I've been driven to succeed and after I succeeded at something, I'd raise the bar and refocus on something new to accomplish. I'd apply a creative mix of problem-solving, building relationships, and thinking about the big picture to get something done.

But a recent New Year's resolution made me contemplate ambition more deeply.

How many New Year's Resolutions have you written down over the years? More importantly, how many resolutions did you intentionally *not* write down or strive to achieve because you were afraid you'd fail to accomplish them anyway?

In the fall of 2021, I wanted to focus on losing weight. While eating fairly well, I still hovered around my heaviest weight ever. By December 2021, I was emboldened to join the millions of people with the New Year's Resolution of *"I want to lose XXX pounds."* I seriously desired to be healthier and a bit lighter too!

As a goal setter and usually a goal achiever, I set a specific goal weight and began my journey with the *Whole30* diet plan. The first two weeks were great, but I had a weekend in the middle where I had a few cheats. One of the commitments of the *Whole30* plan is to stay 100% committed if you are genuinely going to be successful. So after my cheats over the weekend, I seriously considered giving up. But losing pounds was my ultimate goal, and I was determined to stay on the plan for the month's balance.

Some perfectionism started to creep in as I got closer to my goal. If I didn't achieve my goal, I'd be embarrassed to tell everyone I failed. And I'd be frustrated with myself for failing to achieve 100% of my stated objectives. I was worried that people wouldn't appreciate my effort and, by extension, me.

At the end of January 2022, I met a few other friends on the journey with me. We all celebrated our various victories and I realized that, while I still needed to reach my exact goal, I reaped many benefits through the process. While I was not perfect by any means, I completed the entire month, lost weight, felt healthier, slept better, and now I have a great eating plan for the future. Those accomplishments were my true measure of success. Hitting 95% of my original weight loss goal was excellent, and getting that extra 5% to reach 100% perfect wouldn't have changed anything.

My new mindset is to be ambitious and set my goals/objectives very high to push myself and realize that I can never get to 100% (i.e., perfectionism). Otherwise, the result is that I set my goals too low, reach "perfectionism," and don't truly accomplish anything. Now, I take pride in constantly improving without worrying about perfection.

I'm encouraging my same group of friends who met at the end of January 2022 to attempt another *Whole30* months before next January rolls around. Most people are concerned about sustaining their diet plan for a whole month — being perfect. So I've joked we should modify our goals to the Whole 25 or 27 or anything less than the full 30 because reaching 25 out of 30 days is *so much better* than reaching zero.

ENERGIZE

"give vitality and enthusiasm to."

What's your source of internal energy? Besides coffee, of course!

When I first joined ThinqShift, the founder liked to give us an unconventional but individually appropriate title. So part of my original title was *"Energizer."* I was enthusiastic about whatever I was doing. I also loved the idea of vitality. It fit me well, but where did that come from?

When I moved to Sleepy Hollow in fourth grade, I didn't know anyone in my new neighborhood. But I did know I loved baseball and quickly sought up like-minded kids interested in playing baseball on the weekend. But, of course, I'm dating myself here; we didn't have cell phones, social media, or other mobile electronic means of communication. The only "electronics" we could count on was hoping to connect with someone by calling them on a fixed landline and the only mobility was our feet — or, in my case, my bike.

My Saturday mornings in the summer usually consisted of calling my friends or their parents on the phone to ask if they could play some baseball. Mostly, though, I'd get on my bike and start riding around the neighborhood, completely ignorant of big hills and long rides, to get enough kids together to play baseball.

The "standard" baseball game consists of at least nine players on each team. We had 18–20 kids together at once a few times, but more often than not, we usually had fewer than two entire teams.

But I never let that stop us from having a fun time. We'd come up with creative rules and ways to engage — even if it ended up being a game of two versus two baseball games. My initial energy was invested in getting as many kids together as possible for however long as possible. But even more of my energy was focused on giving vitality and enthusiasm to whatever version of baseball we were playing at the time.

What was this energy all about? As I think about myself, the energy I expended getting everyone together provided a platform for me to reach some of my top six values (see my story called **Values** for more context):

1. I needed to leverage my friendships and *relationships* to get everyone together.
2. I was *optimistic* about our ability to develop a game.
3. My *confidence* and competitiveness while playing the game were omnipresent.

If I was on the losing side, my goal was to *persevere* and attempt to win the next time.

Next, we balanced the teams and played by a standard set of rules for *fairness.* And our time together was all about having *fun.*

I've let this state of enthusiasm flourish in all parts of my life. Whether I'm the first one up in the morning or the last one to stop doing something at the end of the day, I'm often the "energy" behind whatever the group is doing and it applies to me as an individual. I love the energy of doing something at the moment. But, most importantly, I've also learned how to channel this energy and more effectively "share it" with others who need it in the moment or over time.

LESSON LEARNED

There usually isn't just one thing that makes you happy and drives you to do more. However, discover at least one thing and let it "feed" you going forward. Don't worry about structure or process or lack of completeness. For me, it ended up being my values. For you, discover whatever gives you life and energy and bring more of it to bear upon yourself and others too!

PERCEPTION

"the ability to see, hear, or become aware of something through the senses."

Hmmm, but what if you don't have those senses?

One of my favorite movies is *Immortal Beloved* starring Gary Oldham. It's the story of the life and death of Ludwig van Beethoven. I always loved listening to his music — especially when I needed something calming and relaxing in the background while studying in college, working as an adult, or just relaxing at any age.

An orchestra usually conducted Beethoven's most classical pieces. For example, a smaller orchestra might be composed of 40–50 different instruments, while a much larger orchestra would be composed of 80–100 other instruments. Beethoven wrote music for each instrument in the orchestra, wove it all together seamlessly, and flawlessly conducted the performances.

I enjoy listening to many of his symphonies. Over and over again. I can hear the various instruments and how well they sound together. The complexity and integration of all of this are incredible. Beethoven's perception of how the music would sound to his audiences was unparalleled.

Did you know that Beethoven wrote several symphonies when he was primarily deaf? Huh? How do you compose something you can't even hear played to understand whether or not it works? That almost feels like riding a bike with no wheels or baking a cake without ingredients. Unbelievable.

Perception is all about using your senses to become aware of something. In Beethoven's case, he needed to focus on other senses, like seeing and writing musical notes or feeling the sound waves from the instruments as someone played his beautiful music.

Here are some other thoughts to expand your ability to perceive what is around you.

Senses

The definition of perception includes the senses, so let's start here. You might not be able to leverage all of your senses. Or, as in Beethoven's case, be able to use a specific sense. Learn how to "turn up the volume" with your other senses to make up for it. A person who is blind learns how to use their senses of touch, sound, and even smell to perceive and "see" where they happen to be. Beethoven could see the notes on the written page, "listen" to the music in his head and feel the music as it was played as the sound waves went through him.

Memory

Think about your previous experiences and any memories you have that might apply. You can increase your awareness of something by using past experiences as building blocks to understand better what you are attempting to perceive. Fortunately, Beethoven could leverage many of his previous works from memory to create many new and beautiful symphonies even after he began to lose his hearing.

Other People's Perceptions

Many times, you can leverage the experiences of others as well. Whether you ask someone for help understanding something or jump into your favorite channel on YouTube or TikTok, many sources of information help you improve your perception of something. For Beethoven, he used his own works but learned from the works of others to enhance his compositions.

Break It Down

If it is possible, break down your problem into smaller parts and then "weave" them back together again. It may be easier to perceive what you need with the smaller pieces and then become aware of the larger problem. In addition, you can use a specific sense on smaller component parts than you might with the whole. For example, Beethoven only wrote part of the symphony at a time, he wrote for one instrument and added a second, a third, and more.

I believe YOU will sense the 4–5 best ways to expand your perceptions going forward.

LESSON LEARNED

Start with your senses to perceive what's in front of you. Then, if possible, use all of your senses to "double-check" each other to confirm your understanding. And don't stop there. You can go beyond the senses to better understand what is confusing or unknown. Whether using your memory, other people's perceptions, breaking down a complex problem, or your new methods, come up with some ways to expand upon only using your senses to perceive everything around you.

FRUSTRATION

"the feeling of being upset or annoyed, especially because of inability to change or achieve something."

There are so many images in my mind right now about frustration. The most prominent is a cartoon image of someone with fire coming out of their head, smoke billowing from their nose, a siren emanating from their ears, and their face all puffy and red.

That's different from what I look like right now. But frustration is what I'm experiencing — literally *right* now as I try to write this very chapter of this very book you are reading.

For each chapter, my process varies a bit each time.

But here's the general flow I shared at the beginning of the book — and my frustration right now!

1. Pick an interesting word or topic (that gets boiled down to a single word). No initial frustration here, but actually finding the "right" word can be a challenge.

2. Take the time to figure out the first time I experienced that word. I go through many aspects of my life — growing up, college, early marriage days, having kids, travel, work experiences, community and neighborhood experiences, etc. Eventually, something comes to me that aligns nicely with the word/topic. This can be the most frustrating part of the process. When did I truly experience this for the first time?

3. Then I do my best to understand the storytelling aspect of my experience. What happened originally? What did I learn from the experience? How did I transform my thinking into a new paradigm? What were some of the thoughts or actions, or ideas I applied to solve those problems? This is also tough sometimes, as I need clarification on whether the transformation was immediate or happened over time.

4. Once I get through that, I boil everything down to a simple lesson learned. Most lessons come to me, but sometimes they feel like a repeat of the "other side" in my story transformation.

But what happens when I have a word that I can't synch up with a good story? I'd drop the word/topic a few times and come up with something else. Ironically, I couldn't give up the word frustration — yes, I got frustrated with frustration!

Okay — what did I do over the past few days to overcome my frustration?

Walk Away and Take a Break

I struggled for a long time over several days to come up with the "right" story. I tried a few but felt they needed to be more genuine. For some reason, I didn't want to give up on this word (see the **Perseverance** story). I kept taking breaks from this word and writing about other topics. It was helpful each time to shift my thinking to something else by taking a break.

Be Patient

Maybe it's just me, but I can't just give up. I knew I could come up with something if I were just patient. I've written about 60% of my chapters thus far and was confident that serendipity would come into play.

Plant That Memory

Once you overcome something, it's essential to plant the memory of the feeling of overcoming something frustrating. I could think about other times when I might have been frustrated and remembered the feeling I got from overcoming that challenge, the lessons learned for getting past it, or the extraordinary new ideas that came out of it. In any case, I think the *huge* smile on my face when I figured out this chapter is my frustration!

Iterations Help Too

What did I want to achieve writing this? But I kept having to remind myself that I'll keep iterating. I'm not worried that my first draft is rough or might get thrown out. I pressed myself to finish the first version, knowing I'd continually iterate on it. Is this chapter now how version one looked? Not. Even. Close.

Change the Process

Sometimes, I would start with the lessons learned. Other times I would dig through the definition in great detail. The most impactful process change was to think about and write the story first — and then pair it up with a word!

You can overcome frustration in a variety of ways. Do your best to be thoughtful about what works for you, and weave in one or two of these lessons.

LESSON LEARNED

Bottom line — I'm not saying don't be frustrated. Instead, I suggest you look for a positive side to every negative experience. Figure out what you can control, don't get in your own way, and look at the big picture while enjoying the journey. The five ideas I shared about my annoyances might be a great starting point for dealing with your frustrations.

SIMPLIFY

"make (something) simpler or easier to do or understand."

KISS = Keep It Simple Stupid. I still need to do this more often.

When Cole was in kindergarten, I worked on a team with my colleagues engaging with Boeing. At the time, we were working on the 787 program — Boeing's newest airplane at the time. The company I worked for had software that helped manage the full lifecycle development process for complex items like an airplane. This version of a Boeing airplane had over 2.3 million parts. That's a lot of stuff to manage!

Much of our role was to help the individual engineers across the Boeing 787 program understand how our software could be used to make their jobs become more efficient. There were numerous opportunities to make something complex more simple. But simple to an adult (using a Phillips-head screwdriver to tighten a screw), who in this case also happened to be a tenured Boeing engineer, is very different from simple to a five-year-old (who might not understand whether to use a nail or screw, what tool to use, which direction to tighten a screw, etc.).

I didn't realize how much I needed to simplify my explanations until I attended a version of "bring your dad to work" day with Cole. How would I simplify everything I got paid to do during the day into something my son and all his classmates would easily understand?

Use an Analogy They Understand

For me, I had the perfect "cheat code." Since I was doing work supporting the actual Boeing 787, I bought a Lego model of the Boeing 787 for my sons to build. Together, they pieced the whole thing, which, to my good fortune, was NOT made up of 2.3 million Lego pieces. So when I told Cole's class about helping Boeing engineers build a 787, I said it was as if I was in this classroom and giving them some directions about how to put their Lego pieces together to form a car or building or whatever they were creating.

Get Visual

Not everyone prefers a visual representation of something, but it's often helpful. For example, I asked how many students had ridden or at least seen an airplane. Almost everyone raised their hands. I suggested they close their eyes and imagine what a plane looked like without wings and that I help

Boeing stick the wings on the side of the plane. That's different from how it really worked, but the kids understood.

Break It Down Into Minor Parts

One of the most effective ways to make things easier for someone to understand is by breaking up a larger, more complex object into smaller parts. I'm doing precisely that with this book — making each story one to three pages and adding succinct lessons learned for each story. Speaking to Cole's class was the same. I had someone sit in the teacher's chair and talk about a seat on the airplane as the focal point of what we were helping Boeing build instead of focusing on the entire aircraft.

Refrain From Assuming YOU Know What Is Simple Versus Being Complicated or Complex

It is up to your audience to decide what is and isn't simple. To the Boeing engineer who worked on the 747 program years earlier, a smaller plane like the 787 might seem simple. When explaining things to Cole's class, I continually asked questions to clarify their understanding. Most of them had flown or seen an airplane. And they knew the differences between the wings and the engine. So I could understand what their perspective of simplicity was and explain my work in terms they would understand.

Keep It Short

If you force yourself to be succinct and concise, you'll discover no other option but to simplify what you share. Some examples would be to tell a story in one paragraph, create a slide deck using only one slide, pretend you have an elevator ride of thirty seconds to explain something to another person, or try explaining something without taking a breath. Anything to keep it short and sweet will likely be simple.

LESSON LEARNED

Analogies. Visuals. Smallest parts. No assumptions. Short. There are many strategies for taking something from complex to complicated to easy in order to simplify just about anything.

Chapter 3

Work so hard you can teach others how

For me, it was my journey with vulnerability and transparency. This happened over the years with a lot of work individually. In the early days of my vulnerability journey, I was too embarrassed to admit that I was trying to be more vulnerable. So I pushed myself hard to work on this daily, weekly, monthly, and it happened through many different perspectives — phone calls, working on my own, in-person discussions, self-study, etc.

I made a lot of mistakes but kept trying to improve. In my younger years, I was nervous about sharing my flaws or mistakes, or challenges I didn't know how to overcome. Now, as someone focused on serving others like a teacher might do with students, I'm in a position with the people I support where I can share my journey with others and help them discover their path toward vulnerability and transparency. When I share my own mistakes or challenges, it makes it easier for others to share with me, and then we co-create solutions to help them address those issues

FREUDENFREUDE

"The lovely enjoyment of another person's success."

Schadenfreude means joy over some harm or misfortune suffered by another. That just sucks in most situations. I'm focused on its opposite, freudenfreude, for this story.

I discovered these words recently while reading Brené Brown's book *Atlas of the Heart*. I did spend a little time pondering what type of people would find joy in the misfortune of others. And maybe we all do this at times. For example, I wouldn't be too sad if a wide receiver dropped a wide-open touchdown pass while playing against my favorite football team.

However, the fun part of reading *Atlas of the Heart* was pondering all the good about freudenfreude. Most of the time, I find much joy or pleasure when someone else is successful. I love to share my appreciation and respect for what they accomplished and I encourage them to continue to enjoy their good fortune.

When I thought further about freudenfreude, I came up with some roles where I've been able to encourage or accelerate that state of being for others. These are great examples of where you can easily find joy in someone else's success in a role versus focusing solely on whether or not YOU are happy in a similar role.

As a Father

When my boys were younger, it was "easy" to enjoy their success nearly daily; there were so many "firsts." The smiles and joy from taking their first steps, getting their driver's license, or being accepted at college made me the proverbial "Proud Papa." And so many of their "failures" that led to many extraordinary accomplishments generated even more freudenfreude. I'm sad that I mostly enjoy my sons' successes from a distance now, since they are both working on their own successes as young adults, but I'm still smiling. At the same time, I recall how often my sons or their friends and classmates discovered a state of freudenfreude while celebrating each other's growth into the young adults they are today.

As a Coach

My coaching career started with tee-ball, basketball, soccer, lacrosse, and more — coaching my sons and their friends. At that level, coaching is easily

90%+ about freudenfreude, and the feedback is incredible. I'm incredibly competitive and love to win, but the smiles I received after seeing a child make their first shot in a basketball game or the cheers from another child scoring their first goal at a soccer match were priceless.

As a Mentor

One of my employers was heavily invested in the idea of a formal mentor program internally. I usually took on the maximum number of mentees to support their growth and development. There are always areas of improvement to focus on and developmental gaps to fill. The best part of being a mentor was diving into freudenfreude with a mentee and celebrating their behavior or mindset shifts in the context of their development. Whether I had the opportunity to share a client's positive feedback on a deliverable my mentee was responsible for or share my excitement with them when they received a promotion, freudenfreude is contagious.

As a ThinqShifter

I'm grateful in my role today at ThinqShift to experience freudenfreude as we help our clients improve their performance, overcome blockers and grow their personal power. I'm always thrilled when someone tells me about something new they attempted or a simple "Ah-Ha" moment they received from a coaching session and how it helped them shift forward. Insert more freudenfreude smiles here!

As a Friend

I often discuss the importance of relationships and networking. When I'm with my friends, I try to understand what's present for them and how they feel. For example, the other day, a friend told me how happy they were after seeing smiles on their daughter's face during college drop-off duty. Sharing a state of freudenfreude with a close friend is a blast.

As a Human on Planet Earth

While I most often experience freudenfreude through the lens of my friends and family, one of my (almost) daily practices is to experience that same feeling with someone I don't know. Whether on social media or television or stories from friends or work colleagues, I love to hear or read about some of the amazing accomplishments of others worldwide. Whether you know them or not, the pleasure or joy you derive from someone else's success or achievement is easily 100 times more powerful than any joy you might gain from someone not doing well.

DAUNTING

"seeming difficult to deal with in anticipation; intimidating."

Standing at the edge of a high dive that's probably 20 feet but seems like 100 feet is another definition of daunting.

When I think about something daunting, it all goes back to Omaha, Nebraska.

I was working for a small software company - InterTrans Logistics. The founder of the company and I were scheduled to meet with 20–25 executives of a Fortune 500 company in Omaha. We were coming from different directions and planned to meet in the afternoon before this important meeting the next day. I landed first and arrived at my hotel late afternoon.

I waited. And I waited. And I waited some more. Finally, around dinner time, I received a phone call from the founder. He wasn't going to make it. Many of these company executives from the Fortune 500 company flew in from other parts of the country for this meeting — and they weren't going to reschedule this meeting just because my company's founder couldn't make it. So I'd be doing this meeting on my own.

One versus twenty-five is a difficult situation to deal with.

In spite of the confident *"you will do fine"* speech from the founder, I was still freaking out a bit. But once I calmed down, here's what I did to overcome this daunting situation.

Serenity

Spending any more time worrying about being alone wasn't valuable. As I hung up the phone, I spent the next half hour or so reaching a state of serenity. In the big picture of life, whatever happens at that meeting won't impact my time on this planet. In fact, it may go so well that I'll write a story about it someday! (hehe)

Get Busy

My next step was to figure out what I needed to do that the founder was planning to cover. And at the same time, I remember everything I was planning to do as well. I quickly got busy practicing his parts and got myself up to the same level with the portions of the meeting I was going to handle already.

Flow

Once I had a sense of everything I needed to do, I reconsidered the overall flow of the meeting. What needs to change since I'm all alone? Or, is there a better way to organize the schedule given the change in circumstances? Thinking about the steps helped me reaffirm I was ready for the day.

Others

Since the founder wasn't there with me, I wondered who else might help me before or during the meeting. I spoke with one of my peers late that night, who answered a few last-minute questions. And there was a great "internal champion" among those 20–25 company executives who I asked to help me during a few parts of the meeting. Lastly, the founder did call me early the following day for one last pep talk. There are usually others to get involved with to make something less daunting.

Go

Many things seem intimidating in anticipation of the actual event. I was actually ready to go later that night and couldn't wait until the following day. I was anxious to get into action and move forward. When the meeting did start, I was definitely ready to go.

The meeting itself went well. Our internal sponsor was extremely happy with our meeting and, even though it's always great to be joined by your founder or top company executive in a meeting, you can survive the process of being alone.

No matter how daunting it seems at the time.

As I think about other daunting scenarios I've faced in my lifetime, some or all of these steps can easily be applied to almost any other situation. That high dive, for example.

1. **Serenity:** Deep breath to calm myself.
2. **Get busy:** Think positively about those 2–3 seconds in the air.
3. **Flow**: My plan? Take one more breath. Jump. Pull arms in. Keep my feet down. Hold my breath.
4. **Others**: Ask my friend for any other last-minute advice.
5. **Go**: Juuummmpppp!

LESSON LEARNED

A lot of situations in your life seem daunting before you try them. Use these steps to shift something that seems intimidating in advance to something that seems much easier to approach after some contemplation. Or take some time to consider what information you need, the vision you'd like to have, or a process you might discover that assists your ability to overcome something daunting.

A lot of situations in your life seem daunting before you try them. Use these steps to shift something that seems intimidating in advance to something that seems much easier to approach after some contemplation.

PRIDE

"a feeling of deep pleasure or satisfaction derived from one's own achievements, the achievements of those with whom one is closely associated, or from qualities or possessions that are widely admired."

Another definition for pride?
Watching a child walk down the aisle for graduation. Wow!

I always thought I had a good idea of what pride meant. I was proud of some of my achievements over the years, or something I had acquired that was unique and I've been proud of many others — my sons, kids I coached, friends, neighbors, relatives, etc. but I didn't feel the impact of pride until I watched my oldest son Ryan walk down the aisle at his college graduation.

At that moment, I understood more deeply what pride was all about and, over the few days that followed, when I had several opportunities to spend some quality one-on-one time with Ryan, my pride for him and his accomplishments grew exponentially. I'll share some examples before I delve into my "after" regarding pride.

Dealing With VUCA

In my role at ThinqShift, I'm supporting seasoned executives through their versions of VUCA (volatility, uncertainty, complexity, and ambiguity). Ryan and his friends had to deal with a pandemic, wars around the world, political strife in the United States, social disruption at many levels, and more — all while focusing on getting through their classes (and many online). Yet, he found the right combination of perseverance, inner strength, and drive to overcome non-stop VUCA while ending up in the top five percent of his class. Amazing.

Personal AND Work/School

Many executives and rising young stars deal with many challenges of work-life integration and Ryan's senior capstone project combined both seamlessly. He showed me a product he created to help young adults (or anyone) deal with their mental health. He combined his four years of experience in Environmental Design/Product Design with personal observations of mental health awareness to deliver an incredible product that will appear on Amazon someday!

Looking Forward and Backward

Ryan is reflecting upon his years at Boulder while at the same time looking forward to the next phase in his career journey. He's excited about his first full-time job but still retains fond memories of his college experience. Unfortunately, many tend to focus on one much more than the other when a solid balance between short-term tactical thinking is best balanced with a longer-term strategic perspective.

And the definition of pride I included above grants a great way to breakdown pride:

One's Achievements

Any time I saw something impressive that Ryan or Cole would accomplish growing up, I would tell them how proud I was. Over time, I shifted my thinking to suggest they should be proud of themselves or their accomplishments. As they established their sense of independence, I wanted them to realize the importance of being proud of themselves — beyond my own parental pride, which was natural.

The Achievements of Others

As I shared above, I was often very proud of my sons. But I've also been proud of so many others over the years. The energy and passion that gets transferred from one person to another in that acknowledgment of their accomplishments are palpable. But your pride in others' achievements must also be super genuine to be felt by the other party.

Qualities or Possessions

The definition notes something being "widely admired." You can definitely be proud of something you own or a quality about yourself. But I'm afraid I have to disagree that they need to be "widely admired." I derive a ton of satisfaction from many items in my place — whether it's a letter from a dear friend, something I discovered on a hike during my travels around the globe, or something I purchased that brings me (and others) joy.

My transformation relative to pride is how to shift from feelings I experience to encouraging others to experience their sense of feeling about something. Think about how you feel when you have a strong sense of pride. What an amazing gift to give to someone else by letting them know they should be proud of something at that moment.

LESSON LEARNED

Pride is a great feeling to experience, and you can generate it from a nearly unlimited number of physical or emotional sources, whether it's something for yourself or others. Pride is something you can experience anytime — think about your recent accomplishments or the accomplishments of others, enjoy the satisfaction then give some of it to others as well.

OBSERVATION

"the action or process of observing something or someone carefully or in order to gain information."

My immediate thought goes back to the first telescope I used to observe the moon and stars. How about you?

Growing up, my parents often took my brother and me on sightseeing trips. We could be in nature, visiting cities, museums, or just about anything. We lived in Ohio and Michigan for the first decade of my life. But at around ten years old, we moved to Illinois. On the surface, it was another midwest town (Sleepy Hollow) surrounded by a lot of cornfields and little towns as neighbors.

We still took some fun trips to see lakes or forest preserves and some longer road trips back to see friends and family in Michigan or Ohio. There were always fun stops along the way — though I've never seen the world's largest ball of twine. Instead, I've seen lakes that seem like an ocean (Lake Michigan), sand dunes that feel like a desert (Indiana Dunes), and a street 103 stories below your feet (Sears/Willis Tower in Chicago).

The first time I felt the full visual impact of these journeys was my first trip to downtown Chicago — before I had even turned eleven years old. Wow! Huge buildings. Lake Michigan. The Chicago River. Grant Park. Field Museum (Natural History). Shedd Aquarium. Adler Planetarium. All within a quick drive or slightly longer walk. Stunning. My eyes couldn't take it in fast enough.

And I really wanted to learn more about *everything* I was seeing. How tall was the Sears Tower? How many bones were in that T-Rex? How many fish were in the center of the aquarium? And once I had those answers, I asked even more questions as I dug in further. I observed as much as I possibly could during each of those encounters.

I'm grateful for the opportunity to have traveled outside of the United States many times, too — including an excellent adventure to Italy.

As I prepared for my time in Italy, I not only read about the journey and sights our family was going to see, but I also read several books about Leonardo da Vinci. I'm a huge fan of Leonardo da Vinci, so when I read about how he approached the world of observation, I was intrigued, and it prompted a recall of my lessons learned about the power of observation.

His list is in bold with my description of each:

Be Curious — Question Everything
Actively listen and absorb the answers/content intently. Then ask more questions and be even more curious. In your travels, many other people — whether travel guides, locals, or friends who have been there before — are often willing to share their perspectives with you.

Retain a Childlike Sense of Wonder
In too many situations, we start to lose our sense of the questions we might ask as a child. As a father, it's been an incredible journey to see the world through the eyes of my children at all ages. I wonder if I would have done a great job of retaining my childlike sense of wonder if not having experienced the opportunity to look at so many things differently with my boys through the years.

Observe
Be aware of everything around you — whether people or objects or animals. Just take in everyday life as often as possible. To me, this amounts to truly being present.

Get Distracted
Some of my most creative thinking happens when I'm not focused on solving a particular problem. Maybe I'm taking my dogs for a long walk, attempting some quiet meditation, or even showering! Getting distracted from the immediate challenge your brain is dealing with is not an intuitive

strategy but an incredibly valuable method to observe something from a different perspective.

Respect Facts

In today's society, many people solely search for information that confirms their thinking. Imagine the power behind having an open mind, asking questions, listening passionately, and seeking out new information to develop incredible new ideas. Chasing facts — especially ones you weren't aware of previously — is a noble approach.

Collaborate

I have to give full credit to Walter Isaacson for his comments about Leonardo's many examples of being collaborative — "Genius starts with individual brilliance. It requires a singular vision. But executing it often entails working with others. Innovation is a team sport. Creativity is a collaborative endeavor." Relationships for life — just sayin'.

Make Lists

My to-do lists include items I need to accomplish one time in a day or consistently over weeks, months, and even years. My lists have some crazy ideas that I came up with by observing, being curious, and asking many questions.

I've been gone from Illinois and my proximity to downtown Chicago for more than a quarter century, but I've still been downtown easily 150–200 times since then. I'll continue to observe and dig in further about something new every time. Take the two-hour architectural tour of downtown Chicago from the boats on the river if you want to learn more about the power and value of observation. And if you've observed everything in Chicago or another city you deeply enjoy, head just outside of that city to explore the suburbs or nearby cities to observe even more.

LESSON LEARNED

More than anything, be curious unless you aren't interested in learning and improving your understanding of the world around us. In addition to being curious, I like the idea of being intentional about what you are observing. Challenge yourself to observe something you've seen dozens or even hundreds of times more deeply, and you'll find something new. When you can observe everything through the lens of da Vinci's list above, you will know you are truly a master observer and advise others on the art of deliberate observation.

Careful observation is an amazing gift you can leverage immediately.

TRANQUILITY

"the quality or state of being tranquil; calm."

Somehow I knew that was my last deep discussion with my father.

My mom called me about a week earlier. My dad was taken to the hospital, and they weren't sure how much time he had. As I figured out how to get back to Illinois to see him, my mom called me again to say the doctors and nurses gave him weeks or more to live. I had enough time to arrange flights for myself and the boys to return to Illinois within the week.

One son was coming from Boulder, and the other one was with me, flying in from Seattle. We met at the airport after all taking red-eye flights. Exhausted, we grabbed a rental car and drove directly to the hospital.

In the days from that first phone call from my mom, things progressively got more difficult for Dad. One of the reasons we took the red-eye flights out was the original estimate of weeks to live was now down to days to live.

My mom was already at the hospital, and my brother Michael had driven back home the day earlier with his two kids. So we arrived early that morning and felt like everything was non-stop; at least, it was for me. There were many decisions to make quickly — both for my father and my mother. I didn't want my mom to have to bear being the one making difficult decisions at this time, so I was getting pulled from doctor to nurse to doctor again — all while trying to see my father and tell him that I love him.

At one point, my father was clearly delirious and not making sense. More importantly, I could tell the boys were doing what they could to calm him down, but nothing was working. I broke away from the doctors and went into my dad's room.

I grabbed my dad's hand, looked him in the eye, and asked him, "*Where would you like your ashes to be spread?*". That question broke his chain of thought. He spent the next hour or more, prompted with my questions, sharing some of the most important places in his life — all against the context that I'd eventually spread his ashes there.

As I think back to that moment, I want to break down everything I did to help my dad reach his state of tranquility — which might be helpful for you at some future time:

Connection
We established a physical connection by grabbing my dad's hand. That sense of touch helped him to understand that I was with him physically.

Direct Eye Contact
I looked directly into my dad's eyes and maintained direct eye contact during most of that intense hour.

Preempted
I refocused his thought process on another subject when I interrupted his statements with a few direct questions. Instead of letting him control the situation, I took control of the discussion.

Positive
What I chose to focus on was a positive story for him. He would be sharing some amazing stories with me regarding where to spread some of his ashes, and he also got to share stories about his life with his two grandsons.

Modeling
I also attempted to model a sense of calmness and tranquility. He began to calm down quickly and followed my pattern of behavior.

There is no happy ending — other than the fact I helped my dad reach his state of tranquility after long periods of confusion and frustration. But, unfortunately, Dad passed away less than 12 hours after that amazing storytelling hour with his grandsons and me. And if there is some sliver of happiness in that story, I got to say "*Goodbye*" to my father, and my sons had the chance to do the same with their Grandpa.

Somehow I knew that was my last deep discussion with my father.

LESSON LEARNED

Tranquility is a state worth achieving — on a daily basis, if possible. Leverage some of the lessons above, or build out some of your own to better enable your own state of tranquility. What better way to practice than to help others reach their own state of tranquility?

OVERWHELM

"bury or drown beneath a huge mass."

Think about the images associated with overwhelm. Hundreds of feet under water with no way up. Someone buried alive and covered with tons of dirt. Some large, amorphous blob that consumes everything in its path.

When I first thought about writing a book, the image that popped into my head was someone buried in a stack of books, piles of papers, broken pens and pencils strewn about, and an office where you couldn't even see the floor. The first few three–four page articles I published on LinkedIn took me anywhere from four–six hours to fully flesh out. How in the hell would I write a whole book if I couldn't get through a single article without feeling overwhelmed?

Over time, I started to publish shorter and more succinct posts. And even added the concept of video posts. Eventually, I realized I had over 100 stories… then over 150 stories. The math started to make sense; one story of 2–3 pages times 100+ stories equals a 250-300 page book.

Other than my "math equation" above, here are some other perspectives I took that helped me "solve" the feeling of overwhelm as I started to dive in and write this book.

Baby Steps

When I look at everything I need to accomplish, I quickly get overwhelmed by the feeling this will never happen because I'm too busy across many other areas of my life. Then I focus on taking a single step (writing one story, rewriting another, identifying a new one, etc) each day and moving forward — no matter how slowly, and if I take TWO baby steps, even better!

Five-Year Plan

One of the frequent processes I explore with my coaching clients is to look at a five-year plan across various aspects of their lives and the energy/focus needed to accomplish their goals. One step in the process is to visualize what you look and feel after accomplishing your goals five years later. Then, when you think about your five year goals, it is easier to visualize what it looks like to order the book on Amazon.com six months from today's overwhelm.

Redefine Failure

Most of my thoughts or feelings about failure relate to my concerns about *"what if the book is horrible?"* or *"what if no one reads it?"* or *"what if no one really cares about these lessons learned — including my two sons?"*. My current thinking includes *all* of those concerns — and many more — but I'm shifting my definition of failure into *"not* writing the book at all." Then I visualize the book on Cole's bookshelf and take another baby step towards writing.

Remember the Fun, Get Amnesia With the Struggles

There are many blocks of time when I get into a total groove and am just having fun. When I struggle, I try to remember the fun stories I've written. And I realize I might just throw out the stories where I struggled. Who knows? Just one fun memory usually outweighs the two–three struggles I sometimes need to overcome.

Define and Celebrate the Little Victories

I've been carving out three or four 60-minute blocks of time to write. Sometimes I'll get done with four or five better stories. Other times it's a struggle to write one or two stories. In either case, I define my "victory" as putting in three to four hours and celebrating that fact.

Maybe this chapter might not seem so overwhelming when I finish my writing. But right now, I'm preparing to hold my breath in case the water I see in Lake Union floods me.

LESSON LEARNED

Like many feelings, part of my growth has been to create awareness of what I'm feeling and remember how I've previously dealt with those feelings. I'll accept the feelings I'm experiencing and put a plan into action about how to deal with them so life is less overwhelming and whatever I'm doing doesn't feel like a "huge mass."

The perspectives I shared above to get through my book-writing process can be used to make just about anything feel much less overwhelming.

CONTENTMENT

"a state of happiness and satisfaction."

For Linus (of Peanuts fame), contentment seems to be a warm blanket. What brings you contentment?

At first, I wasn't sure why I felt so happy and satisfied to kick off the new year. In the course of a week in early January, several friends said that I seemed more "calm, relaxed, and content" than the last time we connected. They noticed my change in demeanor virtually through several Zoom calls versus being in person with them. How did others notice so suddenly that I had peace, tranquility, happiness, appreciation, and satisfaction in such a more obvious way? And when did I shift?

My overall transformation in reaching my own state of contentment occurred over several instances during the week I spent over the holidays with my mom for Christmas 2021 and I've aligned each little story with a word present for me on my overall journey to contentment during that hectic week.

Peace

When I was in Chicago over the holidays, I took my mom to dinner to celebrate her 58th anniversary. And three days later, we attended Christmas Eve service — her first live Christmas church celebration since my dad passed away a few years earlier. It was very sad without my father by our sides for dinner, Christmas Eve service, or the holidays overall. But we were both at peace and quite content as the church service closed with "Silent

Night." Somehow that time with my mom quietly missing my dad gave me some peace. And even my mom was content.

Satisfaction

Unlike Mick and the Stones, I'm getting a LOT of satisfaction across many aspects of my life. My expectations are more realistic, and I'm grateful for many "small things." Life is still hard with the ever-changing conditions of the pandemic and the typical challenges we all face in our lives, but I try to find something to be grateful for multiple times daily — the sun breaking out from the clouds, my dog wagging her tail when she sees me after a long Zoom call or an unexpected text or email from a good friend. Little things everywhere can bring you satisfaction — just keep your eyes open. At church that evening, I recalled many of these little instances to be grateful for over the past few months and how just a little satisfaction contributes to contentment.

Tranquility

Singing "Silent Night, Holy Night" with my mom in the church that night was one of the most tranquil moments in my life. Earlier in the service, the pastor acknowledged that my father was no longer with us. By this point, he's been gone for several years. For whatever reason, the combination of thinking of my dad, being in church with my mom, singing "Silent Night" with everyone, and just being happy in the moment all hit me at once. Content, for sure.

Appreciation

Even a brief time with my sons on Christmas evening after that excellent Christmas Eve service was amazing. They have so much on their plate — experiencing life in college while juggling the challenges of the pandemic, social media, racial injustice, and more is incredibly difficult for young adults. I greatly appreciate how tranquil they seem and how their "enoughness" exuded from each of them during our time together. I can't imagine being as calm, cool, and collected when I was their age. I'm biased as their father, but I was so appreciative of the young adults they've grown into that I observed that evening. Appreciation for others also leads to contentment for yourself.

Happiness

All of this happened as 2021 was coming to an end. On many levels, 2021 was one of my most difficult years personally, professionally, and more. On the flight home, I thought beyond the challenges of 2021 and focused on everything that formed my happiness overall. It was a meditative flight, and I probably had a smile on my face the entire time. Happiness is something that is always with me — even through a rough 2021. There is obviously a good reason that happiness is also part of the definition of contentment and satisfaction.

Whether attending a church service, spending time outside, or relaxing without distraction at home, I hope you can find some activity or experience to help you reach your own levels of contentment.

LESSON LEARNED

We always seem to want more than we have — money, time, relationships, love, or anything else. Take some time to understand your state of contentment or what you need to reach that state. It's calming and probably better than any medicine any doctor could prescribe for you. I hope that some or all of the suggestions above contribute to reaching your own state of contentment.

FORMATIVE

"serving to form something, especially having a profound and lasting influence on a person's development."

Where did you spend your formative years?

Mine were in Illinois — where I started school in fourth grade, continued through high school graduation, stayed in state for school at the University of Illinois, and even remained for my first job with IBM.

It wasn't until I started formally mentoring and coaching others to better understand their formative years that I started to understand the importance of my own formative years. Now I have a much greater appreciation for that time in Illinois. I'm grateful for the many people who influenced me positively — Mom, Dad, teachers, parents, friends, coaches, significant others, etc. — and helped me develop my passions, values, interests, and dreams.

There are certainly many different ways to evaluate and learn more about your formative years.

Here are a few statements or questions that might serve as a guide:

Please Put Your Phone Down for a Minute, and Let's Talk.

Communication is all about how you relate to other people. It can be as specific as how you create posts on Instagram or "talk" via text messaging. Or it can be more general about whether you attempt to call one of your friends or visit them in person.

Another perspective is whether you communicate differently with different people in your life. You might communicate differently with a teacher or a parent than with one of your friends or your sibling's friends. Your location at the time is another influence. How you interact with your friends at a party will vary greatly from how you might engage with a teacher in class or your coach of one of your teams on the practice or game field. Lastly, consider how you communicate your own intentions and actions.

My communication skills were growing exponentially because I was learning to speak to many different types of people about an expanding set of topics through a rapidly developing phase across multiple communication channels.

Do you do what you say you will do? Do you think about how you will complete your chores and homework over the weekend while still carving out time to spend with your friends? Given the prevalence of social media and the many ways to absorb and share information today, I can imagine the challenges young adults face today are very different from what I faced back then, like how long the phone cord was and whether it can stretch into another room to have a private conversation. Learning how to effectively communicate is incredibly impactful throughout your life.

Some evenings my parents couldn't get me off the phone because I loved talking to my friends between homework assignments at night.

Can You Think Like a Rocket Scientist?

There's a great book called *The Seven Secrets of How to Think Like a Rocket Scientist*. The book is about problem-solving and how some of the best scientists in the world come up with amazing solutions to land a man on the moon or send probes to the outer reaches of our galaxy. To **dream** is about thinking big and seeking to understand what seems impossible.

When you **judge**, you narrow your scope into something doable by experimenting and weighing myriad possibilities.

At some point, it is important to **ask** even more questions of yourself and others to diagnose and understand what is truly possible.

Eventually, you need to **check** for alternatives to understand your own assumptions and any possible risks.

Then you should **simplify** your thinking into something tangible and the most likely path to a creative solution to your challenging problem.

To **optimize** your solution, you should gather additional feedback and perspective and clarify that you are solving the problem most effectively.

Finally, you need to pull everything together and *do* what you say you will do. Whether the problem is something to be solved in the next few minutes or might take years to figure out, this is a pretty good way to break down the bigger picture into something more digestible.

How Do You Manage Your to-Do List?

One year for Christmas, I gave everyone in the family a book called *Eat That Frog*. The book addresses how to evaluate everything you need to do, prioritize the activities and stop procrastinating to get it all done. How do these teenagers/young adults get so much done on the weekend?

My high school years involved balancing a to-do list that included homework, after-school sports, work, talking to friends, having fun, and more.

Kids today find a way to balance their chores at home, spend time with friends, delve into sports, experiment with arts and science, do their homework, get some sleep, eat their meals, and still find time to stream shows or simply text or talk on their phones. They figure out how much homework they have and what's needed on the weekend to finish everything by Monday morning. And while they might devise a great plan for the weekend, it might rain when they want to cut the grass or be outside with friends. The result is a change in plans to get something else done.

My observation is that many teenagers and young adults have also embraced thinking about others by adding community service or caring about others to their to-do lists. Parents or other adults need to help teenagers focus on short-term tasks with specific deadlines (take out the garbage before it gets picked up on Monday morning) as well as with their long-term goals (study for the ACT later in the year or plan out your class schedule for next spring).

Teenagers and young adults often do a great job of managing multiple activities. Forming your own process improvements of completing something or many things is what I figured out in my formative years.

How Do You Work With Others?

I often coached others in high school and extracurricular sports who weren't as skilled as I was — helping them improve how to play defense on the basketball court or hit a baseball more effectively against a difficult curveball.

There are many opportunities to help others — especially those less experienced or younger than yourself. Sports have been a great lens for me to observe how teenagers and/or young adults help others. The captains of our high school lacrosse team frequently helped other lacrosse players acclimate to the team — whether working with experienced yet younger players or older players who may have never played lacrosse growing up.

Another observation is how teenagers interact with their friends' younger siblings, and those parents frequently state how helpful a young adult/ teenager is for their younger children. I assume that most parents are not looking forward to the day their child moves out to live on their own, but I'm very confident in their ability to grow into amazing young adults simply by observing how they are coaching and mentoring others across many different aspects of their life.

We are always around other people, and developing ways to positively support and engage with others is a great habit/trait to formulate.

What Are You Up to Tonight?

There are so many possible connections for young adults today that it's nearly impossible to keep track of who is doing what and where, and when. It's great to see how teenagers can leverage communications to effectively connect with their friends. And if they are doing something new, I always enjoy the "sales pitch" of why it should be OK to stay out later or drive a bit farther than they have previously.

Openness, honesty, and trustworthiness are all important characteristics of teenagers as they quickly develop into fine young adults. And it all leads to making great connections early in life that impact you forever.

As the new kid moving into the neighborhood in fourth grade, I quickly learned how to connect with others around me in sports, school, neighborhood, church, and more.

It takes time to mentally "explore" your past to discover some lessons learned during your formative years. For example, I didn't realize my passion for helping others on my baseball or basketball team would be connected to my desire to help others today through leadership services.

Knowing that connection has helped me foster my growth and development across various areas of my life.

LESSON LEARNED

Many aspects of my early developmental years still impact me today. Communication, problem-solving, process improvement, mentoring, coaching others, and connections are core strengths I developed before becoming an adult. Knowing what benefited me in those early years, and still does today, helps me to improve those strengths, identify gaps to enhance them further, and create an awareness of new strengths to build upon going forward.

Think back to your formative years to understand the evolution of your strengths and passions. I share these and others with many of my coaching clients, and I hope you'll also share yours to serve others.

JOURNEY

"an act of traveling from one place to another."

I used to think a journey was only about physical travel, but it is so much more than that.

Maps. The United States. Illinois. Ohio. Michigan. Washington. I picked up several copies of each and cut them up, writing all over them, pasting them on top of each other, ripping them apart, and pasting them back together to understand all forms of my journey.

Okay, let me backtrack a minute. Pariveda Solutions offered an eight-week sabbatical after working with the company for at least five years. Given that we could add another chunk of personal vacation time to the sabbatical, I decided to create an 11-week sabbatical the summer before Ryan went to college at the University of Colorado in Boulder. Roughly a week before my last day of work for 11 weeks, the leader of our office took us through an amazing exercise. Every VP on her leadership team had just 15 minutes on a whiteboard to "tell our story." The idea was to get to know each other even more deeply than we might know each other as VPs in our Seattle office.

One colleague drew out their story as a timeline, with others doing bullet points with subsections under each. It hit me as I struggled to consider *how* to tell my story. Maps. I've moved several times in my life, and it made sense to me suddenly to tell my story based on where I was.

As I shared my own story and heard the stories of others, I realized that a journey is not just a physical journey. It can be emotional, spiritual, psychological, mental, educational, informational and so much more. I couldn't believe it!

A few weeks later, I was house/dog sitting at a friend's and decided to use the weekend to build my new journey map. It was an amazing exercise that even further opened my eyes to the idea of journeys. While the basis of my journey was all about maps and locations, the overall story of my journey spanned well beyond cities and states. Each of these words below has its own connotation about a specific element of my emotional, spiritual, psychological, mental, educational and/or informational journey:

Values

I have a separate exercise about better understanding your own values. The net of my process resulted in my six top values; relationships/friendships, fairness, confidence, perseverance, optimism, and fun. And I looked at the maps to understand where I developed these values.

People

This is where the map came in handy. I identified one or two people who were critical in my life and/or development in that location. It was a blast to piece together when and where I've initiated friendships and relationships with many amazing people.

Passions

My passions included my sons, travel, community service, servant leadership, and learning something new. On my maps, I drew out where my sons were born and where we've traveled worldwide over the years.

Time

Tracking my journey also gave me a slightly different take on time. It was easy to understand my age across various locations. But the impact of that amount of time seemed to vary depending upon that segment of my overall life. There were a ton of lessons learned from the four years of college versus a few lessons during the five years of living in Michigan (no knock on Michigan... I was only four–nine years-old at that time).

Work

Tracking my career journey was one reason for multiple versions of my mapping process. Did I highlight where I actually worked or where my company was located? And what about my responsibility at the time — flying to multiple states and/or countries to engage with clients and prospects? I decided to highlight the employer's location, which was fun because the corporate headquarters and subsequent visits back to HQ also provided many mini journeys.

Growth

I also tried to track significant inflection points of my maturity, growth, and awareness. It was a mix of time, location, and personal development to best understand significant growth areas in my own development. For example, I identified several key lessons learned in my life on the maps.

Happiness

In general, I'm a very happy person. I also noted how my level of happiness varied across these different locations and age levels. Understanding a point of view of my happiness across many different facets of my life was helpful. More than anything, what I learned looking at my past is how to better inform my future going forward. Understanding my journey across so many different perspectives has been extremely helpful in creating new paths for my journey.

LESSON LEARNED

Focusing simply on goals, objectives, and/or tangible actions you want to achieve at some point in your lifetime is all valuable. Focusing on the process, the journey, and what you've learned along the way is immensely valuable. Consider the various perspectives and different types of journeys you might encounter. You will reap many benefits if you pay attention along the way and apply those lessons moving forward versus simply "climbing the mountaintop" — only to see another mountain behind it

---

PLAY

"engage in activity for enjoyment and recreation rather than a serious or practical purpose."

Can (fill in the blank with *every* one of your friends) come out and play?

Until the pandemic exponentially increased the use of the phrase, "You are on mute!", I'm guessing the question "Can you play?" is still one of the most frequently asked questions by people, especially children, around the world. Especially when you dig into the definition and focus on play's enjoyment and recreation aspects versus the serious or practical aspects.

And as much as I'd love to play a game for fun or connect with friends for recreation right now, I'm going to focus on the second half of the definition of play. I believe you can infuse the play with work or almost anything else for a "serious or practical purpose."

I didn't really think a lot of play in the context of work — or for a "serious or practical purpose" until recently. I attended a webinar with someone focused on engaging businesses in the state of play. As we interacted with him, we started to share our own stories of play in the workplace or during something that was for a serious or practical purpose. Here are a few examples where play nicely intersects with work.

Meetings or Events

This one comes to mind first for me. When I facilitate a one or multi-day event, I love the idea of inserting some play time at the beginning of the day. Doing something for "enjoyment" to start the day usually breaks people out of their routines and prepares them for the upcoming sessions. To start a meeting, for example, ask everyone in the meeting for the expectations for the event and share one or two fun facts that they feel no one else knows about them. Even if you are just doing a single presentation, inserting some play in the middle of a meeting helps bring joy to an audience who won't be very interested in slide number 47 of your presentation. Some of my favorite "playful" moments during long presentations include a few extra slides with a cartoon or quick activity everyone needs to participate in.

Relationships

I love using play to introduce new hires or team members. As we figured out how to work remotely during the pandemic, many people used play as an icebreaker or as a fun way to make connections with new people. Examples might include virtual "Rock/Paper/Scissors," asking everyone to grab something in their office/room and tell a quick story about it, or simply sharing one word on your mind in the chat window. Play helps to break down some initial barriers to being the "new person in the room" or the "one person no one has met in person." And play definitely helps with the empathy needed to build relationships over time.   When we intentionally interact through play, we discover connections between individuals that might not have been known without having some fun along the way.

Left/Right Brain

To my friends who know the Rocky Horror Picture Show reference — "It's just a jump to the left… and then a step to the right!". Many of my friends are developers, engineers, and scientists and, in college, I was an engineer. I worked in technology for decades. Most of these folks (including me, big time!) were strongly focused on left-brain thinking. Creativity, interpersonal, vision, empathy, and expression exist in the right brain. Play helps with that "step to the right" and creates awareness of the differences between the two sides of the brain. The more creative folks might want to engage in play via drawings, while more analytical folks enjoy the numbers and words.

Fun. Smiles. Amusement. Pleasure. Enjoyment. Play. My sense is that weaving any/all of these elements into your more serious work or practical efforts will be helpful in the long run. At one of my employers, we used to play games in a conference room at lunch. I'd also have little games and puzzles on my desk for someone to play with during a meeting or discussion. Completing a Rubik's Cube in a meeting usually generates multiple smiles. Maybe the new definition of play should be "engage in activity for enjoyment and recreation *and to enhance* a serious or practical purpose."

LESSON LEARNED

The idea of play as a child, or even as an adult, brings me a smile and warmth in my belly. However, the irony of the definition is play can actually *improve* something you are working on with a serious or practical purpose. I'd strongly encourage you to figure out how to discover the "best of" in terms of mixing recreation and enjoyment with your work or any other activities where having fun isn't the main goal, but it definitely helps.

DOUBTFUL

"feeling uncertain about something."

Despite everyone else's opinion, I never doubted that (fill in your own blank here!). During my senior year in high school, we felt like we had an excellent basketball team with an opportunity to win our conference championship. And this was after a horrible season in my junior year when we were *expected* to win the conference and ended up with a losing record that season.

We started our senior season out well — including excelling in the Thanksgiving and Christmas tournaments we played in. We had a solid winning record against strong competition.

Then, we totally fell flat. We started our conference season games by losing two of our first four games. Our main competition, Woodstock High School, started off 4-0 and looked unbeatable. With a 2-2 record, we were already two games behind them with just eight conference games remaining.

The good news? We still needed to play them twice. The bad news? They soundly defeated two of the teams we had lost to already. Brimming with confidence at the start of the season, we all had significant feelings of doubt at that point.

We persevered. We won our next game to get to 3-2 and then traveled to Woodstock, who was now 5-0, for a *huge* game. If we lost, our record would go to 3-3, and theirs would be 6-0, a three-game deficit with just six more games to play. We played well and won the game — turning a potential three game deficit into just one game. We were now 4-2, and they were 5-1.

Our confidence was better, but there were still lingering doubts because of the two games we had lost previously.

But we won five more games in a row, while Woodstock actually lost another game. The net — we were both now 9-2 with one game to play, fortuitously, in the season's final game and against each other, at home. By now, most of the doubters had jumped on our bandwagon and thought we'd win. And we did. Big time.

What a way to overcome doubt!

As I reflect back upon the transformations my teammates and I experienced at that time, I'll sum them up the following way:

Break It Up Into Smaller Potential Wins
While we wanted to win eight games immediately, the schedule was simply one game after the next. Our goal was broken into many smaller goals by the nature of the basketball schedule. We had to win one game, then the second game, and more. It was a great way to help us focus on a game-by-game basis since we couldn't play all eight games simultaneously. Winning just one game at a time seemed more certain than a much larger goal of eight games in a row.

Deliberate Practice
We broke up our major goal into smaller subsets and deliberately executed a specific game plan against each opponent. We weren't trying to beat Woodstock when we were playing other teams. We simply went to practice, discussed how to execute flawlessly against that specific opponent, and focused on the next game in front of us. Being focused on very specific actions eliminated many doubts on a game-by-game basis.

Make It Public
We told everyone in school and ourselves that we could still win the conference championship — even as the doubters questioned us. While

there is some added pressure when you share something like this publicly, the encouragement we received along the way was incredible. I can't say enough good things about the energy, positivity, and encouragement you get from others when you share something like this publicly. The energy we garnered from friends, family, and fans helped us eliminate many of our doubts.

Join With One or More

Not only did we make it public, but we also had others "join" our quest. The cheerleaders and Pom Pom girls joined our quest. And some kisses may have been offered as incentives to boyfriends on the team! The wrestling team was excelling simultaneously and on their path to a conference championship, and both were winter sports, so we motivated each other during practices in the same gym.

Obviously, we couldn't have others join the team midway through the season, but it was great to have others involved in one way or another. "Groupthink" is another way to attack doubts — whether your own or those of others.

Know Your "Enemies" — and Your Triggers

It's also helpful to understand what could get in our way. I'm pretty sure I didn't realize it then, but there was *nothing* we could do about Woodstock's other games. While seeing them win another game was triggering at the time, we eventually realized we could only win the games we played. Injuries. Tests. Girlfriends are breaking up with us. All of these were "enemies" in our heads we could deal with to reduce or eliminate doubts.

Embrace Failure — and Look at It Differently

Fortunately, we had already experienced major failure the previous season. We knew what it was like to lose. So we could quickly look at what our team could do differently, embrace any current or potential failures, and execute our game plan accordingly. Action in a positive direction often eliminates doubt.

LESSON LEARNED

For every doubt, there is a potential solution, and doubt is a feeling. The examples I shared above are good reference points for different things you can try at any point you are feeling some doubt. Hopefully, one or several or all of them allow you to get past that feeling of uncertainty, move forward, and kick doubt in the butt!

Chapter 4

Bounce Casual Ideas Off Each Other

My friend Mark and I have done the "Biggest Loser" contest several times. We aim to weigh ourselves at the beginning of the "match," encourage each other along the way, and measure who lost the most weight by the percentage lost to determine the winner. As a result, we have both built some good habits by helping each other. We offer each other tips and techniques like using a smaller plate forces you to choose smaller portions of food or how a shorter cardio workout might burn calories more effectively than other forms of exercise. And we "report" how we are progressing against our goals.

It is nice to share what is working or what isn't with someone else in a friendly way. For example, we always supported each other and tried to build new habits by eating, drinking, exercising, etc. We often shared updates like *"I did well with my exercises today, but should NOT have eaten that ice cream after dinner."* There are many different ways to share casual ideas with family or friends.

DEED

"an action that is performed intentionally or consciously."

Did you ever start crying and have ZERO IDEA about why?

The first time I watched the movie *Bohemian Rhapsody*, I started crying in the movie theater when Freddie Mercury said to his father — *"Good Thoughts. Good Words. Good Deeds."* The movie didn't end for another 25–30 minutes, but I couldn't get that scene out of my head. I imagined either Ryan or Cole having the same conversation with me at some point in the future — maybe even about one of the stories I'm sharing in this book! It makes my heart beat faster and puts a smile on my face.

Over the next few months, I watched the movie another dozen times on flights or at home. And I broke out in tears. EVERY. SINGLE. TIME.

Finally, I spent some time breaking it down to understand why those words, coupled together, impacted me. It came down to the same core reason I started writing articles and posts on LinkedIn — which led me to write this book. It's about my sons and what thoughts and words I've shared with them. And what deeds they are doing as a result. The crying is about some deep-seated fear about what I failed to teach them — especially if it's something they desperately need.

This may be typical for a parent. Especially in that phase of life with your children when they are mostly grown up and independent and don't really "need" you any longer?

Here are some of my good thoughts, good words, and good deeds.

Good Thoughts

I hope to share my good thoughts and those of others through my face-to-face interactions, formal coaching clients, sharing good books, participating in community service projects, joining boards, etc. Over the years, I shared many thoughts with my sons — even if they rolled their eyes and responded with a *"Why do I need to know that right now, Dad?"* look. And I'll continue to share my good thoughts in person, on the phone, or in written form.

When I do take a conscious action that someone appreciates or even one that someone doesn't like, I consider what thoughts led me to that specific deed. There may be a circuitous path from your ideas to your deeds, and being fully aware of that path will help you engage future thoughts to improve acts even more consciously.

Good Words

My goal is to write as much as possible about good thoughts, whether they are my own or my interpretations of ideas and perspectives from others. I'm putting something on social media every week in the form of lessons learned or something that would be valuable to others. And I hope to write more than one book in my lifetime, even if the only two copies I publish are for my sons. Lastly, I'm grateful to be in a profession where I can share inspiring and helpful thoughts and words with others through good deeds.

In a way, the words I share with others are an effective way of communicating my thoughts. Whether spoken or written or expressed differently, sharing your words is an important "translation" from the brilliance you might want to share with others, especially for people who need a bit of an instruction manual to convert thoughts or words into specific deeds.

Good Deeds

While I'm not 100% accurate with my intentions, my vision is to perform good deeds daily. Deeds can be small (just smiling to someone who looks sad), medium (carrying someone's heavy package inside for them), large (giving hours of your time to help a nonprofit), and massive (providing significant amounts of time and money to those in need). I focus on the consistency of good deeds to be a role model for my sons.

And that's what the crying was all about, hoping my sons would see me as a good role model who transformed my thoughts into clearly understood words that led to honorable deeds. I know I've made many mistakes in my life and want to ensure the "ledger" of my intentional actions over time leans heavily into the side of many good thoughts, words, and deeds.

MODIFY

"make partial or minor changes to (something), typically so as to improve it or to make it less extreme."

"If it ain't broke, don't fix it." I finally took that phrase out of my lexicon.

When I started writing on LinkedIn for "Lessons Learned for my Sons," I decided that my approach was to write a fuller article (many pages) instead of basic posts (limited to 3,000 characters only). My original idea was to share as much information as possible with each story. Unfortunately, it was almost as if I was trying to empty my brain with a specific subject.

Coming up with a topic was usually the first step. Then, I'd think about something present for me at work that would valuable to share with the boys. After that, there were usually a few different components to what I was working through, leading to thinking about a few potential solutions.

This process might span three to four hours, spread over a few days. And that was just *thinking* about the process. I still needed to start to *write* about the process.

When I'd type these articles out, I'd go to three to four pages in length with five or six different frameworks or solutions or methodologies to help solve those problems.

One article takes eight to ten hours, spread over several weeks. And who had the time to read these articles? I had a few of my friends respond with appreciative comments. I wanted to share more, but it was painful to think

122

about spending another eight–ten hours trying to get something done. What could I modify?

On the positive side, I was conveying the lessons learned not only to my sons but also to anyone who was reading my articles. I continued through the years and slowly fine-tuned my process — getting the article writing process down to two–three hours overall and something I could publish within a week of first thinking about something.

Still, I wanted to modify the process further. What other changes could I make?

As stated above, LinkedIn also has the concept of posts — which are also limited based on the number of characters. Shifting from writing three–four page articles to writing posts of less than three thousand characters would be challenging, but I was up for modifying my approach.

Up to this point in my life, modifications were simple and usually one-time. And also because something might be broken or not working well. In this case, I wanted to fix some things that weren't working well (too much time to write) and make some significant changes/improvements (more succinct and more frequent writing). The idea of multiple, more minor changes was compelling.

Over the next six months, I made a lot of modifications to my writing process — posting more frequently, writing in less than one hour each time, boiling my points down into three or fewer major comments, and making sure the lesson learned not only applied to my sons, but to ANYONE who is reading my posts.

It was a great continual improvement process, and not all of my modifications worked, but I kept working through the process to improve it repeatedly and I constantly solicited feedback from others on what else I could modify.

Oops. Soliciting feedback from others drew me to another suggestion to modify my approach — the world of recording a video instead of writing.

I've kept the same format for my posts — regardless of making a video or writing a post, but now I'm sharing about half of my posts verbally. It's been a fun process. My writing was intact, but my desire for continued improvement encouraged me to modify my process.

"If it ain't broke, still consider how to improve it" might be a better phrase going forward.

LESSON LEARNED

You can slightly improve many things in your life — processes, systems, items around your house or work, etc. Proactively look around your environment, identify what modifications you can make to something in your life, and determine whether or not incremental changes and improvements might result in a better "something" in your life. In most cases, you can always reverse your changes if the result isn't what you were looking for. There are many "somethings" in your life you don't have to modify at all if you prefer. Be selective about what you'd like to improve, consider what modifications you can make and how they might positively impact your actions, and then take action sooner than later.

CHANGE

"make (someone or something) different; alter or modify." or

"replace (something) with something else, especially something of the same kind that is newer or better; substitute one thing for (another)."

What do you do when you are sleepy in the middle of the day?

Some people love to slip into a nap. Others will get up and walk around. At least in the United States, one of the most popular solutions involves caffeine — readily available in many forms, from coffee to tea to energy drinks to soda pops.

I had some late nights during my high school days, but I didn't truly leverage the "benefits" of caffeine until college when I was introduced to the 64 oz Big Gulp from *7-Eleven*. If you haven't had one, it's difficult to describe why that sugary, messy, syrupy liquid mixture I would dump into that giant plastic cup was so rewarding. And drinking it through that long straw was like a delicious syringe delivering incredible flavors into my mouth.

After college, many friends attempted to get me to try coffee. I didn't like the warm liquid on my throat (though hot chocolate or soups didn't count!) and the smell was displeasing. Worst of all, every version of a cup of coffee that I tried made me gag. Icky.

So how does one go about making a significant change?

Become Aware!

Over time, after many discussions with various doctors, I realized (as I should have from day one) that regular or diet sodas are just bad for you. Something had to change!

Break the Old Habit!!

My first step was to cut back on one or two cans of some type of soda pop per day. Or totally eliminate the need to "acquire" caffeine from sodas for one or two days per week. That helped me to break the desire for sodas overall.

Experiment!!!

The next step is a mixed blessing — good news no more dependence upon sodas for my need for caffeine. Bad news — I started to drink those little energy shots. Lots of caffeine. But in a small and harmful little "shot bottle" of chemicals.

Practice!!!!

The significant change was to taste test and explore coffee (again) — using different flavors of coffee, adding sugar, and trying a myriad of different creams. This was *not* possible based on my past and very negative experiences with coffee. But like breaking the habit of sodas, I wanted to try to change my sentiment.

My shift went from always refusing something to pondering a change, breaking the old dependencies, and actually attempting to change, considering the positive ramifications (health) of drinking coffee.

It wasn't that bad and the caffeine hits were definitely helpful. Do I like coffee? Not yet. But it's totally bearable and almost entirely eliminates diet (and regular) sodas from my diet.

Instead of making one massive change, I've also made incremental changes across other areas of my life — personally and professionally. For example, I realized looking at my phone in bed to check emails was not good (aware!). I slowly changed from checking emails in bed late at night (break old habit!!) to checking them just before going into my bedroom (experiment!!!) to not even opening emails after 9 P.M. (practice!!!!). And it is still tricky, like the taste of coffee. Still, I'm sleeping much better, not being connected ten seconds before going to bed!

For the record, I've included this story about Change in Chapter 4 where I believe you can accomplish change mostly on your own. This is *very* intentional for my readers as my thinking is to create building blocks for more complex types of change. There are consulting companies with practices entirely focused on change management. The topic can be highly complex and require a ton of assistance from others. I'm not downplaying the complexity of change; just trying to make it easy for anyone to start with small changes and evolve from there.

LESSON LEARNED

We can all change, take baby steps, be creative, make multiple alterations of something significant, redefine what is "good," and move forward. Ask for help too. You are often not the only one invested in a specific change.

CHOICE

"an act of selecting or making a decision when faced with two or more possibilities"

Heads or tails? What's your favorite pick when flipping a coin?

Growing up, we all make dozens of choices — often daily. Some of them are more challenging than others. Or some seem very simple but become pretty consequential over time. For example, do I want chocolate or caramel syrup on that ice cream? Or what toppings do I want for my pizza? Those are pretty simple choices.

As I considered the idea of choice, the most consequential one that came to me was my selection of colleges. Most of the choices I had made up to this point were inconsequential. I could always get a different syrup topping the next time. Or I could trade one of my pizza slices with my brother if I didn't like all of my selected toppings. But choosing a college felt like a pretty permanent and impactful decision. And looking back on it now — based upon the fact I met the mother of my sons and some of my closest friends in college — making a good choice seemed pretty consequential.

The final two colleges I chose between were Northwestern and the University of Illinois (U of I). Both had strong computer science programs, but U of I had a much stronger and larger engineering program overall in case I discovered a Computer Science degree wasn't for me. Plus, U of I was nearly three hours away from home (felt far away from home), while Northwestern was less than an hour (scared my parents would visit any weekend — or weekday, for that matter). However, Northwestern had a more substantial reputation for education and was ranked higher on most college ranking guides. I needed to make a good choice.

There are probably great little stories for each of these mini-discoveries — effectively, we all crave the "Aha!" moment when understanding what option to select. To clarify the mini-discoveries below, most of these lessons apply to almost *any* choice you need to make — not just which college to attend.

Ask for Help — Sooner Than You Think

It's great to work things out independently, but when you struggle, ask for help sooner than later. It might be the number one suggestion for new employees anywhere. Most people are afraid to ask for help until they learn we *all* asked for help to get where we are today. I made the same mistake repeatedly — it's frustrating and doesn't help you learn other than learning how to ask for help sooner! I spoke with older high school students now attending both Northwestern and U of I to learn about their experiences at each school — but not until I had been accepted by both universities and needed to make a quick decision. I wish I had sought help much earlier in my decision process.

Be Yourself — Don't Just Follow the Crowd

Understand who you are versus trying to "fit in" everywhere. There is a safekeeping mode deeply ingrained in all of us. Returning to our Neanderthal days, it was safer to fit into the tribe versus trying to be unique.

Refrain from trying to fit in. You will discover that most people will appreciate you for who you are. Those who don't are not likely part of the crowd you'd like to spend time with anyway. I didn't know anyone from my high school considering Northwestern, but many of my friends had U of I in their thoughts. My version of being myself was to select U of I to have a crowd around just in case but to live in a dorm with no other high school friends to figure out how to be myself. I didn't choose U of I just because everyone else did — I chose it for my reasons.

Focus on What's Essential Versus What Feels Urgent

Sometimes choices are forced upon you. What happens when one of your options urgently causes a choice upon you when you still haven't figured out entirely what is essential for you? Understanding the relationship between what's necessary and what's urgent will help you prioritize your most critical actions for successful decision-making. For example, Northwestern had an earlier and more urgent deadline to accept their offer to attend school there. When I knew I wanted to wait for the acceptance letter from U of I, I realized that attending U of I was more essential than attending Northwestern and their offer letter with an urgent deadline.

Take Your Time...

When urgency isn't inserted into the overall decision process, take as much time as you need to leverage these other suggestions before making your choice.

...But Know You MUST Make a Decision Eventually

Being thoughtful about the decision process is important, but don't take too much time or effort to gather information. Making *no* decision is worse than making the wrong choice in most cases.

Embrace Your Values

One of my values is fun. Having fun feels like something to do in the present. Look around yourself and enjoy what you are doing right now. Then, jump in, enjoy what others think is fun, and decide whether you are having fun. Northwestern seemed like college 100% of the time. U of I seemed like college 100% of the time — *plus* fun. I tend to assume fun is important to everyone when making choices since it's one of my values. However, you can easily insert one or more of your values here to help you understand the importance of your values between your choices. Embrace your values and make a choice that enables you to stay congruent with them.

Let Your Passions and Interests Reveal Themselves to You As Well

The other side of enjoying yourself in the present is genuinely discovering your longer-term passions and interests. These are lifelong fascinations that will forever be a part of your life. So find your happy place and smile and laugh! There was much more to do at U of I regarding the diversity of interests and opportunities to enjoy life outside my classes.

Learn How To Be Independent and Make Your Own Decisions and Mistakes

Synthesize the many lessons learned, rewarding experiences, challenging situations, difficult decisions, and more into your problem-solving approach. You will make mistakes and improve your ability to make decisions independently. This is different from being yourself, as shared in the example above; this is more about growing your inner strength and exuding confidence in all the steps you take to make a choice. For example, my first mistake: a Computer Science degree was not interesting. Instead, it reinforced my original thinking about U of I and gave me many options to swap to a different engineering program.

Fail Mindfully — and Get Up and Try Again

The bottom line is, do not be afraid to make the wrong choice (because you will make many in your lifetime, just as we all do). Most often, lessons learned come from our failures or inability to meet our original expectations from the decisions we made. Certainly, in my earliest days at school, I still needed to understand what it meant to fail mindfully. At best, I tried to fail without causing too much damage across other parts of my (or others) life.

The value in failure is not just the lessons learned but also your experience in rising up and trying again (differently). My first few failures at college admissions led to a couple of early rejection letters. I changed my process for writing letters to the colleges, which led to my acceptance at both U of I and Northwestern.

STORYTELLING

"the activity of telling or writing stories."... where a story is "an account of imaginary or real people and events told for entertainment."

I think about campfires, s'mores, and crackling flames when I think about storytelling. What about you?

The starting point for me was in my kindergarten days. My mom loves telling the story of me in kindergarten. She would share one of my teacher's comments from my report card: "*David is doing well in class but tends to sit in the back and talk with his friends.*" So basically, I was destined to share my stories with others from my early days.

Over the years, I would mainly share stories with others to get a laugh. But I learned quickly you could tell stories to share information or knowledge or, as the book states, to share lessons learned. I could leverage fun, creativity, and optimism to tell stories.

One year I co-taught several classes with an excellent professor at the University of Washington. The class would go on for many weeks and culminate in a project presentation at the end of the class at the end of the quarter. I suggested to the professor that I share a presentation about storytelling.

Full disclosure here — I'm incredibly appreciative of the support from my storytelling coach, in teaching me how to tell stories much more effectively for my audience. April is my storytelling coach, mentor, and guide. I'll happily share those lessons learned at another time or encourage you to work with April as I have.

My goal is to share some ideas for helping you frame and improve your storytelling. Why? Great storytelling is the most effective way to share information with others — whether in a one-on-one situation, small groups, large audiences, or most forms of social media.

Use Only Visuals or Words

Have you ever played charades? That's the game where you must draw pictures without words. If you are a person who likes words, practice telling stories in only pictures. Or, if you are very visual and love photos and imagery, try writing down a list of words that captures your story. Eventually, you'll find the perfect combination of BOTH to share a story that appeals to everyone.

Grandma/Grandpa

Pretend you are explaining something to your grandma or grandpa. How would you describe the smartphone in your pocket to someone who might still use a landline phone? Unlike my other story, **Simplify**, which talks about explaining something to a bunch of kindergarteners, a grandpa/grandma has many life experiences, and relating your story to something familiar is another storytelling technique.

Elevator Ride

One of my earliest storytelling experiences was to pretend the CEO of the company we were working with jumped in the elevator at the last second. You have just 30 seconds until you reach the executive level to explain your story to the CEO. Hit "Floor 105" for a massive building like the Sears Tower in downtown Chicago, pull together the most succinct version of your story possible, and start talking!

See Into Your Future

How would you describe your story if someone asked you what happened one or three years ago? Imagine your future self describing a situation. What story might you tell knowing what you know today?

Even if your story is mainly in the present or past, sharing an image of the future might make it more relatable as you share it now.

Recipe

For some people, telling a story needs to be like a recipe. You need to deliver the information sequentially. I start by telling someone about the cake. You talk about gathering the ingredients, mixing them up per a specific set of instructions, baking the cake using all the guidelines, and eating the delicious output with family or friends.

Eulogy

Explain something as if you were communicating an eulogy. We tend to be succinct, reflective in a positive manner, and respectful to the individual. You are forced to understand the right balance between the empathies of the audience and the importance of the situation at hand.

Metaphor

This was covered in the KISS (Keep It Simple Stupid) discussion in the story called **Simplify**; find something to describe your story that makes it understandable to the audience.

My goal is to share simple stories from my life that enlighten and entertain and are an effective way to share lessons learned!

LESSON LEARNED

Entertainment is just one "use case" for storytelling. More than anything, come up with a method of storytelling that enables you to share the information most effectively and enables your audience to listen deeply to what you have to say. You will connect with people more effectively, share your point/s more precisely, and potentially help others learn from your own stories. And just as I'm hoping for all of the stories in this book, I hope you can each read my stories and reflect upon your own stories and how the lessons learned you discovered are part of your life.

AUGMENTATION

"the action or process of making or becoming greater in size or amount."

The Lord of the Rings is one of my favorite books *and* movies. I remember several scenes where a very small army grew significantly bigger when augmented by several other armies interested in defeating the army led by the evil Sauron.

I used to think jesters were simply comedians for the King or Queen. However, the original role of the jester was to advise the King or Queen and tell them what he/she needed to hear. I was the jester for an executive at Boeing and learned what augmentation meant along the way.

For most of my career up to this point, I'd focused on sales and business development. In the enterprise software industry, the idea was to sell the software and then bring in a separate team to support the delivery of the software. The salesperson (me) who secured the deal would stay loosely involved in the longer-term relationship — but needed a separate team to be responsible and take on ownership of the project's success.

I joined a team focused on selling and delivering to Boeing when I joined one of the software companies I worked with over the years — PTC. Since Boeing was so huge, we had a focus on various aspects of the company — both organizationally and geographically. My role was to work with a program in Seattle called the Future Combat Systems (FCS) Program.

The initial sale was already completed. My goal was to sell more of the same software and grow the relationship overall — both within this program and across other parts of Boeing based on our success with this program. As I engaged with the key stakeholders from the Boeing side, I quickly understood the best way to support Boeing was to augment their team with some of our people.

The team was terrific and focused on successfully delivering everything Boeing had already purchased, but there was still an opportunity to grow the team further and ensure we maximized our opportunity to identify the long-term value of our software across the program. This included demonstrating that Boeing would benefit and showing how their dozens of partners would benefit. And, most importantly, how the ultimate customer for Boeing, the U.S. Army, would benefit overall.

Within the first year, I provided creative ideas and thoughts to the lead Boeing executive of this program, Rich. He eventually asked me to join his organization as his pseudo-Chief of Staff. Not even pseudo, as Rich added my name to his formal organization chart — directly reporting to him. I was in place to augment his leadership team and do what was needed to support his leadership team, his organization, and, most importantly, their U.S. Army customer.

As an augmented team, we took different actions. We implemented new processes that significantly improved the value of our software to all system users — over 20,000 of them working collaboratively and more effectively because of the team's combined efforts.

After this experience, I realized that augmentation comes in many forms. It might be added ideas to a brainstorming session. It could be someone bringing a new set of tools during a process. It could be adding people to an engagement or adding fuel to the fire in the form of an individual's added energy or passion. In the world of technology, people are talking about Augmented Reality, which adds a digital layer of information to our current physical reality. So making something bigger and better through augmentation is something you should always consider.

LESSON LEARNED

Truly 1 + 1 = 3 or more! Making something bigger and better is usually a good thing. However, augmentation to make something more extensive isn't always the goal.

Consider the purpose of what you are attempting to augment before immediately taking action or applying a specific process to increase something. Becoming more effective or efficient are alternatives to making something bigger. Another thought is to check in with others involved to confirm that augmentation is the "right" thing to do based on the situation at that time. Then remember that augmentation can take many forms beyond physical augmentation — leverage becoming greater in size via incremental IQ, EQ, passion, energy, ideas, and more.

LONELINESS

"sadness because one has no friends or company."

Do you remember what the loneliest number is? Three Dog Night's song says, "One is the loneliest number that you'll ever do."

Ironically, I even think about the idea of loneliness when I'm actually in the opposite state — hanging out with many friends and plenty of company. However, when I truly dug through my memories of loneliness, I happened to be on a busload of Green Bay Packers fans on the way back toward Chicago after seeing my first football game at Lambeau Field. Three of my close friends were with me and we were surrounded by many affable Packers fans. But for some reason, I felt all alone for about 10–15 minutes as the bus cruised back toward Milwaukee, and I thought about other times in my life I was lonely.

At some point, we all experience a state of loneliness. My initial sense of loneliness was during my first few weeks at the University of Illinois (U of I). Granted, I had some friends from high school who also attended U of I, but they were all figuring themselves out, and I felt totally isolated. My roomie was a kind dude — but we were from very different backgrounds, and I wondered whether we'd ever connect beyond living in the same dorm room.

My classes included hundreds of new people, primarily engineers, but only some of them shared some of my interests. I was 17, meaning I couldn't even hit the one bar on campus that allowed 18-year-olds to drink, socialize, and be around a lot of company. So, in the first week or two, I'd be at a school of over thirty thousand people and be on my own. I was despondent and wondered whether or not I had made the right choice of universities.

I kept thinking about the next four years of college and being alone the whole time. It felt as if I should have stayed closer to home to visit with my high school friends. Or to be closer to my family and younger brother. I spent a lot of time reflecting on whether I had made the right decision.

After a few weeks of being somewhat lonely, we moved our dorm room closer to a group of other students I started to spend some time with. I often went to the gym with one of them, played basketball, and built many more relationships on the basketball court. Soon, I connected with a new fraternity, including 20 pledge brothers and another 150 other fraternity brothers. In classes, I got closer to a couple of ceramic engineers.

135

There have been many times, albeit temporarily, when I've experienced a state of loneliness in my life. Here are a few situations that might have resulted in a severe sense of loneliness and what I did to STOP this feeling.

Moving to Illinois (From Michigan)

I didn't know anyone when I moved to Sleepy Hollow in the middle of fourth grade as a nine-year-old. My solution? ***Connecting***. I quickly explored the neighborhood and discovered many kids my age. Some kids noticed me playing basketball in the driveway, came to my house to play one day, and went to many other friends' houses another day. We played baseball, basketball, hide and seek, and a myriad of other games. I established many lifelong friendships and quickly discovered my way of interacting socially. For some reason, I thought the primary way to connect with others at U of I was based upon meeting people in the dorms or my classes. After a few weeks at U of I, I soon realized that connecting happens in many other ways — sports, music venues and being outside were ways to avoid loneliness...just like the days in Sleepy Hollow.

Moving to Seattle (From Illinois)

From the work perspective, I was the first U.S. employee of a company based in Toronto, with my first client in Modesto, CA. I needed to travel weekly to spend time at the corporate headquarters to learn about our products and meet with our clients in person. With no work colleagues, family, or friends in Seattle, I had to ***be intentional*** about discovering connections, whether on the road with my job or during my limited time in Seattle on weekends. Of course, sports was one method of connecting, but I was also intentional about connecting at the theater, sports bars, great restaurants, outdoor concerts, outdoor walks and hikes, fun runs, etc. Being intentional helped me out of my loneliness "funk" at U of I and drove me to meet others unbeknownst to me at the time.

Moving to an Apartment (From my Home)

I moved into an apartment after my divorce. In this phase of my life, I learned about the ***time and situation*** associated with loneliness. Some solitude time is excellent for self-care, whether mentally or physically, and it can be situational and short-term, knowing I'll likely engage with friends later in the week or on the weekend. Unfortunately, my move into an apartment coincided with the pandemic — which seemed to "double down" on my sense of loneliness. But like many of you, I found many different ways to stay connected with others — whether via Zoom, phone calls, or even yelling at a distance in a park or open area. Getting *creative* was a "must have" skill to combat loneliness during the pandemic. Once I got past my first few weeks of being lonely at U of I, I definitely got creative in connecting with others, and have leveraged creativity ever since.

Overall, the sadness connected to loneliness is a temporary state. And it's easily alleviated by connecting with a friend or even going out to be around other people. So, yes — I'm not afraid to go out to a coffee shop or restaurant by myself to be surrounded by many different people.

LESSON LEARNED

If loneliness is a choice, then drop the sadness element. Embrace your time alone. We all have our reasons for feeling lonely at times, whether you are an introvert or an extrovert. Reach out to one person or get out publicly to be around others. Even just getting outside to be around others, where "others" might be defined by animals or plants, can be somewhat therapeutic. Action is key to battling anything related to loneliness. And you can leverage some or all of the other suggestions from above. *Connecting* with others, *being intentional* about what you are doing, understanding being alone might be for a short period of *time* or due to a specific *situation* only, and getting *creative* to move into action to "defeat" any sense of loneliness.

ENVIRONMENT

"the circumstances, objects, or conditions by which one is surrounded."

For this story, I'll use The Earth as the object surrounding us.

Growing up, the environment was simply the "stuff around me", the people or the towns where I grew up. As I got older, I thought more about the environment in the context of nature and how it integrates with everything around us. The most impactful images for me are the before/after photos I've seen in many books where the before is just 10–15 years earlier. The present-day photos are *shocking* in demonstrating how much damage we've caused the earth. When you see a picture of an iceberg from just ten years earlier and then see the image of the same iceberg today, at less than ten percent of its original size, you start to feel the impact of climate change.

Today, I think a lot about sustainability, focusing on the environment as it pertains to the world around us. One idea about sustainability is "the avoidance of the depletion of natural resources to maintain an ecological balance." I'm using that idea to focus on how to save the environment and our ability to inhabit Earth safely. But, I'm also taking the position of leaving something in better shape than I found it, and I'd love the opportunity to leave the earth in a better place for my sons and everyone else living on Planet Earth long after I pass away.

My role at ThinqShift is to support our mission of helping fabulous leaders and their teams succeed and reinvent the world. Now I'm sharing some details about my contribution to how I'll try to "reinvent the world." Sustainability of the environment — in particular, the avoidance of carbon *into* our atmosphere and the removal of existing carbon *from* our atmosphere.

Here are some quick stats from The Nature Conservancy. The average American puts 16 tons of carbon into the atmosphere annually. Globally, the average is closer to four tons of carbon per person. I plan to reduce my carbon footprint significantly, and I also hope to help others reduce theirs while helping to extract some of that existing carbon from the atmosphere. My big picture vision is to avoid AND remove 3.3 million tons of carbon from the atmosphere before I leave this wonderful planet by enabling many others in the following ways:

ThinqShift

As I deliver leadership services to fabulous leaders and their teams, one of my primary areas of focus is to engage with organizations truly focused on sustainability. That includes B Corporations, companies committed to Amazon's Climate Pledge or the Paris Climate Accords, ESG-focused businesses, and companies committed to net zero carbon emissions. While government actions can have an impact, companies and their employees will have the largest and most direct impact.

Me

Personally, I'll appeal to family, friends, work colleagues, clients, and others to take steps toward sustainability — walk or bike instead of driving when possible, reduce your "plastic footprint",x buy used/refurbished, etc. My older son graduated with a degree in Environmental Design to build/design homes with sustainability as the driving focus. My younger son is in Marine Biology, focusing on saving the oceans for marine mammals. Needless to say,

I'm a very proud father of these two amazing young men. I hope many others will make their contributions toward sustainability too, and I'll do what I can to encourage anyone willing to listen to focus in that direction.

GetGreen

I've invested some of my time and money in a software company called Emerald Technology Group in Seattle. I'm hoping individuals and organizations will explore our "GetGreen" app — which focuses on building sustainability habits at an individual level. You can download the app from the app stores. I cannot invest millions in companies like Bill Gates or Jeff Bezos, but I'm hoping to make other investments in business impacting sustainability. Every little bit helps.

At ThinqShift, we often talk about levels of thinking. The meta level of thinking is the highest order of thought and is associated with life and death, philosophy, and the world's natural cycles. The lowest level of thinking is tactical, like remembering to recycle packaging materials. Operational is the next level up from tactical and is more project-based, establishing a weekend of planting trees that will eventually pull carbon out of the atmosphere, for example. Structural thinking is about making more permanent changes to everything around you. For example, install solar panels to decrease your energy footprint (and even put energy back into the energy grid!). Any level of thinking that helps the environment is a good thing.

For me, contributing to the well-being of the environment is an excellent big-picture focus for the balance of my time on Earth.

LESSON LEARNED

There is only one environment when you consider the Meta level of thinking. As defined by Earth, the environment will be about whether humans can survive. This is not only about saving the environment but also about saving an environment that is sustainable for humans. The other lesson here? Find your *own* passion for dedicating time and energy to balance your journey on Planet Earth — especially at the tactical, operational or structural levels. And if you don't have a passion for sustainability, give me a ring, and let me tell you about the environment!

HUMILITY

"a modest or low view of one's own importance; humbleness."

A phrase I've heard about bragging is that you are NOT bragging if you've actually done it. But a great sense of humility is still an honorable trait.

During the first two decades of my career, I mostly lived in an extremely competitive world where we all wanted to meet and exceed our sales targets significantly — most of the time, exceeding expectations led to higher commission checks. But, in some cases, it led to promotions or increased opportunities to work on. And there were downsides, as Margaret shared in the **Introduction**, where my lack of humility negatively impacted business relationships.

Eventually, I transitioned significantly from sales/business development to technology consulting. We received 100% salary and zero commissions. Our performance was judged entirely on our annual performance review process, which included gathering feedback from at least half a dozen colleagues, but more often than not, 10–15 colleagues. In addition to feedback from all different directions, we also provided a self-assessment that presented strong and weak points throughout the year.

My first performance review was terrible. While I had some notable accomplishments throughout the year, much of my review was based upon several significant stumbles. What I thought were strong points were merely "just positive."

And what I felt were fairly minor areas of improvement came back in the review as "must fix before being promoted." After being a high-flier for decades who constantly exceeded expectations, my first performance review was a humbling experience.

It took me months to recover. I worked with my therapist. My company aligned me with an executive coach. My mentor doubled down on specific areas to help me grow and learn. It was definitely a humbling experience.

Up to this point in my life, I always felt that humility would be counted against you when others measured your performance. Why would I tell people about my shortcomings or downplay my strengths? I didn't realize how many relationships I may have negatively impacted or growth opportunities I missed by not sharing openly with others. Therefore, learning about the true definition of humility has been a blessing in my life.

While I'm always interested in new learning, the most important starting point is increasing self-awareness and objectively assessing yourself. Being more humble is a great way to evaluate yourself honestly. You can only adapt and grow if you thoroughly know your starting point. And if you channel humility effectively, you might even slightly judge your starting point behind what it truly is.

Strengths

It is always essential to understand your own "superpowers." Connecting with people, networking in new environments, and being cautiously optimistic are several of my own "superpowers." However, not many people focus as much time on identifying their kryptonite — which is the other side and the origin of your "superpower."

When I was young, I was afraid to admit "I don't know" to other kids. I built up my relationship muscle — figuring out if people like me and share information with me, I'll eventually discover the answer without admitting "I don't know." I missed many opportunities to learn something from a friend instead of pretending I knew what they were talking about or trying to figure it out "on the fly."

Today, I have zero qualms about admitting "I don't know" because I'm confident in my ability to discover the answer or collaborate with others who are in the "know." In addition, I've simply increased my willingness to be vulnerable about not knowing. Over the years, I've been pleasantly surprised by how many people want to help when you say "I don't know" versus my younger point of view that kids might not like or respect me if "I don't know." More importantly, I understand the evolution of my strengths and weaknesses and how to handle both.

As it pertained to my review, I spent a lot of time cultivating my relationship with our client — and paid little attention to the skill I needed in program management or development processes. That's where I failed and created an opportunity to learn and grow. Had I been more humble along the way, I'm certain others would have helped me improve in these areas — instead of fumbling around trying to figure it out on my own.

Imperfections

Let me count the many ways I'm imperfect; hmmm, not enough fingers and toes! For many folks, it is hard to admit what you are not good at, topics you don't understand, or bad habits/behaviors you might exhibit. Realize *everyone* has more than one imperfection — it is what makes us human. Humility is a wonderful equalizer.

My listening skills could have been better — I used to primarily listen to others in a manner to confirm what I thought I already knew. I'm still battling this imperfection, but now I listen more factually (gathering data that does not conform to my beliefs), emotionally, and empathetically to seek a common understanding with a lens of an emerging whole. For example, I didn't listen to my project team, who warned me that we were likely to miss meeting undocumented yet newly important expectations with the customer even though we were 100% aligned with the legal obligations based on their original expectations. And my lack of active listening was peppered across my review. Expectations matter — especially when we should show some humility with our imperfections.

Opportunities for Growth

This is where the most "fun" exists. We *all* have growth opportunities. I'm more aware of potential opportunities for growth across so many parts of my life today than I ever could have imagined two or three decades ago.

One example was my lack of empathy earlier in my life. I shared with many friends and my therapist that I wanted to "build this empathy muscle." I'm not sure empathy is a new "superpower" for me. Still, I love that many friends see me as much more empathetic today from being almost emotionless decades ago. It would help if you attempted to uncover a new habit and let that take root as a way to shift into a new growth area. It takes some humility to agree to begin the formation of a new habit because it assumes your existing habit isn't as good or beneficial. After that first review, my new habit was to ask at least one question about every status report — instead of assuming I knew exactly what was contained in each of them.

I'm not curing cancer or saving the world from climate change, but I know I can serve others in many different ways while staying extremely humble while doing so. Serving others includes an ability to be humble about what you can and can't do for them — and bring in someone else who is better served to support them. It takes a lot of humility to admit to saying, "I don't know.". I wish I had learned that much sooner in my life.

LESSON LEARNED

To grow and develop, you must have an *honest* and *vulnerable* assessment of yourself. Then, get others involved who are interested and invested in helping you be better. Of course, every strength has a kryptonite, and every imperfection has a positive aspect. But it would be best if you embraced the opportunity for growth to grow fully. Humility is the foundation for much of your opportunity to grow and develop. My "almost superpower" of empathy makes me wonder how you might grow your new superpowers.

GENERALIST

"a person competent in several different fields or activities."

How in the hell did I do that? That was my question the first time I tried to catch one of Cole's lacrosse balls with a lacrosse stick on the left side of my body. I'm right-handed in *everything*, so how could I have caught a lacrosse ball in a sport totally new to me, using the *left* side of my body?

I'm a generalist. Hitting a baseball well as a little kid translated into being able to strike a golf ball as an adult. Trying to solve the challenges of the Rubik's Cube turned into a desire to problem-solve with other complex games (and work challenges too). I never played soccer growing up, but I was able to coach many young kids on the concepts of spacing and passing based on my experiences with basketball. And lacrosse? As a right-hander in baseball, I naturally wore my glove on my left hand. And learned how to catch a ball without actually watching it go into my glove. So when I finally gave up on my poor "right side" skills in lacrosse and shifted to my left side, I was shocked at how easy it was to catch.

While I love being a generalist (in most things), the world totally needs specialists in many fields. For example, I don't want a generalist performing life-saving cardiac surgery on me — I'll take the specialist cardiac surgeon 100% of the time. Specialists are critical across so many aspects of our lives. However, after reading a book called *Range: Why Generalists Triumph in a Specialized World* by David Epstein, I shifted even more into the camp of generalists I had already been in.

There are countless examples of how people across all fields (sports, music, art, science, medicine, business, government, etc.) made huge leaps forward in progress because they looked at a problem differently as a generalist than solely as a specialist. I'll share a few examples. One example from *Range* compared Tiger Woods and his success in golf with Roger Federer and his success in tennis. Tiger was a specialist working 100% of the time on anything that would make him a better golfer. Roger played many sports as a kid, even sharing comments that his great footwork in tennis resulted from years of playing soccer growing up. Whereas Tiger was ruthless in his pursuit of being the best, even at age 2, and focused on little else. Roger played multiple sports and didn't take tennis seriously until later in his lifetime. Of course, they are *both* amazing athletes in their fields, but they got there in totally different ways. My sense is Roger's path was more fun and less intense.

Here are three of my favorite passages from this excellent book and my response.

"The cleverest solutions always came from a piece of knowledge that was not part of the normal curriculum."

There were numerous examples in business, science, medicine, etc., where someone outside the field provided the needed perspective to solve a challenging problem. The Einstellung effect is a psychological term for the tendency of problem solvers to employ only familiar methods, even if better ones are available. With the advent of the Internet and global collaboration, there are many opportunities to find ways of merging interesting and more general pieces of knowledge that are widely available but disparate. In my

144

business, many clients in one industry see the benefits of something being applied in a totally different industry they might never have considered. The specialists were deep diving across industry-specific solutions, but the generalists were taking technology-based solutions and applying them to healthcare, for example.

"Birds see farther (more broadly), and frogs see deeper (more depth)."

As someone who thinks he can do a little bit of everything, the "breadth versus depth" discussion was another engaging chapter in the book. Generalists add value by integrating domains — taking knowledge from one area and applying it to another. For example, most people would consider using a brick as a building block in construction. But how many people would use it in a toilet tank to create a "low-flow" toilet?

My favorite example from the book, appealing to my adolescence in the 80s, was about Nintendo using older technologies that were proven in new ways to come up with the GameBoy in the 80s and the Wii many years later. Nintendo looked broadly to take older, more general technology and apply it in totally new ways. Can you name the companies that went deeper and deeper into their specialized niches? They are no longer in business because they couldn't get out of their own way.

"Dropping one's tools is a metaphor for unlearning, for adaptation, for flexibility."

The idea of dropping tools emanates from those brave souls who fight forest fires. Many deaths happen because of the proclivity to keep using the tools on your tool belts to fight a forest fire versus realizing it's time to lighten your load, drop your heavy tool belt, and run to safety. Familiar tools are excellent for dealing with known problems. But in times of ambiguity or unfamiliar challenges, it's best to consider dropping your familiar tools, methods, or frameworks and apply more general thinking processes to solve the problem.

The book shared literal examples of firefighters who dropped their 30–40 pound tool belts and escaped the fires because they were light enough to outrun the fire's pace. Too many others kept their tools and never escaped alive.

Growing up, I always wanted to play every sport. Mostly because I'm highly competitive, but also because I love getting involved with new challenges and being involved with many other folks; those traits seemed to apply to my career progression as well — competing (doing better for my career), constantly seeking new challenges (learning about a new company or solution or offering) and spending a lot of time with other folks (extending existing relationships and forging new ones is a blast). Many of my friends from college are doing amazing work as a specialist in their fields of medicine or technology, for example, but I'm grateful for all the career opportunities being a generalist has afforded me.

If I hadn't learned to be a generalist, many of those lacrosse passes from Cole would have hit me in the head or flown hundreds of feet past me.

LESSON LEARNED

To be clear, I'm not trying to say that being a generalist is better or worse than being a specialist. Both are extremely important. My observations about the world around me are that most people lean into the value of specialization. The idea behind this chapter was to share the lessons learned from generalists and get you to consider how those lessons might be valuable — even if you lean toward being a specialist.

Understand the value of breadth (more of a generalist point of view) versus depth (specialist point of view) with any topic area.

Compare the pros and cons of the *skills* or deep *knowledge* of specialization versus the broader applicability and more significant lessons learned in generalization. The value of generalization is the flexibility to apply your lessons learned more broadly across many other aspects of your life and potentially discover new paths you might not have considered previously.

COOPERATION

"the process of working together to the same end."

What area of your life is it most important to cooperate to reach that end goal?

Let's start with a scenario from a football game. The wide receiver makes a great move to beat the defender off the line and gets wide open in the end zone. The quarterback makes a deep pass, but the ball is thrown a little short. The defender, who was initially left in the dust by the receiver, recovers his position and makes a great diving catch to intercept the ball.

What happens next?

In high school, college, or the National Football League, the quarterback is angry with himself, the wide receiver gets upset with the situation, and the whole team is irritated.

But it doesn't happen this way at the Special Olympics. I observed this exact scenario as a volunteer. The receiver helped the defender get up off the ground, gave him a congratulatory hug, and delivered the defender a tremendous high five. All for basically taking the ball away from him!

My transformation in genuinely understanding the word cooperation was when I volunteered for the Special Olympics for one year.

The Special Olympics celebrated its 50th Anniversary in Seattle a few years ago with the USA Games. I was fortunate to be one of the thousands of volunteers helping behind the scenes to see/help these great athletes compete. Tim Shriver's mother, Eunice Kennedy Shriver, started the Special Olympics over 50 years ago.

I want to share a few important comments Tim Shriver stated publicly that week, but first, let me share the overall mission of the Special Olympics:

The USA Games showcase the abilities of athletes with physical and intellectual disabilities and the impact of the Special Olympics through world-class competition, inspirational experiences, and modeling inclusion for all.

As a volunteer, I observed all aspects of this mission over several days through the behavior of fans, athletes, families, volunteers, vendors, partners, etc. Seeing how happy everyone is around these venues has been a joy. Cooperation runs rampant, and it's incredible to see! Cooperation was also modeled throughout pieces of Tim Shriver's speeches (various snippets in quotes below) and commentary that week:

"Most things that are fun are not important, and most things that are important are not fun."

The USA Games are *both* fun *and* important. And that's the point of these competitions. Competing in these games is very important to many of these athletes. While they are competing at the highest level, I still observed smiles, laughs, joy, and more from these athletes and their interactions with the fans. In this case, the "end" is fun and important, and players from opposite teams are helping each other embrace the fun. Cooperation is the name of the game here.

"They thrive in red states and blue states. They are people of color and mainstream folks, indigenous nations. It brings out the common ground."

I'm not a fan of getting into political discussions in my book, but this is another excellent perspective that Tim offers. Modeling inclusion. What a great phrase. Everyone is included and gets an opportunity to be a part of something larger than themselves. I'm pretty confident none of these athletes think about red states or blue states or purple states, or any other color. They cooperate no matter what.

"I think the culture of Seattle — it's creative, it's about nature, it's about the pioneering spirit — is very much a part of the energy of the Special Olympics movement."

I had to include this quote because I've adopted Seattle as my home though I still have roots in Illinois. The pioneering spirit was alive and well that week in Seattle. There were some great articles about a local athlete named Devon Adelman, who won a gold medal in the first-ever stand-up paddle boarding even after her water shoes were stolen from her car and she was forced to compete barefoot! The other competitors could have stated being barefoot was an unfair advantage. But they all worked together to enable Devon to compete despite this major setback.

"And we are better when we celebrate others' gifts than when we demonize each other's differences."

I love this quote. Too often, we spend time trying to "fix" someone else's problems or shortcomings. Yet, everyone has a gift to offer. Every. Single. Person. We should all focus on leveraging and celebrating the good in others versus focusing too much on the downside. Inspirational experiences were abundant all week at these USA Games. Even minor differences between participants didn't prevent anyone from cooperating with each other.

"I'd love to help people discover the beauty in themselves and others. That's what keeps me growing."

In all the roles I play across my life, I'm focused on helping others, including my kids, my friends, and the people I work with, understand how to see their strengths and leverage them in their personal or career growth. I love Tim's perspective that he grows and develops by helping others grow and develop. The fans, families, coaches, volunteers, and everyone in attendance focused on helping everyone discover the beauty and happiness in themselves and others all week. Of course, this happens with cooperation.

"You have to slow down and pay attention from your heart."

His original context was about observing the athletes in action. Get past the fact this is the Special Olympics USA Games, and don't expect the 100 Meter sprinters to break Usain Bolt's world record. This was still a world class competition. Realize the potential obstacles these athletes have overcome to get here and appreciate the joy they experience in simply competing. However, Tim's quote also applies to life in general *slow down* and *pay attention* from your *heart*. I should leverage this advice daily. Think about how you might feel in your own life as well. You'll crave opportunities to work together with others towards a common goal.

LESSON LEARNED

Start with the last part of the definition — "the same end" — and figure out the most effective way to work with others. You might have competing interests in the short term. Still, you will often discover a common starting point, many mutually beneficial components, and a similar endpoint encouraging strong cooperation across almost any aspect of your life. Then you can start your cooperation immediately.

EXPLORATION

"the action of traveling in or through an unfamiliar area to learn about it." or *"thorough analysis of a subject or theme."*

What do you think of when you hear the word exploration? Are the rockets going into space? Dog sleds heading to the Arctic Circle? A bathyscaphe diving into the deepest parts of the ocean?

Growing up, exploration was simply going into the woods near my Sleepy Hollow, IL house. Whenever I'd go into the woods with my friends, we'd come up with a new discovery. One time it was the perfect sledding hill — including a significant jump at the end. Another time it was an awesome creek filled with all kinds of fish and animals (and insects). During one deep exploratory trip, we found an old car with many shotgun shells surrounding it. It was exhilarating and captivating to think about what we might come up with during our explorations into the woods. My body was full of energy, and I was excited to imagine what we'd discover next.

Reflecting on my early days as an "explorer," I realize we were kids just having a great time. On the one hand, we felt like we were in a totally different world. But our parents knew the truth — we were, at best, just a few miles away from home in a little suburban woods.

What I realize now is that we needed more intent. Not the intent of having fun. But the intent around exploration overall — what were we learning during our adventures? What were we trying to discover? Was there something specific we were searching for in the woods to learn more about?

When you want to explore an area or specific subject, you need to recognize a gap in your knowledge about something intriguing. Here are a few ways I attempted to nurture the idea of exploration in my sons over the years:

Travel

Going to a different city, state, or even country is a great way to explore the unknown on many levels. I remember the first time the boys saw the amazing wildlife in Kenya, learned about a new culture from families in Italy, and jumped into the Pacific Ocean. Not only did they fully embrace the opportunities travel afforded them, but they were inspired to explore various aspects of those trips — before, during, and after the trip itself.

Those trips into the woods were our form of travel, just without a travel agent!

Create Space for Failure

More importantly, create a safe space for experimentation because there will definitely be failures. In the words of Thomas Edison as he invented the light bulb: *"I have not failed. I've just found 10,000 ways that won't work."* He continually explored new ways of approaching the subject of filaments and light bulbs.

For example, I taught the boys how to ride a bike by letting them ride through the grass. When they fell, it didn't hurt nearly as much as falling down on the sidewalk might have hurt. They examined what it required to stay balanced in a comfortable environment on what started as a very uncomfortable form of travel. They studied their own ways of riding the bike and eventually explored the area where they grew up.

Find Your Passion

One part of the definition of exploration is to learn. As I observed the boys having fun and enjoying themselves, I encouraged them to explore what might eventually become one of their passions. Some of those interests were short-term only, while others were skills or knowledge they continue to learn more about. This type of exploration is more about conducting a deeper analysis of yourself and your interests versus physical forms of travel.

Learn From Others

Only some have an opportunity to physically travel or conduct interesting experiments, or truly explore their passions. But you can also learn about something from their explorations of others. Think about school and reading about the extraordinary explorations that so many historical figures took. And the many discoveries so many people made by conducting experiments or simply observing interesting phenomena. Or even just the stories that friends or neighbors might share. Taking the time to learn something from the explorations of others is a great way to explore.

LESSON LEARNED

Exploration can be physical or mental. On the surface, you can easily travel to a new destination or examine a new element, both basic forms of exploration. The key to deeper exploration is understanding the intent behind your exploration, whether to learn something new, analyze something more profoundly or have fun and enjoy yourself. There are so many different ways to explore the world and relationships and everything else on this great planet (and beyond).

PARADOX

"a situation, person, or thing that combines contradictory features or qualities."

I love cheese, but I hate milk, even though cheese is made from milk. Go figure! This is just one of the many paradoxes that play out in my life.

Growing up in Chicago, I became a fan of the Chicago Blackhawks hockey team. And since Seattle had no professional hockey team, it was easy to keep following the Blackhawks when I moved from Chicago to Seattle several decades ago, especially when they won three Stanley Cups over six years.

Then Seattle was awarded their own professional hockey team — the Seattle Kraken. One of my friends took me to my first Kraken game — against the Chicago Blackhawks. I was rooting for Chicago to win, and they did in overtime. I was happy.

I went to my second Kraken game against the Chicago Blackhawks only months later. This time, Seattle won. Chicago lost. But I was still happy. That felt confusing.

We all have many paradoxes in our lives but might not be fully aware of them. Based upon the divisiveness that permeates social media today, I'd love to see everyone experience their sense of multiple paradoxes. Why? Suppose you can experience two conflicting elements in your world. In that case, you can use that experience to assess the tension between two incompatible elements that others might also face.

It seems easy to pick one side or another, especially in a sports contest. Why did I need to choose either the Chicago Blackhawks OR the Seattle Kraken to win? To the point of a paradox — how can I be rooting for BOTH teams?

My transformation was to consider the many other aspects of the situation where there were other commonalities or benefits to merely accepting the paradox. For the Blackhawks versus Kraken, here's what I did:

1. Focus on the *time* that I was spending with a friend.
2. *Appreciate* the fact I was attending a live sporting event.
3. Take a break from work for a *fun* evening out was great.
4. The game itself was very *entertaining*, regardless of who won.
5. *Feeling* the overall energy from the fans was amazing.
6. During the walk to/from the stadium, I got some *fresh air* and a great *exercise*.

By the time I watched the Kraken play the Blackhawks for the third time, I had focused on the other 80-90% of the situation I was enjoying versus fixating on whether I needed to root for Seattle or Chicago. With this simple example, I discovered at least seven common feelings from the paradox versus the one contradictory goal of who might win.

LESSON LEARNED

Start with a simple situation. Get away from the divisiveness and black/white of any situation — there are always shades of gray. We are all complex humans on this earth — each with many of our own paradoxes. Don't focus on the contradictory components; instead, consider the common or other beneficial elements that are both true! In most cases, you will discover the number of common or mutually beneficial elements far outweighs or outnumbers the new differences of the paradoxical situation.

The paradox itself becomes irrelevant primarily over time.

NERVOUS

"easily agitated or alarmed; tending to be anxious; highly strung."

Speaking in front of a large audience. Walking into the classroom two minutes before your final exam. Remembering your locker combination when you have just a few minutes to get to class. Asking someone out for the first time. Doing something you've never done before.

What makes you nervous?

My first time was playing in a "band" for the middle school talent show in sixth grade. I played piano. My two other friends played the trumpet (Jeff Fox) and the drums (Brad Williams).

Our song? The Pink Panther.

We practiced individually, in pairs, and as a group. We were all taking lessons on our respective instruments. We were good — for sixth graders with many other distractions like getting homework done, having fun with friends at parties, exploring the neighborhoods around us, and (attempting to) date some of the girls in our class. It was all leading up to the middle school talent show to be performed in the gym for the ENTIRE school of sixth, seventh, and eighth graders, the teachers, and even some parents.

There were only a few hundred people in the bleachers that afternoon. But to me (I won't speak to whether or not Brad or Jeff were as nervous as I was), I was nervous as I felt we were about to perform in front of thousands of people. Plus, it was a competition, and we wanted to be the talent show winners too!

What would I have said if I could go back and tell my younger self how to handle nervousness?

After years of going through many additional nervous situations, here are some thoughts I share with others about how to combat nervousness.

Name It and Rename It

Admitting to myself that I'm nervous is actually a strength. And I have full awareness of what's happening to me. Now that I know what I'm experiencing, I call my emotion something else — excitement for the unknown. When you feel nervous, think about what might be one or two levels below that emotion and identify with that emotion instead. Exciting, isn't it? For that young piano player, I'd focus on the exhilaration of playing the piano in front of everyone.

Confidence

Thinking about your successes and even recalling lessons learned from past mishaps can increase your confidence level. I remembered that I'd played the Pink Panther on the piano without a mistake many times before. I'd been practicing on and off with Jeff and Brad for weeks and getting feedback in advance from family, friends, and each other.

We were definitely nervous, but we were also probably naively confident in ourselves.

Fun

Everyone has a different definition of fun because we all experience engagement with others in different ways. We reminded ourselves how much fun we had playing together during our sessions. We still helped each other improve during practices but didn't let our mistakes take away the fun element. One of our key outcomes was always measured by the number of claps or cheers during our performance. Enjoy. The. Journey.

If I could go back and tell my sixth-grade self just to have fun and enjoy the moment versus worrying about what everyone else thought, maybe I would have been less nervous.

The Long Game

We were only in sixth grade. If we didn't do well, we could try again as seventh and eighth graders. Thinking this wasn't the first, and possibly only, performance would help alleviate some of the pressure and nervousness.

And it would have been a great reminder that some of the seventh and eighth graders had been in previous talent shows without winning and returned even more confidently.

Breath

How much a long, deep breath can help is incredible. Jeff did this naturally as a trumpet player, and we followed his lead — unbeknownst to us how helpful it would be to calm our nerves.

Imagine Success

Visualization is another way to overcome nervousness. Whether your visualization is about a past success or simply a projection forward about the current situation, keeping a positive attitude about the outcome is also helpful. For example, Jeff, Brad, and I often spoke about how cool it would be to win the talent show as sixth graders.

Comparison

We used a comparison to our advantage: In the talent show, there were only three or four other sixth-grade groups, about the same number of seventh-grade groups, and just one eighth grader. Across a school in the hundreds, we were in a select group of students willing to compete in the talent show. We had already won simply by trying to compete in the talent show compared to others in the middle school population who weren't willing to risk being as nervous as I was.

Subjectivity/Objectivity

As much as competitions try to be as objective as possible, many are extremely subjective. We weren't racing each other to play our music the fastest. We knew we could play all the notes, orchestrate our instruments, and objectively perform well. But we couldn't control the subjectivity of the judges, also known as the student body.

To end this story, we played well, but the eighth graders all voted for the one eighth grader, while the sixth and seventh graders split their votes across everyone else. We actually finished second. Not bad for a nervous situation.

LESSON LEARNED

Understand what you can and can't control and focus on what you can influence directly. The overall idea isn't to eliminate nervousness entirely but to "stamp it down" and give it much less "power" over your actual performance, engagement, activity, or anything else. Consider how you might reframe your nervousness by looking at it from many perspectives. You might realize it is a combination of several, much smaller concerns you can more easily address and get past.

Chapter 5

Dial-a-Friend If You Are In Need or Trouble

When I was younger in software sales, I'd have an accountability partner with whom I could check in and share how many meetings or calls I made in a day or week. He pressed me hard when I didn't reach my weekly goal but encouraged me when I showed that I had met three of my five daily goals. Over time, I wanted to avoid getting pressed and built the habit of making those calls. I could still call him if I needed help, but I wanted to learn to accomplish my goals independently.

BALANCE

"a condition in which different elements are equal or in the correct proportions"

I might be dating myself here, but do you remember what a teeter-totter looks like? Also known as a see-saw, it is my favorite image of balance. Or at least that's what my friends and I always tried to accomplish as kids to be perfectly positioned on the see-saw so we were balanced in the air. I also love that Margaret talked about a see-saw in her **Introduction** story.

"Lessons Learned" originated from our family vacations in Priest Lake. So did my more profound understanding of balance in terms of how it applies to life. You can use the concept of being "balanced" for just about anything; my example is based on the balance between my career and personal life.

There are many different descriptions of work-life balance. Work-life integration. Work-life wobble. Work-life maintenance. We all struggle to define the balancing aspect across the "correct proportions" of work and the rest of our life.

The idea of work-life balance seemed especially ironic while I was working on my vacation. My sons had seen me working on vacations like this over the years, but on this particular trip, I took phone calls in the middle of Priest Lake from our boat, managed a conference call while driving back from an excellent family viewing of a solar eclipse, and woke up early daily to keep up with work issues from our lodge while my family was asleep.

My sons learned during that trip how supportive my employers over the years were of work-life balance. For example, after a long trip, I'd often have breakfast with my family the morning after I returned and go into the office a few hours later than usual, and they realized I often left work early in the afternoon to coach their games, attend school events, or join board meetings to raise money for their schools. I also told the boys how I might break away during the day for a doctor's appointment or take a few days off to travel to a university visit.

More than anything, having the "right" work-life balance is very personal. It varies by individual, the time period of your life, work responsibilities, family obligations, and more.

As you figure out your work-life balance, here are some thoughts to share:

Current Employer

It all starts with understanding the guidelines set forth by your current employer based on your role at work. For example, how much of your work effort can be completed independently versus collaborating with others? What time constraints exist for you to be in your office, working with clients, or engaging with other parties related to your employment? What are your boss's expectations regarding working 8 A.M.– 5 P.M. versus other arrangements? And how is your contribution measured — in terms of billable hours, tasks completed, goals achieved, or something else? Lastly, are there any specific work-life policies in place?

Individual Work and Trade-Offs

There are many examples of individual time — tracking expenses or completing other administrative work, catching up on essential reading materials, documenting critical meetings/engagements, following up with emails or phone calls, etc. One of my favorite trade-offs is meeting a friend for lunch for an hour during the week — knowing that I'll spend that hour on administrative work some evening while the kids do homework.

If I meet a friend for lunch or coffee during the week, I almost always make up for that time, and more in the evenings or weekends to stay caught up with work demands.

Can you make a similar trade-off?

The Time Period in Your Life

A few employees in our office were starting their families. Having kids means you'll likely experience sleepless nights, doctor visits during the week, teacher meetings at school, sports/arts/music practices, and much more. Work with your boss to figure out where your employer will allow you to be flexible based on where you are in your life. Whether you have kids or not or are in a relationship, there will ALWAYS be some demand placed upon your time that conflicts with work, depending on where you are.

For me, I planned on college visits and being part of the board for my son's high school lacrosse club at the time. And my balance changed again the following year when my older son went away to college, and my role on the lacrosse team shifted to a transition out of the board position. My shift was to spend less time on the board and more with work again.

Your work-life balance will vary throughout your lifetime.

Personal Preference

You also need to understand yourself. I'm more inclined to mix in a bit of work with pleasure. When my family was in Kenya for a two-week safari, I got on several conference calls via Skype for work updates. It was less stressful to stay connected for three or four hours on my time rather than trying to spend twice as many hours, or even a few days, in preparations to be entirely disconnected for two weeks.

However, other folks would prefer to get ready for being gone and then get 100% disconnected. Given input from your family/friends, figure out what balance works for you now and adjust as needed in the future.

40-Hour Work Week?

When I started my career, the "typical" work week was 8 A.M. – 5 P.M. with an hour for lunch — five days per week. That's 40 hours per week if you don't want to do the math! I've had periods in my life where I've worked 70–80 hours per week with international travel and other periods where I barely made 40 hours per week because I wanted to be home more often. You need to figure out the balance of investing more time in your work to progress your career more rapidly against the time you'd otherwise spend in your personal life. And know your work hours/week will vary over time.

It's about what you accomplish during that time versus working a specific number of hours in a week or month. Another way is to focus on how much time you want to work over a year instead. Would your employer be OK with you taking a month off if you still worked a full year in just eleven months, for example?

Retirement

I have my retirement plans; you should consider yours as part of your work-life balance. Unless you are financially independent, you probably need to work to retire. Your work-life balance will vary significantly if you want to retire before age 40 versus waiting until 65 or later. I might never "officially retire" and would be fine working into my 80s — so long as I retain 100% control of schedules, time, and more.

In our post-pandemic world, it is heartening to see companies explore concepts like four-day work weeks, hybrid "work-from-home," and many other flexible working arrangements that consider the individual's perspective. People feel more heard and understood by their employers and colleagues and the leadership across many organizations feels more empowered to personalize the work experience for their individual team members.

LESSON LEARNED

Based on the definition, the first lesson is to drop the idea of "equal." Balance is about establishing the "right proportions" given whatever you try to balance. There are tensions on both sides of the teeter-totter, and you can decide how to weigh them. The key is that YOU get to define the "right proportions" and modify them over time, as your circumstances will change at any time.

The story was based on a balance between my work and personal life and I sought perspective from my family, friends, and work colleagues to understand the tradeoffs I was making at the time. But the lessons can apply to the balance you are trying to establish between any elements. Determine the best questions to ask, give equal weight to the answers from both sides and come up with your definition of "equal" if you don't decide to drop that part of the definition altogether.

HOPELESSNESS

"a feeling or state of despair; lack of hope."

I feel it in my heart and soul when someone talks about a hopeless situation. I aim to jump into action, shift into get-stuff-done mode, and help if I can. I hope you do the same for others.

I grew up in the Chicago suburbs and was well insulated from all of the craziness in the world when I was in high school. As a result, I can't remember feeling a true sense of hopelessness while growing up — or even as an adult. I recollect that my value of optimism usually created some hope for me at the time, no matter how dire the circumstances were.

The first time I truly experienced a sense of hopelessness was through my sons. During conversations with my sons and their friends, each had their version of hopelessness about some specific subject. Though I attempted to infuse these young adults with some general feeling of hope, they all had something that gave them a sense of hopelessness.

It was often a fairly significant situation, mainly out of their control. Gun control. Climate change. Social unrest. Homelessness. The potential breakdown of democracy in the U.S. This is just a partial list of what's on the minds of our young adults today. Unfortunately, social media magnifies the more challenging circumstances (sadly, they get more views and advertising dollars that way) while muting what is good in the world.

Through my experiences mentoring and coaching others through deep sadness and genuinely hopeless situations, I discovered a few ways to mollify the sense of hopelessness partially.

Life Events

Some of the best lessons learned are from adverse life events. I used to consider my dad passing away several years ago as "unfair" and a considerable loss. My focus now is to live every day fully and celebrate my dad's life whenever I can versus "enabling" an adverse life event to dominate my experience with my life's journey going forward. Some people consider the death of a loved one as an indicator of their hopelessness about "life is short."

Frankly, life truly is short, so enjoy every moment! Sometimes, I might need to talk to someone about the sadness of losing my father, but I don't allow myself to get into a state of despair.

Thought Patterns

Our brains are masters at taking us down rabbit holes that are not good for us. Give yourself grace. Accept the fact you had a negative thought pattern — we all do. Then pivot your mind to something positive and *break* the pattern! What might look hopeless through one lens could offer several rays of sunshine looking at it another way. Some people even have a daily gratitude journal — an excellent and positive antidote to the many negative thoughts we all have at times in our heads. Other people just need to pick up the phone and ask for help to extract themselves from those rabbit holes.

Inability To Change our Circumstances

When we are in a struggle, it feels like we can't change a thing. When faced with a challenging or hopeless circumstance, my goal is to break down the complexity into small component parts and focus on what I can control and what else I can influence. Then I feel more hopeful since the situation feels much "smaller" in terms of what I can't change or impact. Another perspective is to consider the timing of those circumstances; they might not change in the short term, but if you can get through the struggle, things will improve in the long term. Again, this is where a friend can be supportive.

Hopelessness is typically focused on a specific situation or circumstance. The key is to NOT let yourself slip into a deeper state of despair (despair applies to your entire life and future).

Going back to my dad passing away, one of my own "antidotes" was to take his urn to our favorite family locations and send a photo to my mom and Brother. I celebrated the good memories of my dad there with our family. Whenever I felt myself slip into some sorrowful state, I'd think about one of those visits where I "took" my dad.

The other comment I frequently heard from my sons and their friends was some version of "Our leaders are failing us." They ask themselves how to impact change when they can't influence that individual or group at the top of leadership positions. My hope was to be an adult role model for them to demonstrate that their input was important and influential.

While changes can be most effective top-down (those leaders actually drive the difference), most of the time, I've seen significant changes happen from the bottom up. Getting individuals together in larger and larger groups to take a bunch of very small steps adds up over time. More often than not, a leader decides to drive change when the people under them are forcing them to take a different approach/position. During the pandemic, many leaders demanded their employees come back to work. The employees often pushed back until the leader capitulated to their perspectives and made the appropriate change back to "work-from-home" or hybrid work.

LESSON LEARNED

Accept that life will deliver many complex and challenging situations, and do your best to celebrate the positive side of life and take action to adjust your perspective. Many great stories exist about people facing incredibly dire situations and moving through them successfully. In many cases, there was a family member or friend close at hand as well. No matter how hopeless a situation might appear, understand that almost everything can change for the better over time, and you can start to work on the elements of change within your control to discover some glimmers of hope.

WORRY

"give way to anxiety or unease; allow one's mind to dwell on difficulty or troubles."

I'd say death is a "difficulty or trouble" and it was on my mind the first time I thought I had COVID.

We all have something we might worry about over time — large and small. But, of course, some people are more highly anxious than others. Or just feel very uncomfortable based upon a challenging situation.

But I had just thought about worrying in depth when the pandemic hit. But then, I saw how many people were worried — and it was fully justified. My father had passed away just before the pandemic "officially" hit in the United States, and I was concerned about my mom. But I knew she was being super safe, and we communicated constantly. She was taking every recommended caution, and my concerns significantly subsided.

The first time I feared I had COVID, I peppered myself with a ton of questions:

What is the long-term damage to my system? Could I potentially have it severe enough to die? Where did I get it from, and, more importantly, who else might I have impacted before finding out I was positive? How would my work be affected? What were the long-term ramifications of my life and career if I had some version of long-term COVID that seriously impacted me?

None of this came to fruition because all of my tests returned negative — as they all have been throughout the pandemic and after. Maybe I'm lucky, well prepared, asymptomatic, or have a ton of healthy white blood cells. So there is "mostly" no need to worry for now.

When I'm worried about something, here's what I go through to check in with myself and determine whether or not I should be concerned about something.

Consider the Past

I've successfully addressed various problems in the past and consider what mix of problem-solving might work with the current circumstances. In this case, I had some warm drinks, took ibuprofen, and got some fresh air. As a result, I was already feeling better an hour later. And after getting a great night of sleep, which has always worked for me in the past, was the final "nail in the coffin" about being worried about how I was feeling.

Invest in the Present

I focus on the immediate moment and begin to take actions that I know have worked for me in the past. I'm prepared to adapt quickly and react to whatever is happening. I understand what I can control versus what is entirely outside my control (like the weather outside). In this case, I stopped thinking about future possibilities that may or may never come to fruition. I can only deal with the circumstances I can change now. And I did that step-by-step, and I moved forward without worry.

Rewrite the Future (in a Positive Manner)

Instead of letting my "thinking part of anxiety" get out of control, I simply attempt to script a different and happier future outcome. Instead of assuming the worst will happen, I leverage my actions to push toward the best possible outcome while being aware that "bad things might happen." Many people who are incredibly anxious or uncomfortable with a situation primarily focus on the negative aspects. I'd suggest being AWARE of the negative aspects but concentrating on the positive aspects as much as possible.

Be Careful Where You Can

I still take precautions to avoid difficult situations that might make me uneasy or worried. For example, I often stay downtown in cities I'm visiting for work. Usually, I'll choose to walk somewhere for dinner, but I might end up being routed through a less-than-safe neighborhood to get back to my hotel. In those cases, I might walk twice as far to stay near lighted and busier streets. Or simply take an Uber or taxi home from dinner. Based on my past experiences, this is an easy step to take in the present and enables me to envision a positive experience in the near future.

LESSON LEARNED

Worrying about something is totally understandable and, frankly, largely unavoidable. But letting your mind *dwell* on negative things before they even happen isn't a constructive use of your brain. For sure, you should acknowledge that a situation might cause you anxiety or unease. But treat it like something that comes into your mind during meditation — let it in, acknowledge it is there, and get back to your focus. Instead of dwelling on negativity, use your power of positive thinking, focused action, and fruitful experiences to dampen or eliminate your worries. And, to stay true to this chapter, ask someone close to you for help!

COLLABORATE

"work jointly on an activity, especially to produce or create something."

Acronyms are interesting, but did you ever build one from scratch?

When I first started with one of my employers, I had the opportunity to teach at one of our internal academies. It was a blast — leveraging some amazing materials and mixing in my own experiences to help a group of software developers on their path to becoming managers.

One aspect of this training was called "Deliberate Practice." Across psychological circles, deliberate practice is about doing something that requires a specific and focused effort, with the primary goal being personal development rather than enjoyment. And the only value is to experience incremental improvements versus attaining far-reaching goals.

We discovered that more was needed to help our young developers grow and focus on specific areas of improvement. There had to be a better way. And six to eight individuals around the company were interested in getting together to build a new way.

We decided to collaborate in person for several days. We aimed to understand what worked well with deliberate practice and what could be improved. We came up with a few additions to the idea of deliberate practice — that it should be repetitive and should be continuous and ongoing. We finally devised our new acronym as we collaborated on what was possible. DROP = Deliberate Reflective Ongoing Practice.

And that's when our collaboration *really* began. First, we needed to build out the training materials for the classes. We needed exercises and activities to engage the students and help them learn. Next, we built out manuals for the managers across the company to better understand the goal of a DROP and how to support their people with it. And we needed a cool logo.

I've participated in many teams and worked on many projects with small and large groups. But I'm not sure I've ever been on a team and collaborated so effectively, intending to build out something new that didn't exist before.

And what did I learn about how to effectively and efficiently collaborate?

No Bad Ideas

Many ideas might not be used. But no idea is a bad one. In many cases, one idea can be used as a building block to create a second idea. When individuals attempt to collaborate, they understand that ideas are good and are likelier to share and think out of the box. We probably came up with half a dozen different acronyms before settling on DROP.

Challenge Each Other

We also created a collaborative environment where it was fair to challenge each other professionally. We asked each other hard questions about our ideas and forced each person in the group collaborating to push themselves to come up with better and more robust ideas. I often intentionally start some questions with "Let me play Devil's advocate" as a means of signaling I'm about to ask a challenging question with my collaborative peers.

Democracy Always Rules

When collaborating in a larger group, it's important to enable decisions to be made collaboratively versus having one person dictate the rules or final decisions. If we wanted to run this process in an autocratic manner, we should never have gotten together in the first place. The most senior person in our group not only pressed for a democratic voting process but also voted last in situations where votes were public.

1 + 1 = 3... or More

Like the equation in the story called **Connection**, collaborating often results in answers greater in the group than individual members might come up with on their own. For example, when discussing options for what we needed to do with DROP training, we often had one solution that led to a second... and resulted in a third one. We would have only had two solutions from individuals if we weren't collaborating as a group to notice there was a third one as well. And maybe a fourth or fifth one too!

Future Growth

When you create something collaboratively to start with, it also encourages collaboration downstream in the future. Because everyone knew about the creation of DROP in such a collaborative manner, people were willing to offer suggestions to improve our DROP process. Those suggestions contributed to the project's future growth and the DROP process's overall evolution.

And just because it needs to be said in almost every one of my stories — collaboration is *fun*. Engaging with your peers, friends, or colleagues to create something together is inspirational.

LESSON LEARNED

In almost all situations, the solution that emanates from collaboration across a group is always better, stronger, faster, and more effective than the one created by an individual. Collaboration can be both aspirational and inspirational in whatever you might be co-creating.

Use the suggestions above to better collaborate with others.

PERSPECTIVE

"a particular attitude toward or way of regarding something; a point of view."

How often do you genuinely question yourself or your beliefs? Over time, may you evolve your point of view about some memory you have of an experience?

One of my earliest memories of growing up was during snack time at kindergarten. Everyone would get their little snack and a small carton of milk. You know the carton I'm speaking of. It seemed huge to a five-year-old and looked like a tiny house with a hole in the roof. You'd put that straw into the hole and get your white milk.

I'm unsure how many milk cartons I drank in those first few weeks before trauma struck. At the time, I wasn't even five-years-old. So I use the word "trauma" from the perspective of a little boy still frightened of the unknown.

The teacher passed out our milk cartons and snacks. Eventually, she stopped drinking from her straw and said, "ICKY." Okay, I don't remember what exactly she said. But it was loud enough to get the full attention of 20+ kindergarten students who should have been more interested in devouring their cookies.

The teacher shared with us that her milk had actually curdled. Feel free to search for images of what curdled milk looks like. I remember a chunky white substance that looked like disgusting cottage cheese that would *never* be consumed through a straw.

My initial perspective — I'll never drink milk again.

I never had another carton of milk in that class and I refused to drink milk at home. My mom would go out of her way to pour milk into a clear glass where I could observe there were no chunks in it. I was convinced I didn't like the taste at all. I'm still determining why my mom and dad relented, but I got my dairy from cheese and other sources. This went on for years and years.

Friends would invite me over for dinner. They all had tall glasses of milk. Nope, not for me. All through elementary and middle school, I'd drink water or juice or anything that didn't come in the form of that white, chunky stuff that potentially is on the other end of the straw in that little house-like carton.

Many friends tried to convince me of other options over the years. Chocolate milk — the first sip wasn't sour, but I wouldn't say I liked the taste of it. Tried it after dipping an Oreo or Chips Ahoy into the milk. It still tasted horrible to me. Ice-cold milk on a hot day. Totally gross to me.

As an adult, I finally looked back and tried to understand the connection. It started with the potential of sucking gross chunks of milk through a straw. I turned that into "it doesn't taste good" to me. So finally, I decided to try milk under the best of circumstances, and made many legitimate attempts to try milk ice cold on a warm day, chocolate milk, Oreo cookies, etc. It was better than I remembered, but I still didn't like it.

Over the years, I've continued to try milk here and there. And different types as well — one percent, two percent, soy, almond, etc. I'll definitely enjoy a hot chocolate on a cold evening. And I don't mind a little milk mixed in with my coffee (my new relationship with coffee is a whole other story called **Change**). However, it won't make my top ten (or twenty or thirty) list of favorite drinks.

More importantly, I discovered that for years, if not decades, I was cemented in a perspective that may not have been entirely accurate. Nevertheless, I continued to take in new information and look at my disdain for milk through the perspectives of others and my new points of view.

More recently, I was house-sitting for some friends. I've never enjoyed being around cats — not only am I allergic, but I was scratched pretty badly by a cat at a young age. Anyway, I enjoyed time with my friends' cat (in small doses) without sneezing! New perspectives can be surprising and rewarding.

HEARTBROKEN

"(of a person) suffering from overwhelming distress; very upset."

As I write this story, I'm thinking about some of my friends who just put down their 13+-year-old Labrador Retriever. I'm heartbroken for them. I hope that your hearts are fully operational right now.

For many people, March has the great connotations of spring, no more snow, Spring Break, or something else as you shift from winter to summer. For me, March usually equates to March Madness. And if you are unfamiliar with March Madness, it's the NCAA Basketball season-ending tournament where 64 teams (OK — now 68 with the four play-in games) compete in a winner-take-all tournament. One loss and you are out.

One of the frequent discussions after the first weekend of March Madness is complete (meaning we are now down to the 16 remaining teams) is all about "busted brackets." And whether you had a team you liked, or several teams you picked, another phrase I often hear is "heartbroken." Since my days of filling out my first bracket, most of them have been busted in the first week. I'd never use the word "heartbroken" for my brackets, but the comments made me think about when I was first heartbroken.

It all came down to one word. Pretzels.

More specifically, my pretzels were ruined.

I'm dating myself here, but when I was a senior in high school, phones were often attached to the wall. So if you wanted any privacy, you needed a super long phone cord to sneak into a closet or another room from where your mom, dad, or nosy younger brother might overhear your discussion.

The backstory is that I had been dating someone most of the spring of my senior year. She was a sophomore, and I was about to graduate high school, head off to college and leave her behind for two more years of high school. So it was time to break up with her and "get ready" for whatever the dating scene might look like for me at the University of Illinois.

Immediately following that breakup, I connected with another graduating senior on whom I always had a crush. We got together at a party and kissed in the corner of a room. We were having fun and talked about "going out" over the summer before we both went to college. At that time, "going out" mainly included many phone conversations stretching that phone cord as far away as possible from anyone else in my house.

A few weeks into summer, she called me while I was making pretzels. I figured I could multitask (multitasking is a story for a future book) and talk to my girlfriend while making my pretzels — dragging that phone with the long phone cord around the kitchen with me. Little did I know her call was to break up with me. As far as I can remember, this was the first time I was genuinely heartbroken. The call went long enough that my pretzels were ruined entirely. And I didn't even get to eat those pretzels as an excellent comfort food to help me deal with a broken heart.

What helped me to understand how to process a broken heart best is to know how deeply I loved something. I'm sure at the time, I was heartbroken. But I know now that my love was an early form of the proverbial puppy love. Sadness? Sure. But probably not a broken heart.

Beyond the heartache of my Illinois basketball team losing in the early rounds of March Madness, here are some more serious forms of heartbreak I've experienced.

Losses OF Life

The death of a loved one is brutally heartbreaking. My father. My grandmother. My dear friends Nick and Natalie. My dogs.

My guidance is to celebrate your love and life with them versus focusing on your heartbreak. Even better is a quote from Brené Brown in *Atlas of the*

Heart: "*The brokenhearted are the bravest among us — they dared to love.*" In some ways, without heartbreak, you don't truly understand the depths of love.

Losses IN Life

There are many different losses in life — long-time relationships (a marriage in my case), deep friendships (friends who have moved or are in a different phase of their own life), financial (poor stock choices), travel (flight cancellations leading to missing a whole trip) and more. These each have a varying degree of being heartbroken. And none are as impactful as losing a life. But they should not be overlooked in terms of their impact on you personally.

Losses at "Work"

I've been part of a RIF (reduction in force) and lost my job when my company had to shed over 90% of its workforce. I've been with companies who have been sold to larger organizations — losing the soul of your startup is a bitter pill to swallow as well. Even losing work colleagues who depart or losing deals that were important to you could be heartbreaking. In these cases, you need to consider the situation's unique circumstances, understand the lessons learned and move through your version of heartbreak as quickly as possible.

A broken bracket during March Madness is probably one of the most "gentle" versions of heartbreak, but it can serve as a great way to learn how to overcome being brokenhearted. Maybe you "fell in love" with your great picks only to learn how to move on with some lessons learned.

LESSON LEARNED

My "March Madness lesson learned" here is to have friends who also like to create Sweet 16 pools so we can fall in love with yet another bracket in the same year! But on a serious note, consider the perspective of celebrating your love for something you've lost. Of course, it is OK (and fully expected) to be sad, mournful, sorrowful, dejected, etc. However, what is on the other side of those feelings of heartbreak is an amazing strength and memory that you loved something so deeply in the first place. And know that you can love again. Read **Love** near the end of the book for the other side of being heartbroken.

INSPIRATION

"the process of being mentally stimulated to do or feel something, especially to do something creative."

Over a year after joining ThinqShift, I still didn't have a great answer to the question from my sons regarding the question — *"What do you do at work, Dad?"*.

Sometimes my answer is about helping individuals, teams, or organizations shift their mindsets, beliefs, and habits during a transformation. An individual who is recently promoted. A team that is charged with taking on a new challenge. An organization going through a merger, acquisition, sale, or significant growth inflection point and helping you with the idea that "what worked for you previously won't work for you going forward".

Other times I answered more specific questions about the differences between hard and soft skills. For example, as individuals, teams, and organizations evolve, the hard skills (teachable and quantifiable skills — like getting a certification) are actually easier to learn, and the soft skills (most often thought of as "people" or "inter/intrapersonal" skills — much more ambiguous) are much harder to learn. We usually focus mostly on the much harder development around soft skills.

But when I thought about it, my "what do you do?" goes back to the lessons I learned when I was coaching my sons and their friends in baseball, basketball, lacrosse, soccer, or any other sport they were interested in sharing lessons learned with others. And my desire to share lessons learned with others really kicked in when I was given an opportunity to be a co-teacher for a class of students in the Human Centered Design Engineering (HCDE) program at the University of Washington (U.W.).

I'm simply inspired to help others - through these lessons learned or any other means at my disposal.

Ingenuity

Whether with academics, the arts, sports, or anything else, I've been able to dig deep and figure out how to learn something new, improve something I do well already, or get stimulated to get more creative or inventive. The second class of HCDE students I worked with were graduate students — several of whom were older than me AND worked at notable companies here in Seattle. The fact they were inspired enough to take night classes energized my inspiration. They inspired me to be more inspiring myself — which helped me to focus on how to help others on their path toward inspiration best.

Across the many different roles I play — mentor, coach, trusted advisor, guide, friend, peer, experienced leader, etc. — there are many ways to spread your ideas about ingenuity to others, and I am so grateful for those opportunities to inspire others.

Adaptability

Recognizing the circumstances you face in a specific situation are very different from those you've faced previously in a similar situation — and making the appropriate adjustments to deal with a new set of circumstances. Even more challenging is facing an entirely different situation and figuring out how to pivot and react differently than before. For example, thinking about those kids, I was coaching and changing sports. Can they shift from playing on a basketball court with a team of four others to a huge lacrosse field with a team of nine others (and lots more gear)?

As adults, we all must adapt to constantly changing situations and times. VUCA — volatility, uncertainty, complexity, and ambiguity exist at many levels in our work and personal lives. Therefore, we all must learn to adapt. Those U.W. graduate students were inspired by the stories of others adapting to complex circumstances and hoped to leverage those lessons in their lives.

Creativity

In this case, creativity was about keeping the students having fun while motivating them to improve continually. Doing the same thing over and over is no fun. Creativity in homework sessions, how teams work together during class, and what you are learning between the scheduled classes are all ways of driving interest in your work. Likewise, mixing it up and taking a creative approach to work is also essential. More importantly, creativity often leads to innovation and new perspectives. During several HCDE classes, we delivered exercises meant to instill new creative thinking methods in the class and inspire them to greater ambitions.

And when you are coaching a group of young children, daily creativity is essential to keep their attention and continue to inspire each of them.

Storytelling

Sharing the stories of others is a valuable way to inspire others — especially when you can select a circumstance that might apply to someone's situation. What's even more inspiring is hearing stories from your peer group. For example, I worked with a student before class one day and asked that person to share the story with the group they had just shared with me. I helped them shape the messaging, but the story was 100% theirs to share. They did a great job and motivated others to share their stories later in the quarter.

Sharing marvelous stories from professional sports figures with the kids I was coaching entertained them and inspired them to improve themselves.

Influence

Though I was the "professor" and could tell them explicitly what to do or how to do something, I often tried influencing their actions instead of directing their behavior. Motivation and trust were key here. I wanted them to be interested in what we were doing without it being about "let's do what the professor says." Likewise, leading by influence or example is much more effective than directing or telling someone what to do. I often exerted my influence by NOT answering their questions of "*How should we do this?*" and letting them struggle through in a positive way — another version of self-direction inspiration.

Coaching was no different. Taking off running and asking the kids on the team to catch me before a full lap around the field was a more effective way of inspiring them versus standing on the sidelines, blowing a whistle to get their attention, and yelling at them to "take a lap!".

Teamwork

Inspiring an individual is great, but I love seeing a team communicate and inspire each other. Skills are a plus, and so is knowledge. But when you can motivate an entire team, you will see the levels of inspiration across the group increase exponentially. The group projects were a great example of how other teams can inspire each other. The teams presented their work in progress to each other, gathered feedback from the teams and professors, and were energized to take their projects to the next level.

And sports are the ultimate representation of how excellent teamwork can inspire everyone on the team.

Perspectives

Everyone has their perspective on what inspires them. Solving challenging problems or building new relationships stimulates creativity. Even when what appears to be a challenge to one person might seem "easy" to someone else.

When others have a sense of purpose or vision and can leverage existing processes to move things forward, they inspire each other. We might know what inspires us, so dig into what motivates others.

The U.W. graduate students ranged from recent senior graduates to students in the workforce for decades. It was paramount *not* to teach in one particular manner.

After my experience with the U.W. HCDE students, the answer to the question from my sons is that I *'encourage inspiration in others.'* It happens in many different ways against nearly an unlimited number of backdrops. But it is truly a rewarding experience for me and others as well.

MOM

"woman in relation to her child or children."

Instead of "Dial a friend if you are in need," consider calling your mom after reading this story if you can.

I further appreciated everything my mom did over time as I observed everything my ex-wife did to raise our sons. But then, as a parent, I started to pay a lot more attention to the seemingly unlimited number of roles a mom plays in her child's growth and development. I'm in awe of everything the many mothers I know and all of the moms I don't know have done to raise their sons and daughters.

When my dad passed away, I was much more intentional about calling my mom and flying back to Chicago to spend time with her. It's been wonderful getting to know my mom as an adult. Of course, she's still my mom and asks me to text her when I get home from travel. But now I see her in a very different light.

I started writing this book as a version of "Lessons Learned for My Sons." And it evolved into lessons for everyone and anyone. But as I considered the source of many of these lessons, I wanted to share my appreciation for my mom and the lessons she taught me.

Here are a few lessons I learned *from* my mom the year after my dad passed. There are undoubtedly many other lessons my mom was involved with sprinkled throughout this book.

Resilience

My dad passed away only weeks before the start of the pandemic. Not only did my mom lose her spouse spanning over six decades, but she also had to deal with significant isolation during the crazy pandemic. Yet she always kept positive and moved forward no matter what crossed her path. These observations have helped me with my resilience when faced with difficult circumstances in my own life.

Journey

My mom continued to think about her life journey forward versus any specific goal. She talks about the time she can still spend with her sons and grandchildren. She keeps in touch with old friends and has met new folks in the neighborhood. Mom discovered new interests like pottery and rekindled previous passions like piano playing. My mom is inspirational to me to consider what new passions I might explore down the road as my journey moves forward. Some future passions include learning how to dance, learning another language beyond my poor Spanish, and studying how to play a new instrument.

Happy

Mom stays happy and wants to know whether my brother, me, or others around her are happy too. She is such a positive influence on so many people! If my mom can be happy in light of losing the love of her life, I can definitely be happy in my world.

I hope this story inspires you to tell your mom about the most valuable lessons learned she imparted to you over the years that you leverage today.

LESSON LEARNED

Though I know everyone has a biological mother, not everyone has a mom in their life now. Tell your mom what you love about her and your gratitude for bringing you into this world if you can. In general, if you have some mother figure in your life, let them know how much you appreciate them and the gifts they gave you over the years.

P.S. And apologies to you, the reader, if this doesn't feel like an actual lesson learned. But I wanted at least one story to honor my mom and publicly acknowledge Melanie and all those amazing moms who raised their sons and daughters by including this story!

COMPARISON

"a consideration or estimate of the similarities or dissimilarities between two things or people."

One of my favorite questions is, "How does the technology kids have today compare to what I had when I was their age?".

When I first think about comparison, I think about those "tests" where someone has two images next to each other where only *one little thing* is different, and you need to find it. It makes me crazy sometimes when I can't find it.

My first experience with comparison was concerning the game of chess. My dad taught me how to play chess at a young age. I was learning how to play chess against him and some of his friends before I was in kindergarten. Then, when I was in second grade, my parents entered me into the school chess tournament — many kids from all grades ranging from first to sixth grade. The tournament was structured based on having a champion declared across each grade first and then played out as one-on-one challenges for those champions across all grades.

I can't remember exactly how many matches I won against other second graders, but I beat them all and was declared the champion for the second grade. In my young mind, I compared myself to them all and was better at chess than everyone in my grade.

The next phase started with me against the first grader. After winning that match, I figured I was better at chess than all first and second graders. So I could compare my chess skills and smarts by projection in my young brain. I also won matches against the third, fourth, and fifth graders. Can you imagine where my head was at? Comparing myself against most of the kids in the school?

My luck/skill came up short against the sixth grader, but my skills also compared favorably against most other sixth graders. He didn't beat me by much!

Whether with sports, academics, or other areas of my life, I would compare myself against the progress of others to understand how I could improve myself and do better still. This was with me for the majority of my life growing up until I started to play golf actively.

Until that point, most of my sports activities involved sports where you could play defense against the other team and impact their performance. Golf was the first sport where the game was 90% mental, 10% physical, and 0% playing defense or influencing others. Therefore, the only way to compare me to others was based on how I played alone.

Most of the time, I was focused on comparison from the lens of "What are our differences in performance" and "How am I better?". With golf, I started to appreciate the lens of "What can I learn from our similarities AND our differences?". More importantly, I'd compare myself to where I was previously and measure my success based upon my own progress - versus comparing myself to others.

This permeated through other parts of my life. In high school, we were ranked academically. My only path to improving my ranking was to optimize my development and performance by learning from others and using the positive aspects of comparison. For example, am I studying as much or as effectively as those ranked higher than me? How do those ranked ahead of me participate in class and engage with the teacher? Instead of focusing on the end goal of my final class ranking, I sought to understand how I compared to others across much larger measures. My transformation was to view the idea of comparison through many perspectives, none of which was the "final product." And quite often, the comparison was against my previous performance or achievements - versus against anything others accomplished.

Comparisons are still a helpful tool in my life today, but I use comparisons positively to improve myself or help others through mentoring and coaching. For example, sometimes comparisons help others understand they aren't the only person struggling with a particular situation. Or as an example for someone to learn how they react differently to something versus another person who handled something poorly.

P.S. When you get the "picture comparison test" that I shared in the second chapter of this story above, look at the eyes of the people or animals. That was a favorite "trick" employed by the authors… their eyes were looking in the opposite direction in the two photos!

LESSON LEARNED

Be positive about comparisons. Use comparison to celebrate your similarities with others and even celebrate the differences if they are positive for the other person. And if you compare yourself based on your differences, you can strive to close the gap on those differences by turning them into personal growth or development opportunities. Comparisons should be more than a binary evaluation like I thought they were as a second grader. There are layers and layers of nuance around comparisons. Make sure you evaluate them all as you make comparisons.

EMPOWERMENT

"authority or power given to someone to do something - like the process of becoming stronger and more confident, especially in controlling one's life."

The fact that I have an award named after me, following a stint serving on a board for my sons' lacrosse club, is humbling, to say the least. But the story behind this award is a perfect example of what it looks like to "empower others."

Years before this award recognition, I connected with another father who, like me, had an incoming son who would play lacrosse as a freshman in high school. Lacrosse in the state of Washington is not a school-sponsored sport. As a club, lacrosse needed funding for coaches, equipment, fields, safety equipment, and anything else the kids needed. Michael and I agreed to join the board, which was being formed in its earliest stages, to support the program for the next four years.

Literally, after just one board meeting, two of the original board members left the board. Michael and I looked at each other and said, "*OK — who's going to drive this bus?*". In a way, we both wanted to avoid taking the lead. But, on the other hand, the team was in shambles — with only 13 kids (seven were freshmen, including our two sons) on a varsity team, an inexperienced head coach, and almost zero continuity from the programs of years past.

Our solution was as follows. First, I told Michael that I'd become the V.P. Fundraising (we had less than $5K in our budget), and I'd support him if he was willing to take on the role of President. Plus, I knew I'd likely have to take on the role of President when he departed in a few years when his son graduated with my older son since my younger son was going to be a freshman then. So I knew I would be involved for at least seven years, three more years beyond the original discussion, to see BOTH of my boys go through the program.

Without a ton of "formal" support, we needed to empower others to make decisions and get stuff done to make this program work. We engaged other parents, who were reluctant to join the board, to lead smaller element of the lacrosse club other parents who were reluctant to make the same dedication of time we were driving in their ability to lead smaller parts of the lacrosse club. Over time, they built up their aptitude and confidence in getting the job done and became board members in the future.

After multiple head coaches over our first three years, we were fortunate to connect with a great head coach who wanted to see the program succeed. The great news? His son was in middle school and would be involved in our lacrosse club for another two years, meaning we finally had some stability with our head coach. Michael and I worked hard to empower the head coach to make decisions and take a leadership role for the team — accountabilities we took on over the past few years.

My favorite take on empowerment was with the players on the team themselves. One of our major fundraising activities involved selling car wash tickets. The players were responsible for selling a certain amount of tickets to friends, family, neighbors, and more. To their credit, our two sons largely had taken the lead in motivating the rest of the players. We gave them more and more responsibility, and they thrived.

Over the years, our budget increased significantly, and the team more than tripled in size. We went from one win in our first season to winning the conference championship multiple times several seasons later. And it didn't hurt that both of our sons were all-conference players at their positions during their senior year. That's more of a proud dad moment versus a story about empowerment, but I'm inserting it here because it's my book!

Anyway, we rebuilt the board after Michael "retired." I took the role of president and transitioned my role as V.P. of Fundraising to another father. He did well and felt totally empowered to take the lead there. Knowing that I was leaving in a few years, I quickly worked to empower others to take on roles across the board. Finally, I transitioned out of the president role when my son was injured and didn't play his senior year.

I attended the year-end ceremonies for my younger son's senior year, this time as a parent instead of the V.P. of Fundraising or President. It was great to see the year-end ceremonies from the stands instead of being involved in the front of the proceedings. As they announced various awards, the existing board asked me to present a new award named after me.

The award goes to the player who does the most for the team to work with others *outside* of their efforts on the playing field — basically, which player most empowers others across the team to accomplish other goals beyond success on the field? I was humbled and honored that the board named the award after me, and still am. It's a legacy I'm proud of leaving with the high school lacrosse club. And the only reason it came to fruition was because I enabled others to do so much more than I could have ever accomplished alone.

LESSON LEARNED

Some people might look at empowerment through the lens of delegation only. But that's not what it is about. As a leader, you need to find the right combination of directing, supporting, or coaching individuals to reach their comfort level in taking on more and more responsibility. This combination will vary based on the individual and the task at hand and is a transfer of your power or authority. The decision to direct, support, coach, or delegate also comes down to the individual's competence, willingness, and commitment to owning the accountability for completing the task or ongoing responsibility. And you need to create a "safe space" for them to fail and eventually succeed. Whether they are "controlling one's own life," supporting the efforts of others in a huge organization, or playing a role in a small high-school lacrosse club, the key is empowering others for their benefit versus for self-centered reasons only.

DREAD

"anticipate with great apprehension or fear."

My tummy gets all knotted up when I think about something dreadful.

One of the things I love about golf is that I'm only genuinely competing against myself and the golf course. Yes, I usually play with one to three others during the round. But I'm optimistic that I'll play well individually and to the best of my abilities regardless of how others play.

During a recent trip to Arizona, my friend Steve and I decided to play a more challenging course than we usually might play. The course was rated as one of the toughest courses in the greater Phoenix area, and the starter for the course said, "*You should just leave the driver in the bag unless you have a low single-digit handicap*" Single-digit handicaps indicate a very good golfer. The day I played Troon North Golf Club, my handicap was 15.1 — very much *not* a single-digit handicap, *nor* a very good golfer.

And while the intent of the advice was great, I was on vacation and in NO WAY wanted to leave the driver in the bag. I needed the distance off the tees to play my best. Or so I thought.

Other than the par threes on the front, I missed every fairway I played for the first eight holes. (Truth? I probably missed the greens on the two par threes as well - but I digress!) The first two or three drives went left or right and nowhere near the fairway. It was the third hole where I knowingly experienced a sense of dread for the first time.

Certainly, over my lifetime, I was scared to do something, be it riding a giant roller coaster, asking a girl out for a date, or stepping into a complicated discussion at work. But at those times, I didn't clearly understand what I was experiencing, much less how to deal with it. As a result, there was no true sense of dread.

That definitely changed during my round of golf. After several horrible drives, I was apprehensive and fearful every time I stood on the tee box and thought about where my drives would end up. Dread truly existed for me.

As I thought through the times in my life when I probably experienced a sense of dread (even if I didn't call it that at the time), here are a few thoughts on how to combat dread:

Future

The threat of something being dreadful is a future-based situation. In many cases, you can change the future by taking different actions than you planned to take initially (especially after learning what didn't work a few other times already). I talked about my options with my friend Steve; I put my driver back in my bag, played my three wood, hit my ball into the middle of the fairway, and finished the hole with my first par of the day. I played the first eight holes in a horrific fourteen over par (almost at my handicap before playing our first nine of eighteen holes). Hitting my three wood, just as the starter suggested at the beginning of our round, gave me confidence and eliminated all sense of dread. I played the last ten holes at just three over par. And I had a blast playing with zero dread.

Probability

Who determines how high the probability truly is that something dreadful will happen? If there is something you dread, you give it a much higher chance than it probably deserves. Consider other options that reduce a pending event from high to medium, low, or nearly zero probability of being negative.

For example, I kept hitting my driver in my first few holes and lost my ball somewhere in those rocks and cacti. So there was a high probability that I would hit ALL of my clubs the same way. But by hitting my three wood off the tee, I significantly reduced the likelihood of a negative event happening and significantly reduced my apprehension about teeing off on the next hole.

Negative

Everyone should challenge this assumption. When one of the startups I was with would be sold, I dreaded telling the President I had zero interest in joining the new company. But once we had the conversation, he helped me to find my next role, even being one of my key references for the new job. Something I perceived as a potentially negative event actually turned out to be positive. I initially thought *every* drive would be a negative experience that day. But switching to my three-wood made it a positive experience.

The Other Side of Overcoming Dread Usually Amounts to Some Amazing Memories

There are many ways of mitigating the negative thoughts in your head to turn a dreadful situation into something productive, positive, interesting, and fruitful. Or call someone and ask for their stance on overcoming a dreadful situation from their own experiences.

The roller coaster ride at an amusement park I mentioned above felt exhilarating; dating in college, after I'd finally conquered my fears of asking a girl out on a date, warmed my heart; and difficult conversations at work that turned into something productive instilled me with a great sense of confidence. And playing some amazing golf (for a 15+ handicapper) made me feel like a professional golfer (at least in my head!), originating from what started as a dreadful situation.

LESSON LEARNED

First, break whatever you dread down into small parts — low probability of success, most likely a negative event, and concern for the future. Then, consider what actions you might take proactively to reduce some or all of those factors that make up dread. Finally, once you have a new plan, reevaluate your feelings about the situation and do your best to see the positive "light at the end of the tunnel."

In most cases, dread dissipates into something with little to no fear associated with it. And then you can shift your mindset into something to celebrate down the road.

ENVY

"a feeling of discontented or resentful longing aroused by someone else's possessions, qualities, or luck."

I'm happy this is the only one of the "seven deadly sins" I'm including in my book!

As I took the dogs on a walk one morning in my old neighborhood, I walked along the many waterfront homes with beautiful views of the Cascade Mountains, Lake Washington, and Mount Rainier. Over the years of living in this neighborhood, I heard many people talk about being envious of others who lived with amazing views, incredible homes, and active lifestyles.

The simple definition of envy is to want what someone else has. I have many friends who live in these homes and was fortunate enough to spend time with them, so my thoughts veered in the direction of "I'm happy for my friends... I hope they are well".

While I did not experience any envy with regard to those living in those highly desired homes in particular, I have experienced many different versions of envy over the years.

I first felt and experienced "envy" during middle school. I was envious of several friends who were much more active in the dating scene than I was. They had what appeared to be very romantic relationships — in several cases, with a cheerleader, athlete, or female friend I likely had a crush on. It felt like I was the only one in the class without a boyfriend or girlfriend.

Gut-wrenching at that time.

For me, that first version of envy was all about romantic relationships — effectively *"someone else's possession."* I'm sure we have all been attracted to something or someone another person has. It's natural. My young version of envy via attraction dissipated completely when I developed my relationships and focused on shared happiness, excitement, and joy with my girlfriend. But I sure had a crush on several cheerleaders in high school and a twisted-up gut before I figured it out.

Another category of envy relates to competence, intelligence, knowledge, etc. Basically, this is *someone else's set of qualities.* I was certainly envious of many of my work colleagues when I started a new job in a different organization. One of my goals was to quickly learn as much as possible and perform as well as possible. I knew I was being compensated similarly as they were — but I wasn't adding ANY value. I felt useless, overpaid, and a bit helpless. Over time, I realized I had as much to offer others as they might offer me — especially in the context of my previous experiences before my current role. Collaboration, working together, self-development, and the joy of helping others is much better than envy.

The idea of wealth or one's financial status or lifestyle is frequently a source of envy. Who isn't a bit envious of the person who made millions investing in the "right" company at the optimal time? This sure seems like *someone else's luck.* Seattle has thousands of "Microsoft and Amazon millionaires" — some who worked there and others who invested smartly. To be honest, I might be envious of them when I first hear their story. But within minutes, I'm truly happy for them. They took risks I didn't take and were rewarded; how can I be envious? A true sense of happiness is ten-times more valuable than wealth or lifestyle.

Someone I was on a Zoom call with the other day said they were envious of another person's competence (*qualities*) in a specific area. I reminded this individual of their own "superpowers" and that it was entirely possible this other person might be just as envious of them.

If you find yourself feeling a sense of envy, take a moment to consider everything YOU have before you envy what others have in terms of *possessions, qualities, or luck.*

Instead of being envious of others, I focus on appreciating and enjoying what I have. And if there's something I'd like that someone else might have, I'll figure out how to get my version of that item.

LESSON LEARNED

It's OK to be aware of your envy, and if you have an abundance mindset, you realize there's always more you can get out there. There's plenty to go around. Unearth some *possessions* of your own. Practice to build out your unique *qualities*. And remember the equation that *luck* = hard work plus skill.

I often focus on happiness — both my own and that of others. Instead of being envious of someone, I find it helpful to be happy for them and the joy they experience through their *possessions, qualities,* and/or *luck.* I also remember that I have my own!

What does one of your friends or family have that you might envy? Can you imagine celebrating the happiness that object or situation brings them versus whatever feeling you have?

Chapter 6

Lifelong Friend Who Is in Trouble with You!

The first time I tried the *Whole30* diet, we had a group text of six people on a similar journey. We shared recipes, encouragement, challenges we overcame, and even a few failed days of staying on track. But, as a collective, we got through it together and there were definitely days of no sugar where it felt as if we were ALL in jail sitting next to each other!

Even with a group helping out, I still had one friend I would call if something tempted me. Don't have that glass of wine! Don't eat that ice cream in the fridge, or grab those cookies on the shelf! And when we were in person, it was great to say, "Don't order that," or "Please don't buy that in the store."

BELONGING

"an affinity for a place or situation"

"I don't belong here." I feel sad for people when I hear that statement and I remember many times when I felt the same way about a place or situation. It sucks.

In the one-half century I've been cruising around Earth, I've often felt like I belonged to a group, organization, club, neighborhood, etc. It took me some time to adjust to a new situation, but I usually found a way to belong.

Or I didn't. There were other times when I didn't belong. I'm not criticizing those other places or situations, or circumstances. It's just part of life and reality — we can't belong to everything.

Accept it.

It may be where I am in this stage of life. Or it could be the other people I'm with. Or the specific situation I'm in. Or the mutual circumstances we are all facing. But reflecting on my first two years with ThinqShift, I feel as if I belong more here than I've ever felt before.

What can I share about those feelings? Let me give you some cues to help you understand whether you belong (or not) to a place or situation, or some ideas about how you can improve your situation and strengthen the feeling that you do belong:

Vulnerability

This should be a two-way street. No matter how well I've developed my "vulnerability muscles" over the past decade, I'm still learning to be vulnerable. To an individual person and the whole team at ThinqShift, we are all vulnerable with each other and the group. We readily admit if we don't know something and need help to better understand it. Everyone is open to sharing how personal challenges might impact our mindset and ability to be present right now. And we share our highs and lows equally.

Unlike other companies I've worked with, I could call anyone at any time and be completely open with them without any concerns of repercussions or criticism.

Past Experiences Matter, and They Don't

With some groups, I've belonged to, we can often tie ourselves back to mutual experiences. And often, when you don't have shared experiences, you'll find that you don't belong. At ThinqShift, I discovered that I have a few past or shared experiences with some people but none with almost everyone else, and we all feel we belong together for many other reasons. For example, we are constantly creating new experiences with each other.

Common Mission/Vision/Values

Regardless of the dynamics of the individuals involved in a situation or the unique circumstances surrounding a place or situation, a shared vision or mission or values (or all of the above) can help everyone feel as if they are strongly connected and belong to something. ThinqShift's mission is to assist fabulous people in growing into their definitions of a Fabulous Leader. Of course, there's much more to all that, but everyone at ThinqShift is dedicated to helping "craft fabulous leaders to succeed and reinvent the world." Think about what elements of your organization's or group's mission or vision drive your passion for being there.

Ask for Help

I did *not* feel I truly belonged when I started at ThinqShift. While I had delivered much of the content and executed as a coach and mentor, I had never been focused on those roles as 100% of my job and time. But I persevered and asked for help and guidance from others in and out of ThinqShift. I leaned into assistance from my coach and therapist. I talked to my former work colleagues and had deep conversations with my closest friends. They helped to give me perspective and understand the idea of how I belonged at ThinqShift. It is difficult to "look in the mirror" and understand difficult situations without an outside perspective. Who can you call and ask for help?

Constantly Challenge Yourself

Subjectively often applies when thinking about your perspective. Heck — that is part of the definition. But I objectively question myself and ask hard questions about whether or not I belong at ThinqShift. When the answer comes back, "Yes," I'm relieved and emboldened. If the answer is "No," I try to understand what, if anything, I can do to change those circumstances and shift the answer to "Yes."

Early on, I questioned whether my passion for sales and business development would fully translate into passion and energy for preparation, delivery, execution, and support. When it did — I knew I belonged. Take a quick inventory of your own passions and superpowers and ask yourself, "Is that enough?" or is there more you still want to learn or accomplish?

Stay Curious

Even though I feel as if I totally belong at ThinqShift now, I'll still be curious about what more I can do to fully belong and help others feel as if they belong as well. I'm interested in how the direction of ThinqShift might slightly adapt over the years and explore what I can do to adapt congruently. As we grow, I'll be curious about how new employees feel about belonging and what I can do to help them. Whatever your situation, don't seek out information that simply confirms your existing beliefs. Constantly ask yourself challenging questions to feed your own curiosity.

Fun

A frequent theme for many people and especially me. Whether the word is fun, joy, happiness, enjoyment, wonder, or awe, ensure you get some or all of this as you inquire about belonging.

LESSON LEARNED

YOU get to be the arbiter of whether or not you belong. Clearly, you can't "force fit" yourself into every situation or place. But don't let others dictate the terms of whether or not you belong. Leverage some or all of the ideas above to get an initial indication of how you feel about the situation and then check in with your head, heart, and gut about belonging and ensure they are all in synchronicity.

DEVOTION

"love, loyalty, or enthusiasm for a person, activity, or cause."

Mwenzi was my first dog.

It is pretty remarkable what we can learn from animals.

I didn't grow up with dogs. Instead, my parents allowed us to have fish and, eventually, my brother and I had our own guinea pigs. My little guy was named Pork Chops. He lived a few years, and I had fun taking him outside and letting him "play" in an enclosed space in the yard. Pork Chops was fun to watch, running around the house and climbing the stairs. But I'm not sure how he felt about me.

Did he think about me as his friend?

Mwenzi was a devoted friend.

Yup — that's actually what Mwenzi means in Swahili — friend. Mwenzi was the first dog I ever owned. She was a beautiful black Labrador Retriever. And big, too — pushing nearly 100 pounds and almost all muscle. She had a strong motherly instinct as she was very protective of everyone in the family. I ran and walked and hiked with her everywhere.

Mwenzi taught me all about devotion.

Let's change the word "person" to "mammal/animal" in the definition above because Mwenzi helped me to understand deeply what devotion is all about. It includes love *and* loyalty, *and* enthusiasm. In this case, the person was me. Mwenzi was devoted to everyone in the family and her "sister," Maisha.

My view of devotion transformed into something more deeply than a superficial understanding of devotion based on our interactions during our many walks, hikes, swims, and more.

Unconditional Love

Seriously, how incredible is unconditional love? Just eye contact or a smile from me led to a wagging tail from Mwenzi. And no matter how sad or mad or anything else I felt at that moment, she was always there for me. Seek out a dog if you need to understand unconditional love better.

Energy

If only the power grid could provide energy in the same way labs like Mwenzi shared their energy. Long walks. Uphill hikes. Chasing balls. Non-stop moving. If I only had ten percent of the energy of this infinite source of vigor. No matter how much energy it took to keep moving, she always seemed to have unlimited storage of energy if it meant we'd be spending much more time together. That seemingly endless source of energy fed into our enthusiasm for being together and her devotion to spending time and sharing her energy with me.

Loyalty

Mwenzi was always there for me — regardless of whether I'd been out of town for business for several days or was sick and couldn't get her out for a long run. She was there to support me if I wasn't feeling well. Several times on walks with the boys, she'd place her body between one of the boys and some stranger who might have looked like a threat (to her). Incredible sense of loyalty!

Happiness

I challenge anyone to be sad or mad around a canine ball of energy and unconditional love. Walking outside. Endless games of fetch. Jumping into the water. Eyes that always seem to say, "What are we doing next?". Everything is fun and happy with dogs and Mwenzi seemed to take it to another level.

Of course, I love my sons. I'm devoted to them as well as other causes and activities, but learning what devotion is from Mwenzi took it to a different level for me — even without the wagging tail!

LESSON LEARNED

Go all in. Don't hold back. Use love, passion, enthusiasm, joy, loyalty, and more as much as possible. And let it grow and expand beyond where you started. Let it flourish within you and share that devotion with others. Devotion has two sides — your devotion to someone or something else and the reciprocated love, loyalty and enthusiasm, and you should endeavor to experience both!

FAIRNESS

"impartial and just treatment or behavior without favoritism or discrimination."

Who is the judge of what's fair? I often hear kids playing and someone yelling, "no fair." Frankly, I listen to it a lot as an adult too.

In a different story of this book, I write about my competitiveness and how it has played a significant role in my life. And that story focused on my playing with the older kids and developing my competitive genes. But those older kids weren't always around or available. And there weren't any kids in the immediate neighborhood who were my age. So at those times, I played with my younger brother and his friends. My brother Michael is three years younger than me — not a huge deal at our age today, but when I was eight and he was five, that gap seemed HUGE.

The other side of my competitiveness is that I do *not* like to win anything if the odds appear to be stacked in my favor in any manner. I always wanted to make sure competition was fair — especially when it was competing against my younger brother and his friends. Giving the more youthful kids a head start and racing around the house was fun, but my favorite "competitive event" with the younger kids was canoeing. In some cases, I'd let them have two or three people in one canoe to compete against me (alone). Other times, I'd let them paddle ahead of me before starting a race to the other side of the lake.

I discovered that kids rarely tried to make things fair as I got older. They always wanted to win or play only with their friends, who were often some of the best at whatever was going on. I started to dislike being on the teams that won easily because we had all the best players. It drove me always to want to make the organization of teams, events, or anything else fair to all sides and everyone involved.

As an adult, events get more complex, and the decision about what is and isn't fair gets cloudy. To what level of detail do I track the costs for my sons to attend universities to ensure they each get similar financial support? As a leader, how do you ensure you spend the right amount of time with your individual team members? How do you enable everyone involved to share their perspective on the topic in a meeting with many people? It feels as if fairness continues to get more ambiguous as circumstances become more complicated.

Using the definition of fairness is a great way to break down some ways to make fairness less ambiguous; here's the definition again as a reminder: "impartial and just treatment or behavior without favoritism or discrimination."

Let's use the example of one of my coaching clients who manages a team of over 50 people.

Impartial

Finding someone impartial might be the biggest challenge to start. Identifying a person who can be completely objective is a great way to ensure fairness. You can also create a system of rules and guidelines and create impartiality based mostly on facts and data. Depending upon the circumstances, the leader of that team might be the impartial "judge." But other times, it might make sense for them to bring in an unbiased third party.

Just Treatment

One of my favorite phrases is "treat others how you'd like to be treated." Ensuring you treat everyone the same way is another element of fairness. With a group of fifty people, it would be nearly impossible to treat everyone *exactly* the same way. In this case, fairness would be more about knowing the nuances of what is just for each individual. It isn't easy, but being just is as important across a large team as it is for an individual.

Behavior

We all act in different ways and establishing standard rules or guidelines for everyone to act and behave consistently across the group, game, or situation is crucial. Having a sense of shared values or norms for the team is important and this client is part of a much larger organization, so there were discussions about behaviors appropriate for the team versus what's needed across the corporation. For example, this leader said, "Asking questions during the middle of a meeting is productive." By comparison, in a large Town Hall setting of hundreds of people, the organization preferred questions to be held to the end of the meeting/after the presentation was completed.

Without Favoritism

Whatever the situation, it is entirely unfair to identify the winners or losers or beneficiaries and people who lost out before the situation. "Playing favorites" helps no one. The winners don't truly learn anything, and the losers get frustrated with the odds stacked against them before engaging. Inevitably, some people might feel like they are a "winner" in their leader's view and others are "losers." The leader can't show preferential treatment to any individual or small group versus others.

Discrimination

The scope of discrimination is nearly limitless. You can unintentionally discriminate based on race, religion, sexual orientation, age, size, country of origin, etc. Since the categories are diverse, this may be one of the most challenging aspects of establishing a sense of fairness in a group. This takes talking amongst the group and establishing common ground across all important categories based on the situation or event. The leader of this group of 50 had an extremely diverse team, and there was zero discrimination for any reason. Everyone on the team was equal.

My initial exposure to fairness with a group of children younger than me seems fairly simple now. The idea of fairness can become an extremely complex situation to work through.

Disclaimer: In all fairness to you, the reader, this story could have easily been placed in one of the "Work with a Pro" chapters because it can be a very multi-layered topic.

LESSON LEARNED

Fairness is an excellent value (Yes — I'm biased) and should be "used" selectively. You can't view fairness through a single lens, and you often need to consider many other circumstances and the overall situation to determine what fair means. Most importantly, fairness has two sides — your perception and the perception of others. In most cases, the intention of wanting everything to be as fair as possible is appreciated by others. But realize that some people want to stack the odds in their favor and have no interest in fairness. However, once fairness is established, almost everyone involved will immensely enjoy moving forward.

INUNDATE

"overwhelm (someone) with things or people to be dealt with."

What do you do when you have "too much on your plate"?

Flooding is "the covering or submerging of normally dry land with a large amount of water." Being completely inundated can feel like you are figuratively drowning in tasks, information, facts/data, or to-do lists. The metaphor is that you are the dry land, and all that "stuff" inundating you is the water flood.

With every job promotion, I needed to take on more responsibility to justify my new salary level. So I rarely said "*No*" and jumped into more projects. When the pandemic hit in early 2020, I wanted to help others and continue providing more support. My calendar was flooded with meetings, and I felt overwhelmed with the amount of work I was accountable for.

Here are some quick thoughts about how to recover from this inundation craziness.

Urgent or Important?

We must respond immediately to our boss, client, or someone else. But you can have a discussion with these people and come to an agreement about what is genuinely urgent/essential (only 20% of tasks/requests), what is only important/not urgent (about 60%), what is only urgent/not important (15%) and what is neither (5% — drop it!). Then, figure out your "psychological contract" with the individuals you are working with to let them understand how you will respond to their requests. Don't let an inundation of requests impact hours of productivity — many of which probably support the same boss or client anyway! I continually checked in with my boss to ensure I was focused on what was essential to the business versus what seemed simply like another urgent request.

Tasks/Requests

You can also categorize these potential distractions by better identifying the specifics behind a certain task/request. Do you really need to acknowledge you received an email? Or is it critical to respond to a request when the person making the request won't see your response for hours anyway? Every situation is different, but many tasks/requests can easily be categorized across a team or organization into different "response modes" based upon the details and perceived requirements. For example, I let the people I was working with know how/when I'd respond, which impacted how they flooded me with more (or fewer) tasks/requests.

STAY in Your Groove (Some People Call This Flow)

Keeping your existing momentum is optimal. Think about riding a bike and gliding down a hill. How much longer will it take to get to the bottom if you hit your brakes and come to a complete stop 24 times along the way versus just letting gravity and your momentum lead the way? I learned to focus on specific tasks until completion versus getting caught in the trap of getting 25% done on many different things. Of course, you might need to break a larger job down into smaller tasks to focus on just one at a time. You can't multitask, and context switching is difficult. When you are inundated with so much, staying in your groove to complete one "thing to be dealt with" is easier than returning to it repeatedly.

The exact times vary across studies (research from UC Irvine is one of many), but most agree it takes 15–20 minutes to get back into the same groove of whatever you are doing after an interruption. We seem constantly flooded with email, text, Slack, or social media interruptions. If you consider an eight-hour work day, only 24 interruptions will take eight hours to recover from all of your interruptions. This means you'd get *nothing* done because you are in recovery mode all day. I learned how to get into a flow to get something pushed to completion before moving on to the next flood.

Engage Others

Depending upon your role and how inundated you are, you can engage others and delegate some of what is overwhelming you and, if you are in a leadership role, this might also be viewed as an opportunity to mentor someone else and teach them how to do something that might be "easy" for you but new to them. My goal is to engage others with learning and growth opportunities that allow them to challenge themselves while providing a safe space in case they struggle and need help.

Just Say "No"

This might not always work in corporate America, but there are many things you can say "No" to before getting pulled into something new. Over time, I learned to say "No" with a smile while helping the requester figure out what their Plan B might look like. Another twist is to say "Yes" but with conditions that work for you. For example, saying "Yes" to a task might be acceptable if you tell them *your* deadline is one week, even though their original deadline might be two days. After that, it's up to them to decide.

As I work with my clients today, I share many of these lessons learned. More importantly, I've shared what has worked well for me and others I've mentored and coached. We work closely together to understand which of these lessons might help them in specific situations. Some lessons work well in a particular situation, while others might apply to something overwhelming them differently.

My first comment about having "too much on my plate" makes me think about eating out. Don't you feel a bit overwhelmed when the menu is four or five, or even more pages long? How can you decide when you are inundated with so many choices?

Urgent or Important

Maybe both in this case… it is important that you eat while it might be urgent to decide before your waiter/waitress returns.

Tasks/Requests

Simply make a decision. If you make the wrong decision, you can still order dessert later!

STAY in Your Groove

Do what's comfortable for you. One person might need to read the entire menu, while another would simply say, "I'll take whatever the chef recommends." Many people stay in the groove by coming down to two choices and asking for advice for one or the other.

Engage Others

Ask the waiter/waitress for a recommendation. Or talk to others you are with. If you are bold, ask that table next to you about their food that looks delicious!

Just Say "No"

With five pages, you probably need to say "No" to about 75+ other options. These are just a few of the many different coping mechanisms you can leverage.

RELOCATE

"move to a new place and establish one's home or business there."

I hate packing and unpacking my "stuff"... who wants to live out of boxes when you relocate?

My nephew Jack graduated from the University of Illinois in spring of 2022. He took a job in San Francisco and relocated after two decades of growing up in the Chicago suburbs. The fact he moved away from what's been comfortable for him for two decades reminded me of when I moved to Seattle.

Growing up, I moved several times in my life — from Ohio to Michigan to Illinois. And over the years of living in Illinois, I relocated multiple times — to Champaign for college, to Peoria for work, to the Chicago suburbs as a newlywed, and, finally, to downtown Chicago. But the relocation that was *most* impactful to me was the move from Chicago to Seattle.

So many things changed when I relocated to Seattle nearly three decades ago. My marriage was beginning. I had to start a new job. We needed to discover where to live. We had no close friends who lived here. And the only advice people seemed to want to give us was, *"Don't forget to bring your umbrellas since it rains all the time."*

Looking back, I had trepidation about so many new things hitting me. But I quickly learned to embrace new things — regardless of the result. Of course, there were some failures and bad experiences, but, more often than not, there were so many cool new things to do, it took a long time before we'd repeat anything.

So, hmmm… maybe this relocation thing isn't so bad.

For anyone moving to a new part of the country or world, here are some thoughts and ideas to discover how to embrace the need to relocate.

Enjoy the City...

Living in a big city is a great opportunity. Walk around neighborhoods. Dine at local restaurants. Take in the culture of music, theater, comedy, and more.

Ask everyone, "*Where do the locals hang out?*" And don't be afraid of "being a tourist" as you explore everything.

My experiences were all about Seattle, but they apply to any town, large or small, where you might relocate.

...And Take in the Region Too

Don't forget about all the fantastic adventures you can discover outside the city. It is almost impossible not to see the mountains and want to explore them. Look at ALL elements of nature — the islands, the ocean, mountain lakes, flowing rivers… and a whole other country just a few hours north. I see this in major European cities as well. There's so much culture and newness to embrace in the city that you forget the region just outside of the city is just as (and maybe even more) impressive than the specific place you relocated to. And beyond nature alone, there are usually many smaller and fascinating little cities in the region.

Meet New People...

What an incredible opportunity to build lifelong friendships. Some of my closest relationships started by connecting with new people in my earliest days in Seattle. You find them at work, out socially, playing games, exploring the area, etc., and you'll find creative ways to meet new people. Some folks were long-time residents of Seattle, but just as many relocated to Seattle from elsewhere and shared their success stories.

...And Keep in Touch With Long-Term Relationships

Another strange benefit of moving away is discovering some depth with your existing relationships — whether family or friends. Sadly, a few of my relationships in Chicago dissipated with the distance. The good news is that several of them became stronger/deeper because staying in touch and connected was much more difficult. You'll learn new ways to be close;

today's technology makes it more accessible. And relocation might happen to some of your friends as well; keeping in touch is good no matter who is making a move.

Establish Your Independence...

No matter how independent you might have been post-college, moving a significant distance away from family and friends creates new opportunities to establish independence. Your support systems will change. Your decisions will feel even more independent — just like the one to move away in the first place!

... Don't Forget To Ask for Support

One of the most common mistakes I see in young adults starting is the inability to recognize when to ask for support. That applies to almost everyone as they continue along their paths to independence. Do NOT be afraid to ask questions and seek help as you delve into new and challenging new opportunities. Making mistakes is entirely expected as you learn. Most everyone wants to support you when you ask for help.

LESSON LEARNED

Relocating to a new region is a great "forcing function" to embrace new opportunities. We all want to leverage our past experiences and strengths from our existing location. We need to recall the past challenges of learning new things many years ago when we relocated at some point/s in our life, those same things we lean into today.

Embracing new opportunities when you relocate is a tremendous growth opportunity we should continually seek to discover on our own.

Can you do this all without help from others? Of course. But my experience is that relocating effectively takes a lot of mental, physical, emotional, psychological, and more support from your closest family and friends.

EMPATHY

"the ability to understand and share the feelings of another"

Becoming more empathetic has been a long journey for me. I hope you'll consider where you are on your journey with empathy, as it feels like I can continually improve.

As I was fully present for Ryan's graduation, I had a feeling come over me that I couldn't understand at first. I finally figured it out it was empathy. As I watched Ryan go through the various stages of his graduation process, I understood his feelings and shared my own experiences with those feelings with him in the days following the big graduation day/s. It was a balance of excitement to move onto the next phase of his life against the sadness of moving out of Boulder and back home to Seattle. I shared how I wanted to hang onto my great college memories by staying longer, how much fun I had moving into my first job, and what those experiences were like.

Sitting in the group of proud parents, friends, family, and more, I got curious about where I discovered empathy the first time because we were all sharing stories about "I remember when I graduated" or "I was so excited when I was sitting where my son/daughter is sitting right now." I grew up with kids with shared interests and beliefs. Most of those interests or beliefs about the school, neighborhood, sports, roller skating, music, or whatever were relatively simple. My shift to better understanding, or at least being more aware of empathy, was my first year at the University of Illinois (U of I).

Though we had a common connection in our chosen university, many of us had very little else in common. So I had many opportunities to work on my "empathy muscle."

One way to better understand empathy is through the lens of this emotion's various components.

Perspective

What is the other person's point of view? And what is their experience — *without* making any judgments about the experience? Just listen and don't try to "wear someone else's shoes"... I promise, they rarely fit. Feel what they are feeling and become part of the experience they are sharing.

My first roommate in college was from Singapore, and I had a fantastic experience learning about him and his perspective. It was an incredible opportunity to learn more about an entirely different culture and experience growing up in another country and continent! I'm grateful that Chia-Ling shared so many stories from his perspective. And it was great to hear about his friends' perspective who also came to the U.S. from Singapore.

Emotion

Asking someone questions to deepen your understanding of their emotions is a start. But trying to understand yourself and whether you've experienced similar emotions is key. Matching and understanding someone on their emotional level is a much better "fit" for being empathetic. And even if you can't feel or truly experience their emotion, you can work to understand better how that emotion makes them feel.

Experiencing emotions seemed black and white when I started my days in college — I either understood someone else because I had the same sentiment, or I didn't. Over time, I learned many emotional nuances based on the situation, the individual, the group dynamic, the timing, and more, and, in some cases, I could more deeply understand what someone else was sharing with me back with them. For example, my friend Natalie would share her frustrations with how many guys asked her out all of the time (I didn't have any girls asking me out), and I let her know that I understand her view as to how that might be distracting to what *she* truly wanted (more solitude) partially because our conversation was being interrupted by one or more of those guys at the time!

Reflection

Once you have the other person's perspective and have a good sense of their emotional state, you can reflect on their story and share your perspective that might be aligned with their current state. You can demonstrate how you experienced similar emotions — even if you got there through your process. The most important piece here is ensuring they understand that you "get it" regarding their shared story or experience.

Some long drives back and forth home from school allowed me to reflect (verbally) on my understanding of empathetic situations my passengers would share. Natalie and I had many long talks during these journeys and sometimes we had a third or fourth passenger as well — meaning we'd all have to share perspectives across what, at times, was three or four entirely different points of view. It was great practice, usually with topics that weren't too "heavy" at the time.

As I've learned more about empathy, I discovered that empathy does NOT require that you have experienced exactly what someone else is going through. It is all about listening to the other person's story about the situation and believing them — even if it doesn't match your experience. Empathy also involves compassion and seriously considering your understanding of that individual.

Even if you are struggling to channel your inner empathy, just letting someone else know that you are trying to get there with them is an incredible first step in the process.

LESSON LEARNED

Be present. Listen with ALL your senses — your head, heart, gut, etc. Feel and hear what the other person is saying, feeling, exuding, etc. Learning to empathize more effectively with others will broaden your understanding of yourself while establishing a deeper relationship with the person you are empathizing with. Making it clear that you understand someone else's perspective, sharing your emotional response to their situation, and ultimately reflecting back your thoughtful interpretation of their situation are all building blocks on your empathetic trek.

COGNITION

"the mental action or process of acquiring knowledge and understanding through thought, experience, and the senses."

How often do you think about how you think?

The brain is a pretty cool organ. I remember learning about the brain in school. The most visual representation of the brain I think about is a scene from *Young Frankenstein*. For those uninitiated to Mel Brooks' *Young Frankenstein* movie, I'll let you discover Igor and the "Abbie Normal" brain he brought back to Dr. Frankenstein.

The transformation for me was learning about "The Whole Brain" during one of my training classes at work. We took an assessment and discovered a new way to look at how we learn. If you look at the brain from a structural perspective, there are the left and right brains. There are also critical components of the brain in the upper and lower sections of the brain. Ned Hermann, decades ago, used this physical paradigm to create what's known as The Whole Brain and the four quadrants.

Here's a Quick Summary of the Four Quadrants:

1. The visionary quadrant asks, "Why?"; think about this as an experimental voice in your head
2. Analytical quadrant; asks the question "What?"; analytical voice
3. The action quadrant; asks the questions "How & When?"; safekeeping voice
4. The personalization quadrant asks the question "Who?"; relational voice

Given this new perspective of how I might learn, I re-examined different methods of learning I've leveraged over the years.

The Left Brain and the Right Brain

There is no correct answer about whether left-brained or right-brained thinking is better — we all need both sides to survive. However, knowing I grew up with a much stronger left-brained thinking style, I've worked hard with my therapists and coaches to engage my right-brain thinking.

My mom taught math, and my dad was a chemist. So both my genetic background and learning environment were heavily focused on left-brain thinking. I worked for several manufacturing companies for college internships and moved into information technology quickly after that. After almost a decade with technology and management consulting, which favors left-brain thinking, I finally moved into a role where I am 100% focused on helping others, whether family or friends or work colleagues or customers, to understand how to leverage their strong left-brain skills best while enhancing the right brain essential abilities. Or vice versa.

It is a great exercise to attempt to learn something from *both* sides of the brain - and be fully aware of what you are doing.

Design

What is your best experience with great design? Is it a product that you fell in love with immediately? Or the layout of a store or restaurant that inspires you? When I opened a package with a new MacBook Pro inside, I was highly impressed. Apple even thought about great design in the context of the packaging for my new laptop. User-centered design is about ensuring the people using the systems daily that we are architecting and designing will address their primary requirements and use cases.

The engagement process with one of my former customers is a great example. We start the year with an agreement for a specific amount of work to happen throughout the year. At the end of the year, we would review what we accomplished and typically found that we had modified 50-70% of our original plan. The customer was always happy that we worked closely with them on making real-time design changes weekly or even daily. And we were pleased to deliver exactly what was most important to our customer — because the definition of "most important" changed rapidly through the year as their business conditions and priorities changed.

More simply, I moved the furniture in my room around two–three times yearly. Sometimes the changes were significant, but other times they were simple. More importantly, as my use cases changed over the years, so did the need to "redesign" my room. For example, who needed a whole table for a record player and records when you had tapes or CDs for your Walkman? And no design space is required today for record or DVD players with streaming services so prevalent.

Great design forces you to understand what thoughts, experiences, or the senses will impact yourself or others. And I often acquired new knowledge while coming up with new design options.

Stories

For centuries, most of our experiences, knowledge, and thinking were conveyed through stories. They are a helpful way to turn information into context and are easier to remember. What are some of your favorite stories? I can think back to stories I have heard from others, read on my own, or even shared with my boys as I tried to get them to sleep at night. Great stories resonate with me more than a list of facts or data.

Almost every chapter I am writing in this book starts with me telling a story. It began initially when I wanted to document my stories for my two sons and share my "lessons learned" with them. This book allows me to document the story for my sons and share it with YOU, hoping you'll find them valuable.

Storytelling is a great way to synthesize facts into a more specific context and mix in an emotional element. And I hope these chapters make the information I am sharing much more personal, memorable, and, most importantly, *actionable* for my sons and you, the reader.

Listening to or reading great stories is a wonderful information-gathering technique.

Symphony

One of my favorite musicians is Beethoven. When I listen to his music, I am amazed that anyone can combine many different instruments and musicians into a beautifully coordinated piece of music. Creating a (literal and figurative) symphony is about clearly understanding the relationships among the various components of a system and how to synchronize them.

I remember coaching my kids and their friends in soccer over the years. Some of my favorite moments came when I helped the kids "see" the bigger picture of what they just accomplished. They were excited when someone scored a goal, but they needed to see the fuller process of what happened collaboratively to lead to that goal. The goalie made a great save and passed the ball to one of the defenders. Several defenders passed the ball beyond the opposing teams' attackers to move it to midfield. On a team of eleven players (in case you do not know soccer), the coaches and I watched how eight or nine different players touched the ball, passed it among each other, and set up their teammate for that goal. Listening to Beethoven's Ninth Symphony is amazing, but watching a group of eight and nine year-old boys work together was their version of a fantastic symphony.

Understanding something as complex as a symphony can make it easier to understand other complexities and improve your cognition.

Empathy

Have you ever been in a group where one person yawned, and then *you* started to yawn? Several studies at ncbi.nlm.nih.gov/pmc/articles/PMC3678674/ demonstrate that yawning when others yawn around you is a primitive form of empathy. Sympathy is feeling something *for* someone else… empathy is feeling something *with* something else. And I'm definitely empathetic for sleep when someone else yawns!

So many people were incredibly supportive of my family and me when my father passed away in 2020. I am grateful that many people offered their sympathies through phone calls, text messages, Zoom interactions, nice cards or letters, and more.

My most meaningful interactions were with truly empathetic friends about my situation. In some cases, they described their journeys with the death of a loved one and inferred how I was feeling. In other cases, they could "step into my shoes" and understand the emotions I was experiencing as if they were going through the grieving process with me. Being sympathetic to a problematic situation is wonderful, but being genuinely empathetic takes it to another level.

Empathy is the way to go when it comes to understanding people more deeply.

Play

Games are one of my favorite team-building or people-bonding exercises. Whether it is a basic board game, a fun game of cards, or a more interactive game like an escape room, games are a great way to bring a group of individuals together to solve problems and express themselves.

Humor is another way to interact creatively with friends, family, or work colleagues. Telling jokes is a way to lighten the mood during a stressful day. My friend prank-called me the other day for fun, and the funniest part of the call was my friends busting out laughing half-way through the call. I am smiling again, just thinking about that phone call.

Joyfulness is a great way to demonstrate and experience happiness. One time when I was with some of my childhood friends, a song we all remembered from middle school came on, and we immediately started to dance (poorly) and sing (even worse). My face hurt from smiling and laughing for hours afterward.

Play is an interesting form of discovery and a great feed into cognition. And you can also find another story in the book called **Play**.

Meaning

Man's Search for Meaning by Viktor Frankl includes a great quote about his theory that "*man's main concern is not to gain pleasure or to avoid pain but rather to see a meaning in his life*." His larger point is that the purpose of life is about the journey itself. The journey is something that often comes up with Buddhism as well. I love the idea of focusing on the journey.

I am finding more meaning in my life by sharing lessons I've learned and helping others develop their leadership qualities. Coaching a group of eight- and nine-year-old boys was always a great time. But it is so much more rewarding to be a part of teaching, developing, and nurturing the next generation of leaders — what an incredible journey!

Cognition includes many words/topics spread across this book, whether exploration, collaboration, or discovery. Track down whatever method is most effective for you to acquire additional knowledge and understanding to learn more. Or experiment with bits and pieces of each and come up with your own formula!

LESSON LEARNED

Create awareness of your cognition. How you understand, process, empathize, strategize, etc. We all learn and understand differently. The key is to understand and continually improve your awareness, understanding, processing, and feelings associated with acquiring knowledge, understanding, and wisdom, and I hope some of the methods I shared above — left/right brain thinking, design, stories, symphony, empathy, play, and meaning — are useful and you continually improve your cognition.

SUCCOR

"assistance and support in times of hardship and distress."

How many words do you hear and think, "*What in the heck does that mean*"?

I learned the word succor one week in English class, remembered the definition for the quiz at the end of the week, and (hopefully) remembered it weeks later as I was taking the year-end final. Full disclosure — I just searched for "how to take care of someone," and succor was one of the words. The definition is "*to assist in times of need or distress*." Succor is outside my daily vocabulary, but I plan to use it more frequently.

I've been helping those in need of assistance over the years but it didn't hit me until my second son was born. If you aren't getting enough sleep, a crying baby is one of the loudest "distress" calls you will ever experience. Being unable to calm down, self-soothe, and fall asleep gave Cole hardship and distress at the time.

One of my favorite books to read to boys was *Dr. Seuss's ABC*. The rhythms and playfulness of the words led me to read them repeatedly to Ryan during our bedtime ritual. I memorized portions of the book and "read" part of the book to Ryan in the dark.

By the time Cole was a baby, I had memorized the entire book. And I could "read" it to him to comfort him in the dark and get him to fall asleep on my shoulder. Then, whenever Cole was still awake after reading a book or two with the lights on, I'd turn the lights off and "read" the ABC book to him in the dark. Not only did I want to comfort Cole, but I also didn't want his crying to wake up Ryan!

On the surface, it seems as if I learned a new skill — memorizing a book — and I clearly wasn't looking to memorize a book for the sake of memorizing a book. But, it was what Cole needed regarding "assistance and support." I learned how to tune into Cole's needs (falling asleep in the dark) versus my own (needing a lamp to read) and provide him with the level of succor he required at the time.

Bottom line — I asked myself these questions (based on the definition of succor):

1. What is the *distress* someone else is facing? (Cole couldn't fall asleep on his own yet.)

2. Is this *hardship* a one-time situation or an ongoing challenge? (He certainly wasn't going to learn in a single instance — this was an ongoing challenge that needed attention).

3. Do I have the ability to provide some or all of the *assistance*? Meaning, is there something I can actually do in this case? (Yes… learning how to "read in the dark" was something I could take on personally.)

4. Or do I only have the opportunity to *support* someone else? (If it was something like breastfeeding, I clearly could only support my ex-wife, but it was about indirectly providing succor to Cole.)

LESSON LEARNED

You need to tune deeply into the needs of others to help them during times of stress. Think about how to get creative in a time of need and come up with a solution that focuses on the needs of others versus what you "think" that person might need. Ask yourself some or all of the questions I've outlined above to confirm their definition of assistance and whether it might differ from what you believe, and when you deliver the desirable level of comfort, they'll be grateful for helping them through their distress or hardship.

STRESS

"constraining force or influence."

There are many manifestations of stress. For this story, I'm focusing on "a physical, chemical, or emotional factor that causes bodily or mental tension and may even be a factor in disease causation."

Like many other words in this book, I've also experienced stress in my lifetime. However, stress is one of the words I haven't considered deeply. Let me recount some of my past stressful experiences:

1. Playing piano at my first recital.

2. Standing in the batter's box and waiting for the pitcher to throw the ball when we are down by one run, in the last inning, with two outs and two strikes.

3. Needing an A on my final exam, at a grade of 95/100 or higher, to shift from a B+ to an A- in a college class.

4. I hoped my girlfriend at the time didn't even consider during our nice dinner out that I was going to propose to her later that evening.

5. Wishing beyond all belief that both of my sons are healthy as I watched them being born and become part of humankind.

6. More recently, hoping that the person coughing on the plane next to me didn't give me COVID.

At the time, any of these events, and so many more, could be stressful. However, the event that got me thinking a lot more about stress was the need to start my own business as part of my work with ThinqShift. I've always wanted to start my own business, but it never happened (insert many excuses here).

Starting my own business made me stressed thinking about marketing, sales, networking, legal, accounting, bookkeeping, general administration, etc. While I've been involved in these activities throughout my work life, I've never had to be 100% responsible for each of them. STRESS big time!

Stress can include unpredictability, uncontrollability, and a feeling of being overloaded, among other things. I'll break down those three below.

Unpredictability

Life, whether home or work, changes constantly. Why be stressed about something that hasn't happened yet? The focus here should be on adaptability and learning to deal with ambiguity in real time. One of my favorite quotes about being in the moment is from *The Last Dance* with Michael Jordan: "*How can I worry about a shot I haven't even taken yet?*". Don't try to predict what might happen; just be ready for anything to happen.

I've successfully applied this principle to my work with ThinqShift. For example, I couldn't have predicted how many forms I needed to complete to start a business in the State of Washington, but my bookkeeper worked with me closely and helped me through the process. Another helpful thought is to be adaptable because no one can predict the future.

Uncontrollability

This is another frequent "contributor" to stress. And there are a LOT of elements in our lives that are 100% out of our control. Instead of getting stressed out about something you can't control, focus on the specific things happening that you can control. And for those uncontrollable issues, figure out how to prepare for them in advance or do something differently.

For example, I can't control if it rains, but I can bring an umbrella or stay inside an extra hour and wait for it to stop raining.

With ThinqShift, I often focus on how I can help an individual I'm coaching or a leadership team I'm energizing. While I can't control their specific outcomes, I can share enough success stories or frameworks as applied to their particular circumstances, and I know they'll feel more in control themselves.

Feeling Overloaded

One of my coaches likes to say that we tend to underestimate what we can get done in a year and overestimate what we can get done in a day or week. Granted, you can't control if your boss, spouse, or somebody else adds more to your to-do list. But you can learn to prioritize by determining what is urgent and important and what you should drop altogether. Or even add a time element — my guess is that some of that list does not need to be finished or even started immediately.

So, if I ever feel overloaded with my accountabilities at ThinqShift, I balance what is necessary with what is urgent — coupled with the timing (days, weeks, months, years, etc.).

Lastly, I want to quickly address the component of mental stress that leads to difficulties with someone's mental health. I will NOT try to provide some quick fixes or lessons learned for those in need.

Please find a therapist knowledgeable about best supporting someone with mental illness. If you don't have access to a therapist, consider leveraging the 988 Suicide & Crisis Lifeline as a means of seeking support and help for yourself.

I like to do a mini-retrospective on what was stressing me to remind myself, "That wasn't so bad now, was it?".

So, for example, here are the "answers" to my stressful events from above:

1. I played Fur Elise without any mistakes.

2. I singled and tied the game (and scored after two more hits by my teammates).

3. I got a 96 and that A- in my Ceramic Engineering class.

4. She didn't, and we got engaged that night.

5. They were and have been (Yes — still wishing they *remain* healthy).

6. Still, no COVID — 100% of my tests have been negative.

Almost as if I didn't need to be stressed out at all.

There are many common stress relievers out there: hug your dog, call a friend, take a walk, get a massage, squeeze a stress ball, close your eyes and breathe deeply.

LESSON LEARNED

The starting point is the self-awareness that your mind or body is feeling something caused by a person, situation, or unique circumstance. Then try to understand the impact of this stressful situation and determine what, if anything, you can do to mitigate it in any way. In many cases, the stress we feel is related to something improbable occurring anyway. Try to look at the stressful situation through the lens of unpredictability, uncontrollability, and your feeling of being overloaded. Solve those as best you can to significantly reduce, and maybe even eliminate, the stress you are feeling.

WONDER

"a feeling of surprise mingled with admiration, caused by something beautiful, unexpected, unfamiliar, or inexplicable."

How many movies have you watched dozens of times?

Or, how often have you watched a specific scene dozens of times? My answer is probably no more than half a dozen, with the movie *The Secret Life of Walter Mitty* being one of them.

The reason why is probably tied to situational bias. I first watched the movie on my way to Kenya with my family. I loved it so much, I told both of my sons to watch it, and then I started it a second time, and a third time, and a fourth. Granted, I dozed off throughout several viewings over two flights of 10–12 hours each.

During one of my recent viewings of Mitty, I started thinking about the idea of wonder. His experiences include:

- Escaping a volcano eruption.
- Avoiding a shark attack.
- Jumping out of a helicopter.
- Climbing in the Himalayas and more.

These scenes and adventures are beautiful, unfamiliar, and difficult to explain without watching the movie. I wrote a couple of different LinkedIn posts about Wonder, but as it relates to this book, I had to think back and evaluate when I first experienced a sense of wonder.

It was likely the confluence of two significant events in my life — a trip to Spain (see the chapter on **Introspection**) and, more importantly, my first significant travel *without* my parents. Over the years, I've been lucky to travel around the United States and into Canada and Mexico with my parents, but Spain was my first trip overseas and the first time I'd traveled without my mom and dad.

I went to Spain alone to live for six–seven weeks with a family I'd gotten connected with through my dad's work. The family I lived with was excellent, and they lived in the center of downtown Guernica. It was a beautiful little town in the Basque region of Northern Spain. Over the six–seven weeks I was in Spain, I experienced one wonderful moment after another.

The best way to share my experience and consider all aspects of wonder is by breaking down the second half of the definition: "...*caused by something beautiful, unexpected, unfamiliar, or inexplicable.*"

Beautiful

My "summer break" family picked me up at the airport, and instead of going home to relax, we immediately went to the base of the Pyrenees Mountains. Talk about beautiful views! I've seen some mountain ranges before, but seeing the Pyrenees on my first full day in Spain was absolutely incredible. There are beautiful things all around us — both natural and manufactured. Take a minute to appreciate them fully.

Unexpected

Freshly grilled octopus — unexpected how amazing it was. Of course, the setting was in a little place called San Sebastián — a resort town on the Bay of Biscay in Northern Spain. My hosts would take me to a restaurant/bar on the water; we'd order beer or wine. Yes — I was only 18, so being able to have a drink in a restaurant/bar was also unexpected. Olga, the daughter in the family who was my age, and her boyfriend shared some freshly grilled octopus — which had just been delivered within an hour from a catch that occurred just an hour before. Even if you aren't a "foodie," you must enjoy a sense of wonder — at least gastronomically! Welcome the unexpected with open arms.

Unfamiliar

One of our "side trips" was a week in Paris. An eight-hour drive goes by quickly when you are driving through the Pyrenees, along the ocean coast, and planning to end up in Paris. By now, I was nearly fully fluent in Spanish. How does that help me in a country and language I'm 100% unfamiliar with?

Again, a wonderful experience was to quickly discover how "easy" it was to pretend I was not the "Ugly American" who spoke loudly in English but rather the "blond-haired Spaniard" who was trying to connect his almost fluent Spanish with their articulate French.

Unfamiliar with the culture, language, expectations, and more, it was an amazing experience as a direct result of being willing to find my sense of wonder in a totally unfamiliar environment.

Inexplicable

The Lascaux cave paintings. Yes — I saw them. Yes — I took pictures (and wasn't supposed to). Yes — even after I describe them below, they are still inexplicable. Getting out of the summer heat and traversing our way into a set of caves to see some "dibujos geniales" (cool drawings) was a wonderful experience. Wonderful while inexplicable — I'll explain a bit. Lascaux is famous for its Paleolithic cave paintings, found in a complex of caves in the Dordogne region of southwestern France. They are rare and unique because of their exceptional quality, size, sophistication, and antiquity. Estimated to be up to 20,000 years old, the paintings consist primarily of large animals once native to the region. Even after some research, imagining that I had seen them in person was still inexplicable.

When I first wrote this, I almost described this last one as "Inconceivable." I might give the Oxford Dictionary a ring and ask them to add inconceivable to the definition of wonder. I'm sure it popped into my head because that word is part of a famous scene from *The Princess Bride* — another one of those movies I've watched dozens of times.

But I digress.

After my trip to Spain and many amazing experiences, I greatly appreciated the concept of wonder. During my travels since then, I've been able to specifically seek out wonder and enjoy it more deeply and meaningfully at the moment I'm taking it in. And wonder applies to general experiences, time with friends and family, and many other aspects of our busy lives.

LESSON LEARNED

Wonder comes in all shapes and sizes. You can feel surprised by something incredible in nature or built by many. It can come to you through any of your senses and touch you in many different ways. So do everything you can to "capture" the wonder at that moment. Savor the feeling and deeply embed the memory into your psyche. I hope you also discover a sense of wonder with something in your life. More importantly, do the work to fully embrace wonder across all of your senses, feelings, emotions, and passions and share those wonderful experiences with others.

CONVICTION

"a firmly held belief or opinion."

"Like a dog with a bone"... I know my dog Suki never likes to give up her bones. I can also be the same way in terms of not giving up on something.

We had been consulting for years with a large client in the Seattle area. Our relationship went back many years, and this client formed a foundational piece of our Seattle office (and revenues) for years.

The lead of the Seattle office "owned" the original relationship with this client. But as he successfully grew our office, he had less and less time to invest in managing the overall relationship with this client. The concern was that there would be much less time and effort invested in what could be a great, long-term client relationship. Within a few weeks of joining the office as a new vice president, we agreed it would make sense for me to manage the relationship going forward.

Since I had much more time to invest in the client relationship, I spent more time on-site learning a lot more about the client overall and how our younger consultants were doing with the client. Bottom line — I quickly discovered that our team didn't enjoy the work we were doing. From a dollar and cents perspective, we needed to maintain this client relationship. From a people perspective, we should disengage entirely. And many people across the company and our office felt we should also walk away from this client.

However, I held a different opinion. I felt we could grow our overall relationship with the client while removing ourselves from this less-than-interesting line of business. Unfortunately, only some others across my company believed it was possible. However, the team at the client site agreed with my assessment and fully substantiated our conviction that we could make a significant transformation.

Over the next two years, we nearly doubled the number of people working with the client while simultaneously removing ourselves from the less-than-desirable work on a specific set of projects. As a result, not only were the employees at the client thrilled, but the client and the very cool projects we were working on became a "destination request" in terms of other consultants wanting to work with this client as well.

Did I have a clear idea of how this would happen when I kept holding onto my belief we could transform? Not. At. All. There were a few factors that bolstered my conviction that we could make a change:

Be Aware of Confirmation Bias

There were many signs we could be successful in other parts of the business. We started multiple pilots, leading to small projects that grew into larger ones. Our employees were having fun in other parts of the business and identified more and more places where we could expand. Certainly, I made every attempt to interpret ALL new information as supporting my opinion, but I also sought out information contrary to my conviction — that we should simply walk away from the overall relationship or that walking away from that one less-than-desirable project would cause the client to end our relationship. Instead of continually looking for reasons (and data) to validate that we should remain in our current situation with no changes, we looked for contradictory reasons to invest elsewhere.

Ask Provoking Questions

Whether it was me challenging the team, the team challenging me, my peers questioning our strategy, or outside advisors informing us of other options, we continued to ask hard questions and seek objective answers. Several times, we were still determining if the new projects would grow large enough to support the extraction from the less-than-desirable project. We continually asked each other provocative questions that led to new opportunities. Would that three-person project ever grow beyond three people? Would a one-month engagement expand into more of an annual opportunity? And are any of these other projects actually more fun for our employees than the one we were on at the time? It felt as if we asked one good question, it would inevitably lead to two additional questions. They all helped us to challenge and simultaneously validate our convictions.

Search for Comparables

We also looked for other examples across our company where similar transformations had occurred. We learned what works for them and what doesn't. We applied the lessons learned. For example, we used another contract from a different client as a baseline for us to use to build out a new statement of work going forward. It led to a new project at this client based upon a comparable elsewhere. Let's say you have a strong belief about an ambiguous situation. One way to confirm your conviction is to find similar situations where others had a similar belief about the potential outcomes.

Challenge Your Assumptions

In this case, most people assumed that walking away from one piece of business would negatively impact the client relationship and result in us losing the client entirely. Or that we could even flourish in other parts of the company outside of our past comfort zone with a specific business unit. We quickly identified the data, experiences, and observations behind these assumptions, adjusted them to our new potential reality, and moved forward with our conviction.

Be Willing To Admit You Are Wrong

As much as I wanted this to be successful, I was also prepared to walk away entirely if my conviction was inaccurate. We continually modeled different scenarios to ask the hard question about walking away and the impact on our long-term client relationship, our people on the ground, and the Seattle office's finances. We continued to provide solid answers to the "What if?" questions — for example, we'd redeploy our eleven people across these three other clients if we walked away. We had worked through potential secondary and tertiary options for this team if we were forced to admit we were wrong and had to walk away from the client.

LESSON LEARNED

Stay strong when you firmly hold beliefs or opinions, but not blindly. Challenge yourself. Ask others to challenge you. No one can be your "Devil's Advocate" better than yourself. But others can help you discover blind spots. Act like a scientist and test your opinions and beliefs with the intent to dispel them first. Convictions are great — but keep them from dominating your thinking.

HAPPINESS

"the state of feeling or showing pleasure or contentment"

Ever get a song in your head that you can't, or won't, let go of? One of my favorites was Bobby McFerrin's "Don't Worry, Be Happy." I always smile and enjoy watching the music video with McFerrin, Robin Williams, and Bill Irwin.

Throughout most of my life, I've considered myself a happy person. I love to laugh, smile, enjoy life, and bring energy to help others experience the same. However, I only fully embraced happiness once I understood it much better later in life.

A few years ago, a Professor at the University of Washington (UW) offered me the opportunity to co-teach a class with him in the Human Centered Design & Engineering (HCDE) program. Most of our discussions were about systems thinking, design thinking, and how to apply various frameworks and methodologies to the concept of HCDE. He was incredibly flexible in his willingness to consider my suggestions for the course, including my desire to dig into happiness and how that played into the world of HCDE.

We ended up meeting with another UW Ph.D. in the Psych Department who teaches several courses on happiness. She was wonderful enough to present her materials about happiness during our HCDE course. She also gave a presentation to my company. The message was about "Learning Happiness," this is my take on the various topics she discussed about being happy — as well as some of my own.

Mindfulness

As Mother Teresa states, happiness is about being in the moment. And the next moment. And the one after that. Mindfulness focuses on the present — the immediate present and that specific moment.

I'm still learning how to be mindful. Sometimes I try to clear my mind — which feels nearly impossible during a hectic day. Instead, I often think about unforgettable memories with my sons, friends, or work colleagues. I know I've reached my sense of mindfulness when I feel myself smile. There are dozens of apps, hundreds of books, and endless videos about mindfulness. Find what works for you, and be mindful of being happy in your moment.

Gratitude

Any day of the year is a perfect one to be grateful for, but Thanksgiving is one of those days (in the U.S.) of the year that allows everyone to slow down and consider what they are grateful for. More importantly than just *considering* gratitude, you can share your gratitude with others. I love to take a few minutes with others and tell them what I appreciate about them or our relationship or how they have made me feel in the past (or present). Of course, many people will say "Thank You" for your comments. And YOU will likely smile and gain some sense of happiness in response.

Awe

Be aware of what's around you. Life is amazing. Nature is incredible. People are good, caring, and loving. The world is a very cool place. Music is inspiring. Art is stimulating. Take a minute to think about something much bigger than yourself and experience the awe. Happiness is all around us.

Sleep

How do you feel after a great nap or an incredible night of sleep? One of the roles of sleep is to create new memories and "throw out" the garbage in your brain that's no longer needed. The brain works to retain as many happy memories, thoughts, lessons learned, and more as possible. Even closing your eyes for a few minutes without falling asleep can enable you to channel one or two happy memories.

Movement

Exercise comes in many forms — riding a bike, walking, running outside, using exercise equipment, doing yoga, stretching in general, etc. Think about what works for you and move around when the timing works. I probably don't often smile as I'm getting ready to exercise and about the only time I'll smile during exercise is if I happen to be talking to friends or family while taking a walk, but after some exercise or movement — I often move the facial muscles needed to form a great smile. Happiness can be felt throughout your body.

Social Connections

Find someone to socialize with, whether with family, friends, work colleagues, pets, or strangers. The "Learning Happiness" presentation included a great quote by Aristotle: "Man by nature is a social animal." I crave being social. During my sabbatical one summer, I optimized the time I spent with others. While I was diligent about spending some productive time alone reading or learning something new, my smile/day volume was always highest when I was with others. Whether you prefer to be more introverted/empathic with just one or a few people, or be around more extroverted/social with many people, happiness expands exponentially with other connections.

Servant Leadership

Doing something for others usually elicits a warm feeling inside of you. Some people take mission trips. Others visit other parts of the world or the country to help those in need. Think of all of the natural disasters you read about, and the "best" stories are those about how one set of people helps another set of people through a difficult situation. I think about those firefighters battling forest fires to save hundreds or thousands of families from losing their homes or even their lives. Seeing the difference you can make in someone else's life is a definite recipe for happiness just like seeing someone else impact others, as those firefighters do.

Prosocial Spending

The holidays are a great time to give to others in need. Most people are generally happier when they spend money on other people. My company provided a training stipend this year to use in any way we wanted to improve ourselves. I used my stipend to offer a grant to the professor who created this "Learning Happiness" presentation so she could present it to all of the employees in our office one afternoon. As I observed my colleagues engage in the presentation and the activities, I probably smiled several dozen times during the two-hour session. Happiness is infectious and prosocial spending is contagious.

LESSON LEARNED

There are dozens of different paths to happiness. You only need to discover one or two to spark your desire to traverse the third, fourth, or fifth path. The more paths, the merrier. Being happy at the moment is excellent and provides immediate joy. Happiness is a permanent state of body and mind we can all strive to achieve during our journey on this planet. Know that the journey to genuinely embracing happiness is a long and never-ending process. I've gotten help from many people, and I continue to work on adding more happiness paths to my trek across Mother Earth.

MACROCOSM

"the whole of a complex structure, especially the world or the universe, contrasted with a small or representative part of it."

What is the biggest natural structure or building or something else huge you've ever seen? I remember seeing Mount Kilimanjaro as the backdrop for a herd of elephants and thinking how huge it must be to make those elephants look so tiny.

In the years between the passing of two of my favorite people, my dad and my long-time friend Nick, I've been very focused on the macrocosm of my life on Planet Earth. At the time, I was in a state of an incredibly complex mix of sadness, frustration, depression, dejection, and more, but I eventually realized that those emotions were just a tiny part of the fuller, more complex me.

My advice as a coach/leader/mentor/guide/advisor frequently involves taking something complex or challenging and breaking it down into smaller components. With macrocosm, it is the opposite — you avoid thinking about the more minor details and only consider the whole. As difficult as it was to consider the passing of Nick or my dad as "small," I focused on the much bigger picture (of the world) and life (the decades left in my journey) that helped me get through those situations.

The most effective way to focus on the whole is to understand the relationship of the components to the whole initially and then only focus on the whole. Here are a few of the shifts I'm making to consider life from a macroscopic perspective instead of the specific, individual components.

My Sons as Young Adults

My shift is from being a father only for these young kids to becoming an advisor, guide, friend, counselor, teacher, coach, *and* father as my sons move from young adults in college into the next phase of their lives. They are already thinking about their roles on Planet Earth, and I hope to convey any lessons learned that can supplement and enhance their career and life journey. This book is one way I'm sharing those lessons.

Relationships

My shift here is to continue to go deeper and deeper with my closest friends and family — considering our lifelong connection versus simply getting together for dinner one night. While I'm always open and excited about cultivating new relationships, my focus is strengthening existing relationships and exploring how I can help others understand the macrocosm of Earth and how they fit into the bigger picture of the universe. Relationships can be one-to-one, one-to-many, or many-to-many.

Art and Science

The Vitruvian Man is the ultimate combination of art and science. More than anyone before him (and most after him), Leonardo da Vinci figured out how to optimize the connection between the left (analytical, detailed, logical) brain with the right (expressive, creative, holistic, feeling) brain. The geometry of the circle and the square perfectly mesh with the personal aspects of the human body.

My shift is to help others discover their strengths and growth opportunities in each part of the brain coupled with the dependencies across them and their overall relationship to their long-term ambitions in life. To evaluate their fullest potential versus some specific skill or piece of knowledge only.

Sustainability

One of my passions is to support individuals, companies and others involved in battling the challenges of climate change (see **Environment**). My context is to create a viable world for my grandchildren and *their* grandchildren to thrive in forever. Your passion might not be sustainability; maybe it's social justice or the impact religion can have on others worldwide. Find one big and audacious passion that feels like a much greater "whole" instead of working on something from a tactical-only perspective!

Many Versus One

Most of my decisions now concern how many people I can impact. We all get one journey on this planet, and I hope more people can have a more extensive and longer-lasting impact on what's happening worldwide. That feeling of helping others makes my own life feel more whole in the macro sense. The idea that one is significantly smaller than the many is certainly macro-thinking.

Visualization

Some people learn through words, while others learn through visualization. Whenever I get lost in the details, I attempt to visualize something *huge* to help me transform my thinking into more macro-based perspectives. When considering their "role" in the larger world, problems or challenges seem small or meaningless. Even if you haven't been to Kenya, you can probably shift your focus in your mind from a single elephant to a herd of elephants to the backdrop of a massive mountain in the background.

These are some of my shifts; I hope they inspire you to consider what your shifts might be.

LESSON LEARNED

Slowing down and thinking about the bigger picture provides a lot of fulfillment. Of course, we each have interests or passions, but I love considering my role on Planet Earth and how I can be a better steward of our little planet across this massive universe. Day-to-day tactical activities are necessary and usually never-ending. Putting those daily activities into context by focusing on the bigger picture will help you understand the role macrocosm plays in your life.

Chapter 7

Been There, Done/ Seen That

I was fairly new to project and program management when I shifted from technology sales to consulting. As a result, I frequently leaned into the experiences of other professionals who had been doing this for years to build the habits I needed to be successful. Since many of them had spent their careers working through project and program management challenges, they were well prepared to share their lessons learned with me.

READINESS

"the state of being fully prepared for something."

Quote from my hide-and-seek days, "Ready or not… here we come!"

Imagine walking out of the hospital with your day-old, newborn baby. The nurse is with you to ensure you know how to load your son into the car seat, but there is no car seat.

I thought I was ready for Ryan to come home. Oops. Our state of mind focused solely on everything we needed to do within the hospital's four walls. Given this was our first child, we knew there was a lot to prepare for, but when Ryan was born, all other states of mind were non-existent.

Needless to say, I learned my lessons about readiness. As a result, we had no problems with Cole three years later and were extremely prepared because we got into the right state of mind. Our readiness plan included what we needed before, during, *and* after the visit to the hospital.

Less than two decades later, when Ryan took off for college, I shared some of the lessons learned about readiness for him in the context of going away to Boulder, CO - and many of these could have easily worked for ME getting ready to bring Ryan home from the hospital many years earlier:

Ask for Help

Learning to become independent is one of the most frequent comments I hear from young adults regarding what they are most looking for. I'm a huge fan of these kids establishing themselves and becoming independent. My concern is that some kids might take that too far and attempt to do *everything* on their own. The tough challenge is when to ask for help versus trying to do it all on your own. There are many great lessons that young adults should learn on their own. Try to find when it makes much more sense to ask for help. For example, there is no need to spend hours building a bed frame when you can ask the Resident Assistant how to do it in five–ten minutes.

Be Yourself

There are literally hundreds of different clubs at a major university like Colorado. There are fraternities and sororities. Clubs for academics. Clubs for outside interests. Clubs for just about anything you can imagine. And there are thousands of new people to meet — all with different interests and curiosities. There will be a lot of pressure to "fit in" with other people, clubs, etc. One of the most difficult challenges young adults might face is being themselves. However, to be yourself, you first must…

…Understand Who You Are

The subtle difference here is that you'll learn who you truly are and what you desire in college. As a parent, I observe many children acting in a certain way because that's how they feel their mom, dad, or high school friends want them to act. In college, that pressure is off since you are living on your own and getting to make your own decisions. So dive into your passions further. Explore new passions you may have never checked out. Figure out what's interesting to you versus others. Maybe your family didn't embrace music, and you'd love to explore an instrument. Or you spent most of your time in a sport in high school, yet you wanted to try something different (that wasn't offered), like rock climbing. Experiment to discover who you are.

Build Your (Readiness) Plan

Homework will stack up quickly, as will the many potential (very fun and enjoyable) distractions to studying, and many students need to have a part-time or full-time job to get through school — meaning your time is already partially booked. Consider how you'll handle all of the demands on your time that could deter you from getting classwork done effectively or meeting the responsibilities of your job shifts. Your plan can include fun, relaxing times, studying, class preparation, and working hard, and please remember to get a little sleep mixed into that plan!

Plan and Prioritize Your Fun Appropriately

Part of your plan should absolutely include having fun and enjoying yourself. As you learn more about your passions, you'll learn how to prioritize your time to optimize your fun and non-study or non-work time. Heavy homework assignments, midterms, working overtime, pop quizzes, and final exams will always prevent you from getting to 100% of your fun times. Just figure out how to mix this up most effectively.

What Do You Want To Be When You Grow Up?

Honestly, I have friends and colleagues who are still asking themselves this question. My best friend from high school knew he wanted to be a pilot in elementary school — and still is a pilot 40 years later.

However, he's the exception to the rule. So dig into your classes and determine where you'd like to be after college. It's not a decision to make in the first year or so. But feel free to experiment and learn what's interesting to you. Maybe asking what you want to be when you grow up is too tough a perspective — perhaps figure out what you want to do after college?

Meet Everyone

Classes. Dorms. Quad. Walking around campus. Football games. Cafeterias. There are endless opportunities to meet new people. They will each have their perspectives, passions, interests, and curiosities. Go for it! Explore as much as you can with all of these folks. There's an endless supply of entertainment and enjoyment out there. Explore it with others and discover some new ones through their eyes.

Learn How To Be Independent.

Yes, you should still learn how to be independent when it comes to all of this. It's an accumulation of many lessons learned, rewarding experiences, challenging situations, difficult decisions, and more than you'll encounter over the years. However, you'll learn to assimilate all this information with the excellent starting point you've built over the past eighteen years.

Fail Mindfully

Failure is one of the greatest sources of lessons learned and knowledge. Be transparent about your failures. Be willing to show humility and what went wrong with yourself and others. If you are vulnerable with yourself and others, your failures will quickly lead to future successes. I'll add another, more famous, perspective about failure: Thomas Edison didn't fail to make the light bulb thousands of times; he learned what didn't work, leading him to success.

Though the ideas above focused on that little baby boy with the missing car seat, now on his way to college, many apply to getting ready for almost any situation.

RESILIENCE

"the capacity to recover quickly from difficulties; toughness."

RIF. Reduction in Force. That's a nice way for a company to avoid having to say, "We are firing a bunch of employees." I've been there. It's tough.

I survived the Internet crash of 2001 when many companies declared bankruptcy, closed their doors, or got gobbled up by more stable companies. During that time, I returned to a company I had previously worked for. Even though the overall landscape had changed and I was stepping into a different role, I was in my element and looking forward to working with an established software company after nearly three tumultuous and exciting years with an Internet startup.

Then my boss called me one day and said, "You are being let go," as part of a broader RIF. Over 90% of the employees were getting similar phone calls from their bosses. We were all shocked and devastated to get this difficult news.

And only a few weeks later, I had another job with a great organization, an amazing team, and an incredible manager. So how did I pull that off?

Resilience.

I don't remember the exact sequence of events when I was told I was part of a major RIF, but here's my approach to recovering quickly from a challenging situation.

Understand the Circumstances

While the initial phone call and aftershock were challenging to understand, I took the time to assess the situation objectively. My performance was not the issue. I did everything correctly. In fact, I was actually thriving after nine months in the new role. Once I realized I could do nothing to control the circumstances, I felt much better about my situation. The bottom line, the company was severely mismanaged globally. I assessed the situation based upon the circumstances, learned the lessons I could and moved on.

Architect a Plan Forward

I needed a job quickly to address my family's finances, healthcare, etc. Therefore, I aimed to identify interesting companies where my skills and interests would align. In parallel, I actively networked with friends in the industry to understand what they enjoyed about their jobs with their companies and whether or not I'd be a fit. Though the overall market economy was still recovering, I felt confident about my prospects and quickly discovered two or three potentially interesting opportunities.

Move Into Action Mode

Less than a day after getting that phone call, I devised my plan and started to move into action. I kept thinking about moving forward with a job search versus "looking in the rearview mirror" and contemplating what had happened with the previous company. Phone calls and emails led to interviews and further investigation of select companies. Within a few weeks, I had several opportunities and needed to down-select what I felt most interesting.

Keep Checking in With Myself...

Though I knew the circumstances were out of my control and it helped pull together a plan and take action quickly, I still wanted to be honest with myself. I needed to pause and honestly assess my feelings about the situation. I was aware of my emotions — sadness, anger, frustration, confusion, etc. — but didn't let them prevent me from moving forward.

...And With Others

This situation was unique in that many of my peers faced the same difficult challenge. So it was beneficial to stay connected with so many others to help them with their resilience going forward. And even if you face a similar situation alone, you can still engage with others for support and help along the way.

Nature

It was also helpful for me to look to other sources of inspiration. Nature tends to be extraordinarily unpredictable yet also very resilient. So if I ever found myself in a rut, I'd think about how nature recovered from natural disasters over the years. For example, if an entire forest could recover from devastating fires, I should be able to find a new job after being part of a RIF.

Looking back, getting that RIF phone call was one of the best things that happened to me from a career perspective. I ended up in such a better place. Happy. Productive. Great people. Working for the author of the **Introduction** to my book (thanks Margaret!). And I only got there with resilience.

LESSON LEARNED

A key component of resilience is like driving a car — keep your eyes forward versus looking in the rearview mirror. You can either dwell in the past, looking backward at your current circumstances, or do something to change them looking forward. Keep looking forward and work on making the changes you need to recover, and you will need time to react and recover from whatever feelings you are experiencing. Some or all of these approaches might resonate with you, and I'd love to hear from you about what other approaches would be helpful with your resilience. Pick what works best for you, mix in anything else that you like, and bounce back quickly!

COMPETITION

"the activity or condition of competing."

Compete — *"strive to gain or win something by defeating or establishing superiority over others who are trying to do the same."*

No. It's not another story that involves sports.

As I write this book, Amazon.com is one of the world's largest companies. If you asked anyone, they would be hard-pressed to identify a line of business that Amazon.com was *not* involved in. But that was only sometimes the case.

A few decades earlier, when Amazon was just a few years old, and Jeff Bezos was actively involved in the company, they were known as the "World's Biggest Bookstore". Used books. New books. Any book. Just order it online, and you'll get it.

They had an idea to shift their business model. Most people thought they were crazy. Instead of just books, maybe they should also try selling and shipping CDs and DVDs to your home. Trying to challenge the paradigm that we rented videos or DVDs from a Blockbuster store or purchased CDs from somewhere like Tower Records might not seem insane now, given the prevalence of streaming services today, but, from a business perspective at the time, it was a major shift in their business model and they needed to somehow support this new business model to compete against the status quo.

That's where we came in. At the time, I worked for a software company called i2 Technologies. We had some incredible software that enabled companies to match the supply of whatever they were selling most effectively against the potential customer demand. Our focus was to help our customers lower the cost of doing business by optimizing how many warehouses they utilized, what they placed in those warehouses, and how they ultimately shipped products to their end customers from those warehouses.

I'm clearly biased that i2 Technologies was the best in the industry. However, there were two or three other companies that had similar technologies and Amazon wanted to evaluate all of them. So we had to *compete* to win the business.

I won't bore you with the details; I probably don't remember most of them. We had an incredible team who was extremely knowledgeable about all our solutions. The net — we won the competition against the other competitors. Why did Amazon select us?

Relationships

We established professional and personal relationships with each other. We understood what was important to the key players at Amazon and built a strong sense of trust. There was a sense that we would ensure that Amazon's ultimate objectives were truly addressed. And we infused the process with our passion and energy to let them know we are with them on this journey into a completely new business model.

Execution

There was also a strong sense of how we would engage with Amazon and what we would do with them daily, weekly, and monthly. We described how we had been successful and how we'd implement those strategies to ensure Amazon's solution would work well. And we committed to helping them meet their deadlines as the world shifted some of their holiday spending from Black Friday to Cyber Monday. They wanted to send more than books out that holiday season!

Requirements

A lot of time was spent clearly understanding Amazon's precise needs. Previously, all books were stored and shipped from one warehouse. They wanted to move into CDs and DVDs, and they also wanted to ship from a second warehouse. If this worked, they might consider adding another warehouse or two and shipping out other products. Hmmm… did that work out for them?

Future

As I briefly foreshadowed above, we also discussed how the current solution would scale to help them with a future vision. Ten warehouses versus two. Fifty different types of products versus three. Changing economic conditions and increased demand across the U.S., North America, and the whole world. We spent a lot of time thinking about far beyond their existing requirements.

Other Options (for Them To Consider)

While we spent time on all the factors above, we also needed to consider the other technology companies in our space. What were their strengths and weaknesses? How did our solutions compare to their strong points and weaknesses? Did they align better with Amazon's needs in any way? Understanding what other companies in your space offer besides the above factors is important.

As I shared already, we won the deal. Our engagement was so effective that they decided to work with us fairly straightforwardly. So, in a way, it wasn't a competition when it was all over, though it was important to treat it that way during the process.

CURIOSITY

"a strong desire to know or learn something."

Who do you think are more curious creatures: babies, puppies, or kittens?

Both my son and nephew graduated from college in May 2022. The most frequently asked question was, "What will you do next?". They both had jobs lined up and were excited to think about what their first days at work might look like. As I tried to get into their heads about their next phase of life, I was curious about their first work interactions.

I thought back to my first job at IBM and one of my first sales calls. I was meeting with the founder of a small transportation company in Peoria, IL. I diligently prepared for the meeting by figuring out everything I needed about the cool technologies that IBM offered. Within about five minutes of our meeting, the proud founder of this company asked me what I knew about *his* company.

I was not prepared to be curious about what was important to him or his business. He could have kicked me out of his office and refused an opportunity for me to come back. Fortunately, the founder took me under his wing and shared information that I should have researched before our meeting — or at least shown a desire to learn about it during our meeting. He was generous with his time, walked around the trucking yard, and pointed out the many different types of trucks he owned and the purpose of each. It started to spark my curiosity.

Learning so much about trucks fascinated me, and my inner child took over and I started to ask more questions. The founder was so proud of what he had built that we spent nearly two hours together talking about his business, the future of trucking, what he's hoping to accomplish soon, etc.

After that meeting, I vowed to be prepared for every meeting I had coming up. When I was first starting my career, we needed to go to a library or leverage some business services to garner information about companies at that time. Even if we were curious before a meeting, learning much about a company or individual wasn't easy. Today it's "easy" to be super curious in advance — explore a company's website, LinkedIn profiles of the individuals, and more. But the key — *spend the time* upfront learning as much as possible. Be curious in advance.

Your questions will be more pointed and relevant and most people will be impressed and greatly appreciate that you took the time to consider them and their company. Looking back, I approached this meeting incorrectly, but it led to learning the four lessons below. These lessons all have one thing in common: curious questions.

Prepare Properly in Advance

I prepared for the first meeting with the founder of this transportation company the only way I knew how. I learned everything I needed to know about the technology I wanted to share with him regarding the project, but I did *not* prepare to understand his company, industry, or anything about him as a founder. I knew it was a transportation company but little else. If I had been more focused on his business rather than my technology offerings, I would have been able to prepare in advance with some questions about his company and be much more curious. There are many ways to research companies, industries, or individuals — even back then. For example, I could have learned more about the different kinds of trucks and which ones his company typically required.

Find Who Can Give You Answers

I was fortunate that the founder I met with was willing to give a curious kid a lot more of his time than he probably should have. I frequently think of this experience as I prepare for meetings today. I not only correctly prepare through research to answer questions about the company in advance but also consider with whom I'm meeting, whether that be a CIO, CMO, or CFO, and what curious questions are best suited for them. And consider who you might seek information from before the meeting — other clients, partners, people knowledgeable about the industry, etc.

Be Genuinely Curious, and Don't Make Assumptions

Not only was the company founder willing to give me more time to ask questions about his business, but he also took the time to give me a tour of the whole facility. We walked around the transportation yard, and he showed me the different kinds of trucks (I assumed all of them were basically the same) his company used. Asking even more questions quickly became infectious and, to my surprise, really opened up the founder to share even more information with me as we walked through the truck yard. I learned NOT to make assumptions as I could never have understood how many different types of trucks existed... I knew them all as simply "18 wheelers".

There Is no Such Thing as a Dumb Question

Back then, I was naïve enough to ask the founder of a transportation company, someone who has been in the industry for 25+ years, questions like "How many different types of trucks are there?" I sense that many people today shy away from asking questions of people because they are afraid it might seem like a dumb inquiry. Instead, you should be bold because you never know what you could learn or where it could take you — like, in my case, on a facility tour.

I've learned that when you spend the time to prepare properly in advance, figure out who you want to ask questions and show that you are truly curious, you'll find the answers you are looking for and definitely some experience along the way.

LESSON LEARNED

There are literally *zero* reasons for not being fully prepared for a meeting by digging into your curiosity about an individual, a specific subject, or any other topic. You can do much research in advance to create more space for curiosity. And then leverage that information to prepare a strategically focused discussion. Even if you don't have time in advance to prepare, you can still ask questions and avoid making assumptions to increase your level of curiosity.

As I shared in my story above, curiosity goes *far* beyond being prepared for a meeting. The four lessons I've shared above will apply to any circumstances where you strongly desire to learn more about something. Be curious and develop your understanding of almost anything you desire!

THERAPY

"treatment intended to relieve or heal a disorder."

Would I walk again? The answer is "Yes, but...".

At the time, it didn't feel like it. I was playing basketball with my friends. We played on a smaller court than I grew up playing in high school, but we still managed to get in games of five-on-five and play full court. I stole the ball from someone on the other team and sprinted while dribbling to our basket on the other end of the court. I remember going up for a layup and remembering my friends trying to help me up from the floor. What happened?

I didn't realize then that my patellar tendon had been pulled off my bone 100%. Not to get too graphical here, but imagine your lower leg no longer having the major tendon attached to your upper leg. "Ouch" doesn't begin to explain the situation.

Fortunately, I lived in Seattle and got rushed to the hospital at the University of Washington. In the next few days, I would have surgery to reattach my patellar tendon. Everything went exceptionally well from the surgery, but I couldn't put any weight on my left leg for at least six weeks — and then only delicately after that.

And only after a *lot* of physical therapy.

I couldn't even bend my left leg for the first six weeks because I needed to let my newly constructed "tendons" get used to their new responsibility of holding my knee in place. After that, we did some therapy to recover from the atrophy of my muscles. But there was much more in store.

Over the next six weeks, I bent my left leg slightly — 15 degrees, 30, 45, 60, and 90. My therapist was thrilled the day we finally broke the 90-degree barrier and got almost 100 degrees! The pain was brutal, but I wanted to walk again.

Finally, I was approved to start walking — though my leg muscles had atrophied significantly since my injury. More therapy to re-learn how to walk. How to bend my knees, and what exercises I can do at home to accelerate my therapy and what mental hurdles I needed to overcome, like maybe I could never play full-court basketball again.

The process was long and challenging at times, but I'm grateful for my therapists and the hard work they did to help me recover. I'm a huge fan of therapy today — and all kinds. Mental. Physical. Emotional. Psychological. Cognitive. Behavioral. Holistic. And many more.

My recovery from blowing out my knee took a long time and required perspective from many different angles during therapy.

Be Patient

Recovery can be minutes or decades. It all depends on what you are dealing with, but patience with the process, the people involved, and the actual healing process on the way to recovery is important. I couldn't bear weight on my left leg for more than a month; there was *nothing* I could do to speed up the process, so I needed to be patient.

Rely Upon Others

Whether those others are the expert therapists who can help you along your journey to recovery or friends who can share lessons learned, don't try to do this all on your own. In my case, there was NO WAY I would get through this without experts. That helped me to overcome any stigma associated with going to physiological and cognitive therapists later in my life.

Follow Instructions

Some recovery processes can be extremely complex. Not only should you rely upon others, but you should also leverage past processes that have worked for so many others previously. If someone gives you specific instructions, FOLLOW THEM! When I was frustrated, my recovery process was slower than I expected, and my therapist pointed out that I wasn't following the instructions to exercise correctly. I got it!

Find Your Fit

Not all therapists are a perfect fit the first time. There is a personal element to the therapist-patient relationship. Don't be afraid to explore other options if your first option for therapy doesn't work for you. I ended up going to several different physical therapists until I found one who helped me to focus on a specific recovery process that fit what I imagined I wanted to be able to do in the future.

Envision What's Next

Therapy can definitely have ups and downs. Consider your destination's endpoint to stay positive during the process. It was extremely helpful to think about skiing or playing basketball with my sons when they got older. That was my motivation to push through difficult times.

And I've been involved in several other "flavors" of therapy and applied these same guidelines to mental and/or emotional therapy as well. Whether you or someone you know can benefit from any therapy, I hope these steps help you or them get through the process successfully.

LESSON LEARNED

Ignore the word "disorder" in the definition. That contributes to the negative connotations and stigmas about going into therapy — especially for mental, emotional or psychological challenges. Therapy is an amazing elixir for your head, heart, body, and soul. There's more power in asking for help than trying to do something alone. Therapists can help you recover and assist your growth going forward.

COMPREHENSION

"the action or capability of understanding something."

What's 2,300,000 multiplied by 5,000? And that's not even the most challenging thing to comprehend.

My ex-wife and I spoke many times about traveling to Africa. She was a huge fan of Kenya and exploring what it might be like to go on a safari and I was totally up for it. We had an amazing trip, and at the very end started to talk about where to go next. She wanted to go to Morocco next, but it was my turn to pick our next adventure.

Where to go? What's most interesting? Fresh from some amazing experiences across Kenya with unbelievable wildlife, I wanted to go back in time instead. Growing up, I visited some incredible Mayan ruins during trips to Mexico with my parents, and, while it was a blast for my brother and me to climb the stairs to the top of Chichén Itzá, I wanted to go bigger. There was only one choice.

Egypt and the pyramids.

We worked through the various travel options to decide upon a tour that fit our needs. We planned to cover all of the top places to visit in Egypt — Aswan, Cairo, Luxor, travel down the Nile, tombs of Nefertiti/Tut/etc., Abu Simbel and more. The list seemed endless. But at the very top of the list for me were the Great Pyramids of Giza.

Growing up in Chicago as a kid and traveling to New York City as an adult afforded me the opportunity to see and go into some of the tallest buildings in the world. The Great Pyramids of Giza aren't that tall in comparison. The Eiffel Tower in Paris is about double the height of the Great Pyramids. Closer to home, the Great Pyramids are about the same height as the Space Needle.

But you cannot comprehend how massive the pyramids look until you are standing at their base and looking at one of them. Just one stone is 2.5 tons or 5,000 pounds. And over 2.3 million of those stones are stacked on each other. Completing the math equation above, the stones that comprise one pyramid weigh over 11.5 *billion* pounds.

That would be a big job for someone to build in today's world. We have massive earth-moving equipment and the heavy machinery needed to move something that large. Over and over again. But can you imagine how that was done over 6,000 years ago?

Incomprehensible.

One of my favorite stories over the years was about the aliens landing in Cairo, and they used advanced technologies to move the stones into place. In one of my college Ceramic Engineering classes, there was a discussion about the plausibility of building each stone as if they were large, concrete bricks — meaning you only had to move the materials in place to create a large "stone."

Our guides, experts in the region, told us they were mined nearby, moved with many people/animals/wheels/carts/etc., and even lifted into place sometimes when the nearby Nile flooded. They would actually "float" the stones carried on platforms into place. So bottom line — a very plausible explanation behind how the pyramids were built exists.

But it was still hard to comprehend. Just seeing how big these stones were and then looking up to the top of the pyramids, and it wasn't just about stacking a bunch of heavy stones on top of each other. These were extremely complex structures — situated perfectly so light entered small openings in the pyramids on specific days of the year, aligned so tightly together centuries of earthquakes and other natural disasters didn't move them an inch and filled with complex tunnels and hidden areas to protect the mummies and great wealth of the deceased Egyptian Kings and Queens on the inside.

Hold it — did it just become even *harder* to comprehend? Yes.

The good news about something difficult to comprehend is that, in most cases, you can further educate yourself on the situation. There are countless books and reference guides about the pyramids. While some of the information might be conflicting and speculative since they were built over 6,000 years ago and no one was present to take pictures with their cell phones, I could better comprehend how they were made. I asked people and listened intently, and I learned how the Egyptians built so many other impressive structures during our trip — and how those lessons learned applied to the Great Pyramids of Giza.

I don't know whether or not you have a bucket list, but if you do, this is a great addition!

LESSON LEARNED

Ask questions. Be inquisitive. Don't make any assumptions and check and double-check what you learn. For the most part, you can seek to understand more and more about a situation to comprehend it better.

I strongly encourage you to accept that when you can't comprehend something, admit it, and then follow the guidance to understand better. We all get in trouble when we can't admit we don't understand something and make (wrong) assumptions.

Too many people today are simply downloading information to confirm what they already believe. Take on the challenge of seeking factual information and some comprehension with empathy to learn more about something you don't truly understand.

VISION

"the ability to think about or plan the future with imagination or wisdom."

How cool would it be to have x-ray vision like a superhero?

I wish this story was a lesson learned about acquiring X-ray vision; it's not, but it is about creating and sharing a vision with others.

When I first thought about the word vision, I thought of sight. As I matured, I realized that vision is something more — like Steve Jobs telling the world we needed hundreds of songs on a little device that fits our pockets instead of a new CD player to play the ten songs on my favorite CD. My creative strength is more about taking existing pieces and pulling them together uniquely to demonstrate "the future with imagination or wisdom."

I first understood the impact of sharing a vision with a company who became a great customer and long-time business partner when I was with Pariveda Solutions.

During our "get to know you" presentation for a potential client, we had the opportunity to differentiate ourselves by sharing our unique vision for creating a long-term partnership. One presentation component was discussing their possible future vision using 3-D printers. The idea was for their customers to be able to print out small versions of their products on a 3-D printer. To support this assertion of their future, we showed a 1/10th scale example 3-D printed I-beam, one of their major products. We speculated about their ability to deliver products printed out of wood in this manner in the future. I had never used a 3-D printer before and only had basic knowledge about an I-beam. But I got creative and figured out how to combine both into a vision for this new customer.

In the early years of our relationship, several executives told me they had heard of the story of the 3-D printed I-beam we shared during that presentation. I don't recall exactly, but I'm sure we answered most of the questions the leadership team asked throughout a three to four hour meeting. I know for sure they all remembered the 3-D I-beam.

This was my transformation — how the power of a vision had the potential to significantly impact others — meaning they committed to a long-term relationship with us and are still great customers over eight years later!

My lessons learned about the importance of vision?

The Future

No one knows what the future might bring. Our team took an understanding of the current state of the customer's environment and speculated on what a potential future might look like. For many in the room that day, the concept of 3-D printers was something new in terms of printing wood products for clients in the future. We helped them to glimpse that potential future. They loved our ingenuity.

Imagine A Solution

We definitely used our imaginations to come up with the idea as well. We also mixed in the wisdom of what customers needed at the time coupled with the future direction of their industry. We combined all of this and came up with the idea of showing them what's possible — a 3-D printed I-beam. Then we printed a small prototype — which they passed around the room with wonder to give them a real feeling of what is possible. Very quickly, our imaginations became their imaginations for the future.

People and Process

We also shared stories about how our people, in similar situations (new technologies with new clients), built out creative solutions to solve complex business problems and how our methodologies and processes would support a similar problem-solving process for them as a potential client — even though printing 3-D I-beams out of wood didn't exist then. People and processes are needed to make the future solution possible. To fully support the vision, we also needed to explain the process of reaching that vision at a more granular level.

When thinking about and sharing a vision, consider that some folks need to see just two or three steps along the way while others might need to see eight to ten steps in a 20+ step process. Still, others need to see an example of what's possible. Everyone has a different "help-needed" in seeing a possible future — including stories of people and examples of new methods being used. Your job is to provide as many aids as possible to help others see their version of the vision you might have solidly entrenched in your head.

LESSON LEARNED

Having and sharing a vision is excellent — especially when you can quickly "transfer" that vision to others and allow them to embrace it as their own. Make it real by articulating the vision clearly, sharing examples of what's possible, and guiding them through some reasonable steps to achieve that vision. Just remember that some people want to work on the plan for the vision while others want to think about it on their own. Still, some need to "see" it in their minds, while others might want to explore their feelings about the future vision. Bottom line — it is a unique "recipe" of all these components that will help you convey a vision.

CONJECTURE

"an opinion or conclusion formed on the basis of incomplete information"

This story is *not* about irony, but the irony is that it randomly follows the story about Vision and happens to be about my involvement with the same company one year after the story about vision occurred.

One of my biggest professional missteps might have cost me my job at a different company. Fortunately, I recovered from the misstep and helped turn it into a long-lasting positive thing.

For the first two decades of my career, I was primarily responsible for client relationships' business development and sales. While I would stay very involved with the delivery, execution, and long-term support of the projects I sold to specific clients, I didn't have direct accountability for the ultimate success of our clients.

The expectation for a Vice President at Pariveda was to sell (what I've done most of my career), become the lead executive for the relationship AND own accountability for the ultimate solution delivery. From a customer perspective, the VP was known as the "Officer in Charge" (OIC). Pariveda was a company that expected to engage with clients throughout dozens of projects and many years. This OIC perspective was a new role for me, and I was learning on the job.

For the first few months, I spent most of my time understanding how we have supported other long-time clients. There were many clients with well-known names like Expedia, T-Mobile, Southwest Airlines, and Chevron, to name a few.

Then we got a phone call from someone at Boise Cascade. They used to be well known for their office products — reams of paper, for example, but they sold that part of the business and were mainly focused on engineered wood products — building materials for homes and small companies.

Unlike most of our long-time clients, Boise Cascade was brand new to Pariveda. The client contacted us out of the blue, and I had the opportunity to be the VP who engaged. We went through a lengthy evaluation process (on their part). Eventually, we reached a mutual understanding that our companies would be great partners — and we'd fully deliver upon their critical project on time and within budget. Flip back a few pages for **Vision**, if you didn't get to this story sequentially!

My client was great to work with. His team was engaging. Our employees were having fun doing something very different. My perspective was that everything was going well.

My "relationship muscle" informed me that we were executing effectively and we were on track to deliver everything the client wanted. But my point of view at the time was entirely conjecture. My "program management," "problem-solving," and "big picture" muscles weren't fully engaged at this point in my career - I was lacking a lot of critical information about the project.

Bottom line, though we delivered a lot of work that was *not* in the original agreement that far exceeded our original scope, I should have informed our client that we would *not* be delivering some of the less-than-important capabilities the client felt were part of the original agreement. My mistake (one of many) was that I effectively approved adding a bunch of great capabilities that the client really prioritized without saying anything about what we needed to take away to make up for this extra effort.

I needed to ask more questions or dig into the available information to make decisions based on complete information. My conclusion was that "everything is great," the "client is loving us," and "we will definitely continue working together next year." More conjecture.

My client felt otherwise and was fully justified in doing so.

Without getting into the details, we made some concessions going into the following year. I was removed temporarily from the client relationship, and we slowly got the relationship and project back on track. After a few months, I retook the lead and learned my lessons about managing the overall client relationship going forward.

Relationships are great but aren't 100% of the equation. Upon reflection, I realized that I was simply downloading only the information I felt was relative (confirmation bias) versus digging into the other sources of information I needed to assess the situation accurately.

I needed to ask more questions and seek a better understanding of the short and long-term strategy for the client; ensure our team is addressing their requirements and solving the "right" problems for the customer; determine whether or not the correct timing and processes are in place to keep the client happy; and, even though I had a solid relationship with one sponsor — I wasn't even checking in with other meaningful relationships.

CAREER

"an occupation undertaken for a significant period of a person's life and with opportunities for progress."

How many changes in careers have you had?

I first thought about my career in the sense of a "significant period of life" when I started at IBM. My college days were over, and it was time to be focused on my career. At that time, many people worked 25+ years for the same company they joined after graduating from college. So I told many people I would "get my 25-year Rolex" working with a great company like IBM. Needless to say, the watch I'm wearing right now comes from Apple and has nothing to do with my days at IBM. Therefore, my focus for this story is more about the second half of the definition - "opportunities for progress" - which I'll call more of a transition.

Just a few days before his wedding, I spent an afternoon with a great high school friend. He had been in the financial services industry most of his career and was in the middle of leaping into the world of technology. In our mid-50s, making such a huge career transition was significant. A major change in your career is significant at *any* time. Transitions are tough.

I shared with Dan my journey in making a significant career change. I've done it twice and shared some stories and lessons about both.

What makes up a career transition anyway beyond "opportunities for progress"? For this story, I'll define it by making a significant change in your industry *and* the role you play within that new industry. Many other transitions along your career journey involve your growth from an individual

252

contributor to a first-line manager to a leader of tens or hundreds or more, and many people move from one company to another — shifting their geographic focus. All of these are valid in their own right regarding career journeys as you seek "opportunities for progress".

In 2013, I had an opportunity to move into the consulting world. During the first two decades of my career, I was mainly focused on specific technology solutions and concentrated on targeted industries and my primary role was some mix of sales and business development. However, this new opportunity as a Vice President included many roles beyond sales and business development, like becoming an enterprise architect, program/project manager, coach, mentor, recruiter, marketer, advisor, leader, and more. We literally had unlimited solutions with no concentration on specific industries. It was an amazing opportunity, and I'm grateful to this day for those who helped me through that career transition.

My first "Aha" moment came when I had to sign a contract with my first client. And it was more than an "Aha" moment; my company called my VP role with our client the "Officer in Charge." It was truly the first time I felt 100% accountable and legally responsible for everything happening with that client and it was only the start of my transformation.

From there, my days/weeks/months became a non-stop learning process. Many people view the concept of Imposter Syndrome as a negative experience. I view Imposter Syndrome as an opportunity to get onto my learning edge, grow, and develop. But how did I do it?

Engage Trusted Colleagues

My first step was to lean into the experiences of others with whom I could be vulnerable and trust. I didn't want to admit to everyone that I felt like I was in over my head. My "inner circle" was a great set of trusted advisors, my fellow VPs, to lean into.

Collaborate With Your Peers

Eventually, I learned I could also be vulnerable and open with my peers around the country. We were all facing different challenges in our markets, and it was easy to share our challenges and learn from the experience of others.

Do Your Research

I also spent a lot of time researching behind the scenes. Obviously, the Internet provides a wealth of access to information about all topics. I went old school and purchased and devoured books on specific topics I wanted to learn more about. I also found some beneficial online courses to help my growth as well. Even listening to podcasts, which I'm generally not a huge fan of, found its way into my mix for research purposes in this new career.

Share my Superpowers

When I realized that I had something to offer others, it became even easier for me to learn and be vulnerable. I had been successful in technology sales for over two decades, and I shared numerous lessons learned with many folks with whom I worked and had little experience with complex sales. And even the breakdown of technology was different here. My previous focus was on enterprise software that solved business problems, while many of our projects were consulting solutions that solved more technical issues. I shared my business point of view and learned from others' technical points of view.

Learn From Those Who Work With You

Over time, I became so comfortable with being vulnerable that I was willing to fully admit what I didn't know, which was a lot. The younger people who worked for or with me were more than willing to share their experiences, knowledge, and skills. And none of them expected me to be an expert software developer; they just wanted me to "have their back" as their leader. They appreciated that this "old guy" was willing to learn from them and their experiences.

Be Open With Your Vulnerability — Always

All of these steps I took make it easy for me to see the power of vulnerability. Being open and honest, and transparent with *everyone* about what I'm good at and where I need to get help has been instrumental in my growth.

Constantly Seek Happiness

Most of us need to have our careers to make money and pay our bills versus "chasing your passion" for a career. I'm generally a happy person, but my level of happiness went up exponentially with each of the two career transitions I've made in my lifetime.

Then, at the start of 2021, I decided to make a second career change and move to ThinqShift. While I also leveraged many of the lessons learned above, you can learn more about that story in another chapter called **Adapt**.

It was an amazing few hours sharing some of these lessons learned with my friend just days before yet another opportunity for progress for him (getting married). And I was happy to validate that most of the lessons I learned from my first to second career helped me shift into my third career. P.S. His wedding was a great time and he's doing great in his new career too!

While these lessons were focused on a career transition, these lessons work for many other transitions as well - being a doctor for years and becoming a nonprofit leader; professional athletes moving into their next career after retirement; the many mothers who return to work after raising their children; and so many more.

LESSON LEARNED

The last part of the definition includes "opportunities for progress." Of course, anyone can stay in the same career their entire life, be happy and successful, and have many "opportunities for progress,". Whether you want to grow and develop yourself in your current career or make a significant career transition, realize there's a wealth of "help needed" across many aspects of your life — whether people or information or simply your internal fortitude.

AVOIDANCE

"the action of keeping away from or not doing something"

Spending time with friends outside on a sunny afternoon or studying for a final exam? It might even be raining outside, and I'd find a way to be outside still to avoid studying.

I'm grateful that the University of Illinois accepted me to join another 35,000+ students in Champaign/Urbana, IL. The campus is huge, and the student population is diverse. Needless to say, there were always so many other things to occupy my time *other* than studying.

Quizzes and tests during the semester are hard enough. Final exams were scheduled well before the actual date, but it was easy to find almost anything else to do on campus to avoid studying for the exam.

In my first semester at school, I quickly learned that "cramming" is not a good strategy. Essentially, there was never enough time to study for the final exam if you started after dinner the night before your test.

Sometimes transformations happen immediately; sometimes they happen quickly, but you only realize it has happened later; and sometimes they happen over an extended period.

In this case, the first half of my understanding of avoidance happened in college. Most of the lessons I learned about not avoiding something were related to studying for final exams in college. Those were great lessons I could apply to many other use cases in the early stages of my career and personal life.

The second half of my transformation happened when I started to lead teams of teams. There were many other situations even more complex than studying for final exams — where my early lessons learned didn't always work. I learned several additional lessons to deal with these more complex situations and how to defeat the enemy called avoidance!

As I look back on my learning experiences around avoidance, there are a few tips I can share to make your process smoother and swifter.

Break It Up Into Smaller Parts

Evaluate your whole task and determine how to break it into smaller components. For example, one final exam was based on the book we used for the entire class. Instead of stressing about digging into the whole book, I worked to understand the first chapter fully and then moved into chapter number two. And three. And more — until I got through the whole book part by part. Leading several teams across a complex engagement and dozens of individuals involved, we needed to break up the work across multiple, interconnected teams to more efficiently deliver against our client's requirements.

Spread It out Over Time

This aligns nicely with the previous suggestion. Clearly, there were better strategies than studying the night before for eight–ten hours and not sleeping. But studying for an hour or two every afternoon or evening over two or more weeks leading up to the final exam worked well. Likewise, there were critical inflection points in the delivery of a complex project at specific weekly, monthly and quarterly milestones. No way could we build this complex solution the night before - ha!

Seek Help From Others, if Possible

Collaboration is usually a great idea when working through something you are avoiding. Whether I studied with another classmate for the same exam or studied with a friend who also had their own exam, it was always motivational to connect with another person. And as a new executive at Pariveda, I often asked for help from my team as well as others who had led complex programs previously and sought their guidance.

Take on the Hardest or Biggest Challenge at the Beginning of the Day

When you have a busy schedule and many tasks looming, it is often helpful to take on the biggest, hairiest, and ugliest tasks to start the day versus avoiding them until the end of the day. Usually, I'd share with my team what my biggest challenge of the day was and finish that one first. It was excellent role modeling to demonstrate how to avoid — avoidance!

Okay, I get that not everyone is a "morning person." If you don't like the suggestion above, here's another one for you…

Align the Hardest Tasks With Your Highest Energy Times of the Day

There are many times when I need to work on a process or methodology-heavy tasks — my least favorite kind of work. Sometimes these efforts look insurmountable, and they are easy to consider avoiding, but I know I'm usually in a great flow early A.M. or late P.M. — that's when I try to take on these challenges. As a coach, I help my coachees understand how to align their biggest challenges with their highest energy times. Don't avoid the challenge - intentionally schedule it based upon your energy being most ready to take on the challenge.

Ask Myself, "Why?"

There might be some anxiety, concern, worry, or fear about the work I'm avoiding. But I'll stop to ask myself, "Why?" I'm avoiding something and working to alleviate those concerns. For example, I might fear taking on a task without knowing all the information. Once I identify that fear and how to mitigate it, I'll move forward with that task. As a leader, asking "Why are you trying to avoid something?" was an easy question of anyone on my team. It became an even more valuable question when I'd ask myself "Why?" was I avoiding an issue.

Can I Reschedule It?

There are some legitimate times when avoidance is actually the correct course of action. That's totally fine. Sometimes something else comes up that was unplanned — forcing you to reevaluate your overall schedule. I'll intentionally move a task to another day or weekend when those situations arise — called it "planned avoidance." Adding more and more and more doesn't work. I try to get as much done as possible, but sometimes rescheduling makes the most sense.

LESSON LEARNED

When you feel anxious or concerned about something and determine avoidance is your "best" strategy, think about past successes… and how you felt *after* completing the task or accomplishing your goal. Then, channel that feeling, use one or more of the strategies I offered or others that work for you, and get it done! Cramming for a test or trying to get work done at the last second can be extremely stressful and result in a less-than-ideal result. In most cases, avoidance only delays what you need to finish anyway. Get one or more strategies that work for you, and STOP avoiding the inevitable.

COMPETITIVE

"as good as or better than others of a comparable nature."

What drives you? Whether competing against others or your own goals, how do you get yourself motivated to be successful at something?

I was born in Cincinnati, Ohio, in 1967. Less than six years later, my family moved to a suburb of Detroit, Michigan. Not only were my parents both Cincinnati natives, but they were also fans of baseball, and the best team in baseball at the time (with all apologies to the Oakland A's) was the Cincinnati Reds — also known as the Big Red Machine. As a budding baseball player myself, I'd want to hit huge home runs like George Foster, run the bases with passion like Pete Rose, make amazing running catches in the outfield like Ken Griffey (he didn't become Sr. until his son, Ken Griffey Junior, joined the Seattle Mariners many years later), play flawless fielding like Joe Morgan or clearly lead the team like Johnny Bench — one of the greatest catchers in the history of the game.

When I moved to Michigan, I found myself among mostly Detroit Tiger fans. All the baseball games I played with my friends would be Detroit versus Cincinnati, and most of the kids I played with were several years older than me, but I didn't care since I was Johnny Bench or Little Joe Morgan or George Foster when I came up to bat against whatever "Detroit pitcher" they happened to be pretending to be.

I'm sure I lost more games than I won. But I remember never wanting to give up playing against these older kids. As I observed what they did well, I learned as many lessons as possible from them. But I also played organized baseball on an actual baseball field and quickly improved during practices and games in whatever baseball league I played. My competitive drive was growing quickly.

Fast forward to several years ago, my mentor at the time asked me what my values were. I went through a process to develop six values that were most important to me. Unsurprisingly, one of the values on my list was confidence — which often manifests through my competitiveness.

When I went on a three-month sabbatical not long after that discovery, I traced the origins of my values to when I first remembered them being important to me. If I'm honest, my competitiveness evolved from not having kids my age in my immediate neighborhood and wanting the other kids to keep inviting me to play with them. I had to be good enough to play the games and keep improving to keep pace with them.

Over time, I really discovered a "new" definition of competitiveness. I love to play games of any type — sports, cards, puzzles, and you name it — and I love to win. But my definition of competitiveness now centers on my growth and development and evolution, versus the need to win. Continual improvement is important to me — or performing at my best in any situation. So, my measure of competitiveness is all about how I've done against my measurements.

Golf is my favorite example. You don't get to play defense on the other players in your foursome. You can't yell when they are driving or trying to sink a putt. You have zero control over their ability to hit a great shot. You can only control your game by driving the ball from the tee box, hitting irons from the fairway (hopefully), chipping onto the green, and putting the ball in the hole. Focus on your own game and do as well as you can possibly do on each hole while applying your lessons learned from the previous holes to the next ones.

I still play tons of games and love to win. But I realize now that I usually compete against myself as much as anything. So my competitive juices are always present but less current than my time with others.

P.S. In case you didn't notice, I have another story about **Competition**. I enjoy the topic so much, I had to write about it twice and couldn't pick just one winner.

LESSON LEARNED

Another definition of being competitive is "possessing a strong desire to be more successful than others." And I'm sure that's how I started. I consider competitiveness an important attribute today because I have my definition and understanding of what's important to me in terms of being competitive. I'm not advocating that you send new meanings of words to Mr. Webster or Wikipedia. Peel away layers of words and understand what something truly means to you, competing with yourself internally versus against others externally. Or, even better, across our life's journey, consider how your current self compares against who you were five, ten, or more years ago. Now that is the best way to be competitive!

GRIEF

"deep sorrow, especially that caused by someone's death."

I've lost several people in my life over the years.

My grandma died when I was 24 years old. By this point in my life, I had several friends who had lost a grandparent (or two). And her death wasn't sudden; it progressed over a period of time.

Likewise, my father passed away after months, if not years, of slowly losing his good health. It was not a surprise at the very end, but it was still sorrowful.

My friend Nick passed away when I was 47 years old. Even though Nick had been battling cancer for over a decade, it was still a bit of a shock and extremely sorrowful when he finally gave in to that horrible thing called cancer, and it probably impacted me heavily because I thought of his role as a father as much as his role as a friend — how would his kids deal with their father's death? Also, Nick's wife is extremely resilient, but I also grieved for her.

But the person I think of most when I genuinely feel a sense of grief is my friend Natalie. She passed away at the age of 23. Not only was it a surprise when she passed away, but she was also my first experience with death.

Natalie and I first met in middle school as sixth graders trying to figure out the world — or at least this new paradigm of going to different classrooms throughout the day. We were in some classes together. We crossed over in various sports, and we sometimes hung out after school, on weekends, and during the summer.

In high school, Natalie fully blossomed into a beautiful young woman. She was popular and fun to be around. And many of my male friends wanted to date her over the years (and did). I'm unsure if I lacked the confidence to ask her out or simply knew we were meant to be friends, but that's the status we maintained throughout our days in high school.

While at the University of Illinois, Natalie and I truly got to know each other. She ended up at one of the most prestigious sororities on campus. So many people around campus recognized her, and she rarely went out without someone noticing her.

261

I was lucky enough to join one of the most prestigious fraternities on campus, and our two houses were frequently linked together. We often had football tailgate parties, sat at football and basketball games in large blocks, hosted joint parties, and attended each other's events many times during the year.

Somehow, I must have been a bit of a "relief valve" for her. Though we saw each other frequently through our sorority-fraternity connections, we also found a lot of time to spend one-on-one with each other outside of that world. For example, we'd often play tennis together - her favorite sport and a sport she had to teach me. Fortunately, I could leverage my athleticism to (mostly) keep up with her and stay competitive. We had hours of fun and often followed up with a beer or drink after, paid for by the loser, of course.

Other times, we would find ourselves at a busy bar with many of our friends. Yet we'd somehow find time to grab a drink together and still manage to engage in a deep, 1-1 conversation while dozens of guys were trying to get her attention, loud music was blasting in the background, and numerous other late-night interruptions tried to stop us.

Some of our most fun adventures were driving home once or twice a semester during the school year. I'm not sure we even used the radio as we'd talk about a myriad of subjects for hours as we drove home on a Friday and back on a Sunday.

After we graduated from college, we didn't get the same time together as I moved to Peoria, IL, and Natalie was several hours north of me in the Chicago suburbs. So when I learned that Natalie was in an accident and might not survive, it was a serious gut punch for me.

The definition of grief includes the word sorrow, but it should also include suffering, agony, torment, pain, and more. I'm sure I felt all these emotions and more when Natalie finally passed away about a week later.

And her funeral was even more sorrowful. I'm grateful that her mom asked me to be a pallbearer. I remember speaking to almost everyone in attendance since I knew her close high school friends and many of her closest college friends. Tears. Hugs. Tissues. Storytelling. More tears. Grief sucks.

While many people speak about the linear progression of the stages of grief, I've come to experience that we all weave in and out of all of these stages in our progression. We even experience some of the elements/stages of grief years later. Many people refer to these stages of grief (and did) denial, anger, bargaining, depression, and acceptance. While those are helpful, I prefer to think about grief based on its foundational elements:

Loss

While this includes death or separation, many other types exist. It could be the loss of a vision or dream or a long-time relationship. And it might be something as basic as your sense of what you consider normal regarding something or someone. To initially process grief, it is important to dig deeper to understand what loss you are experiencing.

Losing Natalie meant losing a dear friend and my closest female friend. I've rarely played tennis since those amazing days in college.

Longing

To me, this is the most challenging component of grief. Longing is spontaneous. I'll cry about something and not realize why until I realize I'm longing for something or someone I've lost in my life. Whether it is the passing of a dear friend or relative or something tangible, many of us wish we could reconnect with what we lost once more. While longing doesn't help me to process my grief, it does remind me to live in the moment and celebrate my relationships and sense of normalcy.

Today, I long to have just one more discussion with Natalie and talk about how our lives have progressed since those days 30+ years ago in college together. As I've shared through other stories in this book, I keep connected with her family, which helps with some of my longings.

Feeling Lost

Feeling lost might persist for years or more. Part of our process is establishing our sense of normalcy given a new set of circumstances. We need to reorient ourselves mentally, physically, intellectually, emotionally, etc. As most of us have experienced through the pandemic, this is part of creating the "new normal" for ourselves after a loss.

Though we didn't live near each other after college, we often found time to connect during the holidays. After she died, however, I felt lost during my first few trips back home, knowing I couldn't have lunch with Natalie or laugh and talk during our drives to and from U of I together.

LESSON LEARNED

In many ways, grief may never leave us. My strongest cures for dealing with the grief I've experienced in my life is to understand my loss clearly (Natalie passed away, and I lost someone who was probably my closest female friend at the time), celebrate the positive times regarding what I've lost (I keep in touch with many of my friends from high school and we often bring up stories about Natalie that make me smile) and do my best to live in the moment (I love reaching out to Natalie's mom or her friends from high school and college) while continually adapting.

Sadly, as I'm currently working through this version of this specific story, I learned that my friends had just lost one of their beloved Labrador Retrievers. I cried when I heard the news and plan to grieve with them tonight. The definition of grief talks about "someone's death," but we might all grieve for our beloved pets or relationships or many other things across our life's journey. These lessons can be applied to anything you grieve in your life.

Chapter 8

Match.com — Be Selective About Your Pro

For me, I met with four therapists until I finally settled upon the therapist I've been working with for the past decade. I was extremely selective. The first three therapists I spent some time with were intellectually brilliant. But I didn't "connect" with them. Not only is my current therapist intellectually challenging, but we've also connected on many other levels. I feel we've gotten to both the heart ("feeling") connection as well as the soul ("bigger picture" and lifelong learning) connection and not just the head/brain ("thinking") as I had with previous therapists.

SUFFERING

"the state of undergoing pain, distress, or hardship."

I usually focus on fun and happiness, but we should also discuss the opposite side.

I'm grateful for my mom and dad's efforts to care for my brother and me. We were in a stable environment with minimal suffering. Sure, there were a few painful incidents here and there, but I don't recall anything that relates to distress or hardship.

Before I progress, let's define those three elements of suffering:

Pain: physical suffering or discomfort caused by illness or injury.

Distress: extreme anxiety, sorrow, or pain.

Hardship: severe suffering or privation, where "privation" means "a state in which things that are essential for human well-being such as food and warmth are scarce or lacking."

As I stated above, I was fortunate growing up, but I heard stories at church, in school, around the neighborhood, or on the news about how other people might be suffering.

Suffering didn't really "hit me" until I traveled to Kenya for the first time. Of course, there are many amazing aspects of Kenya. But it was the first time in my life I observed people suffering from pain, distress, AND hardship simultaneously.

The lack of clean drinking water and difficult living conditions overall in some of these villages resulted in many illnesses borne by the residents.

And not having a job or knowing where money might come from brought about extreme anxiety and distress in many villagers.

Lastly, shelter wasn't readily or easily available to everyone. There were just too many basic human needs that needed to be met.

Fortunately, many amazing people in the world want to help others who are suffering, and many different organizations are established to support others suffering in one way or another.

For example, I've been involved with several nonprofits created to help others suffering in Kenya and other countries worldwide — including the United States of America.

But... What helps those suffering?

Money

The most obvious answer. Every nonprofit organization I've worked for or with needs money to operate. Whether through donations, fundraising activities, grants, or something else, money helps bring the mission of helping those suffering to life.

Time

I've often been in the role of working with nonprofit organizations or asking people or companies for money. If they aren't able or willing to donate money, I'll often ask for the donation of time. Volunteers usually make these nonprofits work and are a critical need to help those suffering worldwide. I've often volunteered my time to help with fundraising in circumstances when I didn't have significant sums of money to donate.

Empathy

When you truly understand the feelings of others, you will have a much better idea of ways to help them through their suffering.

Positive Energy

Giving some of your power and energy to a nonprofit could also be helpful. As I've attended board meetings or fundraising events, I'd come in with positive energy to influence others to make more significant donations of money or time. I can think of multiple times at a fundraiser where I raised the energy level of others — and resulted in them increasing their bids or donations or willingness to volunteer.

Collaboration

Finding other companies or organizations to collaborate with often has great benefits. For example, I acquired used laptops at five percent of the list price from my company and donated them to a nonprofit organization helping those in need.

Network

Reaching out to networks to discover others who might know how to solve some of those complex problems relating to pain, distress, and hardship is also helpful. For example, one nonprofit I worked with helped to build a well to source clean water for the local village — instead of having the villagers carry back questionable water from sources where animals drink and bathe.

Just Ask

What might appear to be hardship, pain, or distress to you might not be how other people are experiencing that situation. It often helps to ask what people are going through and whether or not they are genuinely suffering.

As I've shared throughout this book, we will all experience some form of suffering in our lifetimes. Be compassionate to the suffering of others as you wish others might be with you. But compassion is just the first step. Taking steps to help someone suffering actively is the key step. Selfishly, I feel better about myself when I've helped others. But, more importantly, observing how other people restore their situation or circumstances is even more rewarding.

LESSON LEARNED

Knowing that others might be suffering is important as you travel through the various phases of your life. I strongly believe in helping others who are suffering — be good to others, but also because you'll find yourself suffering at some level at some point in your life and appreciate help from others along the way. It might take a lot of work with more experienced people to understand whether or not someone else is suffering. The subtle hints and data points might not initially make sense, and it takes an astute and experienced problem solver in many cases to kindly assess if someone else is suffering and whether you or someone you know can help them.

GRATITUDE

"the quality of being thankful; readiness to show appreciation for and to return kindness."

When did you first start thinking about grades in school?

When I was in fourth and fifth grade at Sleepy Hollow Elementary School, my most vivid memories were of the playground. We had the amazing monkey bars (not allowed any longer). And lots of swings and other playground equipment. But the big game was kickball. Boys and girls were just having fun. To the best of my recall, there were no grades nor discussions about A's, B's, or worse. If we returned to class after being on the playground, that was probably enough for the teacher!

As I progressed to Dundee Middle School, I had some vague recollections that we were being "graded," but those memories are few and far between. My middle school days were more about being around many different students and figuring out what classes we had to take versus what classes were optional. It was the first time I could recall being thoughtful about my classes. But grades weren't truly top of mind.

Finally, in high school, I became fully aware that we were being graded. Homework, quizzes, and tests took on more relevance. My freshman and sophomore years, however, were still about having fun with friends, prioritizing whatever sport I was playing then, and mixing in other fun activities like a jazz club, chorus, or other interesting activities.

I am trying to remember exactly when, but at some point in my freshman or sophomore year, I became aware that we were not only being graded but also being compared to and ranked against everyone else. My actual class ranking wasn't the point. The fact that I wasn't considered "one of the best" or "one of the smartest" kids in school really got to me.

In parallel, I recall having teachers I enjoyed and others that weren't so much fun. But why was that? Did they challenge me in specific ways that I didn't appreciate? Or did I just not enjoy those subjects? So again, my recollection is vague. But I never really remember having a teacher that I truly respected (though, in fairness, I probably didn't understand what that word meant at the time, either).

269

Until I met my high school chemistry teacher, James Borello. Mr. Borello challenged me to be a better student. He pushed me when I didn't even know I needed pushing. He strongly encouraged me to work harder in and after class — being diligent about my homework, preparing for all the quizzes he gave, and ensuring I was ready for his most challenging exams, especially pushing me hard to prepare for that final exam.

My most poignant memory was taking the final exam, knowing I needed a specific grade to ultimately get an "A" in the class. I did well but ended up a point or two short of the total points needed that semester to make the grade.

Now that I had finally embraced the idea of "getting good grades," I was deflated that I had worked so hard and just missed the grade I sought. I went through my final exam, all of my quizzes, and each of my homework assignments to discover whether or not there was a point or two somewhere else that I might fight for.

I went into Mr. Borello's office before the end of the school year and shared with him my point of view. We started diving into the details, and we jointly agreed there were a few extra points here and there — just enough for him to be willing to change my B+ to an A- (in those days, the + or - didn't make a difference to the GPA as it does today). That change was HUGE, and I was extremely grateful to Mr. Borello for being willing to listen to my perspective and give me the A-.

Reflecting on that time, I'm actually grateful for many other reasons than just the A-. Mr. Borello suggested that if I were to apply myself a bit harder during the year and be more diligent about what's needed all of the time, including for the final exam, we wouldn't be in the same position in the future. I took his advice to heart and got straight A's throughout the balance of my junior and senior years.

Though I left Chicago 25+ years ago, I've often traveled back to Illinois to visit family and friends. And several times, I've made an effort to go back and thank Mr. Borello for his confidence in me and his ability to challenge me to be better. I constantly tell him that he's my favorite and most influential teacher.

LESSON LEARNED

Gratitude can be very layered. You can be thankful for something at the moment and show kindness in return. But there is often a secondary or tertiary benefit to gratitude. I've experienced gratitude on many levels with others and constantly ensured that they receive the appreciation they deserve.

Gratitude also has a rebound effect — the more you give it to others, the more you feel positive and warm about yourself.

Lastly, I've even felt gratitude when I share *observed* gratitude with others. Not everyone gets it, and there have been many times when I watched someone else do something nice for another person *without* getting a "Thank You," and I'll walk up to them after and share gratitude with them. Tell you what... I've never *not* gotten a huge smile from that person. And I smiled right back.

TRANSITION

"the process or a period of changing from one state or condition to another"

Wow! That's a lot to break down. I can't even imagine how many different transitions I've experienced in my lifetime. I've moved from Ohio to Michigan many times and across multiple locations in Illinois and among several locations in Seattle. And I've made many job transitions as well as I touched upon the story called Career.

But the one that stands out the most to me is my transition from college graduation to starting in the "real world" working for IBM and it was a compound transition — parents paying for college versus me paying for 100% of my life; college versus work (do I need to explain more here?); living in a fraternity or "college apartment" (an extension of the fraternity) versus my own apartment; hanging out with friends for fun versus networking for career aspirations.

When I watched my son Ryan and my nephew Jack graduate from college on back-to-back weekends, the concept of transition hit me hard. Here are some of the stories and ideas I shared with them as they embed their major transitions:

Independence

The word I use most often with Ryan is independence. When I was his age, I'm not sure I realized how many little decisions happen daily. Unintentionally or not, many of those decisions were made by a family member during college. Going forward, he'll learn how to make all these little decisions independently. I'm excited for him to develop his method of making decisions and establishing his sense of independence as he transitions into a role that challenges him in new ways.

Time Management

All that comes to mind is how many wonderful distractions there are in college. I won't list them here for many reasons! Needless to say, there are an exponential number of new and interesting opportunities as you transition to the working world. Managing your time preparing for a college final can be difficult. But understanding how to manage your time in your first job can be overwhelming when everything seems like an urgent priority. Be prepared, fail early and often, and learn from your missteps in managing time as you transition to the work world.

Sleep

This might seem like an odd category, but I wish I had learned how to sleep more effectively. No more sleeping in until noon or 1 P.M.! My roommate in college was from Singapore, and he was brilliant at taking the 15-minute "power nap." He pulled many all-night sessions (and graduated in four years with a master's degree), and he found a way to take naps as a refresher.

That's a bit more challenging to execute at work - but keep it as a potential option. A better focus would be getting enough sleep and learning how and when to sleep effectively while in bed. For the record, sleeping or napping during one of your boring work meetings does not count! Mainly because you can't nap at your desk as you transition into the working world. Solid sleep in the "right" amount for your body nightly will make you more productive the following day — without exception.

Technology

I started my first job 33 years ago — we didn't have laptops or cell phones. However, I'm not so old that we couldn't leverage computers, the earliest stages of the Internet, phones, music players (do you remember the Walkman or a boom box?), etc. At its core, technology, especially today, can be critical in your transition from college to your first job. While this technology can be distracting to some, it can also be used for good. Now I'll have to "borrow" a quote from Spider-Man that goes something like this *"With great power comes great responsibility."* I'd apply that axiom to leveraging technology to its maximum benefit, even if that includes relaxing and winding down with Netflix or texting your parents. Make sure you understand when you are crossing the line from productive uses of technology versus falling into major "rabbit holes" with zero productivity.

Relationships

Your relationships may be diverse at this point in your life. They emanate from an extended base, including your school, neighborhood, parent's friends, sports or extracurricular programs, etc. You can establish so many brand new relationships on your terms and based upon your interests. Thirty years later, some of my best, life-long relationships evolved from my first job after graduation. Learning how to build new relationships post-college college while maintaining existing relationships from high school or earlier is a great baseline. Your transition to the work world will provide many opportunities to build new and strengthen existing relationships. There is little downside to investing in relationships during your life — humans are naturally meant to be social creatures.

Temptation

Some folks might not want to acknowledge all the temptations, especially after the many temptations you might have experienced in college or high school. Temptations are prevalent across all walks of life, but they all seem so close up and real when you transition from college life to being on your own, blowing off work for a day of fun, and spending too much money on "fun" items. I remember there being so many new and different temptations. Learning how to say no, experiment in moderation, try things with the safety of others present, or ask many more questions before trying something are all ways of dealing with the many temptations you might face as you transition.

Big Picture

Too much pressure exists to decide "what do you want to do when you grow up?". The transition to your first job should be considered an experiment. Keep aware of your big-picture interests, but don't try to come up with an exact solution to your long-term plan because you took your first job. There will be more job transitions in your life — trust me. Your longer-term vision is about learning who you are and who you want to become over the next few years versus immediately following your initial transition from college to work.

Shoulders of Giants

I often reflect upon all of the things my dad and mom did for me growing up. I hope I'm not stating an alternate fact here when I quote Issac Newton: *"If I have seen further than others, it is by standing on the shoulders of giants."* Anyway, I'd consider my parents two of those giants. But there were many others — key teachers, coaches, friends, relatives, neighbors, and, just in case my brother is paying attention, siblings! So as you transition into something totally new and different, consider who might help you in that journey and allow you to stand on their shoulders.

While many of these ideas are applied to your first transition into work after four years of college, most apply to almost any transition you might face in your life. And there are undoubtedly other ideas about transitions that you can add to the list above as well.

LESSON LEARNED

Being adaptable is key. You can apply lots of lessons learned from your past and others. Still, your adaptability is essential to dealing with a transition process at any stage in your life. The eight ideas shared above — independence, time management, sleep, technology, relationships, temptation, the big picture, and the shoulders of giants — should be helpful as you discover your own ideas for handling transitions. And you'll likely come up with others to help you adapt to the transition; email me your additional thoughts. I'd love to hear about them!

ANGER

"a strong feeling of annoyance, displeasure, or hostility."

Imagine an image of a cartoon character, red-faced, with puffing cheeks, and steam coming out of their ears.

274

For years, my ex-wife and I were going through couples therapy. During some of those times when the therapist was asking me about my feelings, I usually started by saying I was angry. But, to her credit, she always pushed me to uncover what was "one layer below" anger because most of the time, I would follow up with, "And I have no idea why I'm angry."

Most of the time, I had no idea what she was talking about in terms of looking "one layer below." She showed us an image of concentric circles with anger at the center and other emotions circling anger, but I still didn't totally get it. Over time, I slowly started to understand there was a more specific emotion (or several) below the surface of my anger. Sadly, I couldn't process it on my own. I needed my therapist to help me understand what might genuinely be present for me.

The significant shift came after reading *Atlas of the Heart* by Brené Brown. An image in the book clearly showed many of the emotions that might be below the surface of anger. Everything my therapist had been teaching me over the years made complete sense. Just considering all of the different emotions that might be behind my anger was jaw-dropping. Over time, and with a lot of help from my therapist and coach, we uncovered many different emotions that were present for me when my first instinct was to say, "I'm angry."

Here's a subset of emotions I realized was behind my anger. I'm sure there are many others you can add to your own list. These are just a list of emotions I've actually tended to discuss with my therapist and/or coach at some point. Some of these emotions may actually be what is behind your sense of anger:

- Fear
- Anxiety
- Frustration
- Confusion
- Hurt
- Grief
- Sadness
- Isolation
- Shame
- Guilt
- Jealousy
- Outrage at injustice
- Helplessness

- Overwhelming stress
- Humiliation
- Embarrassment
- Depression
- Rejection
- Loneliness

I could write a whole book about many different "flavors" of anger (or maybe someone a *lot* smarter than me should write it) and how I've experienced them. But thinking about anger, looking at this list, *and* trying to identify the actual emotion/s I'm experiencing is a great starting point when I'm not with my therapist. There were so many times I was just sad, hurting, lonely, or afraid, and those emotions manifested in me as anger. Ironically, I wasn't angry at all…but I had no idea how to explain my feelings.

It was super helpful for me to recall the many times when I felt anger in the past. I looked at this list of words and many other words related to anger to understand my feelings. Over time, I slowly built up my understanding (and vocabulary) of what it means when I'm angry.

I'll share a few quick stories about what might have felt like anger to start but were something else. Why am I sharing these stories? Because understanding what is actually "behind" your anger can help you process your actual feelings and emotions more effectively.

Sadness

Sadness should be another another story in this book, but I'll save it for Lessons Learned #2. I experienced a lot of sadness after Melanie and I ultimately agreed to end our 30-year marriage. I'm still sad and hurting and not 100% through the classic stages of grief (another of the 19 emotions). But I try to focus on the next 30+ years and stay optimistic about what I can create in the following stages of my life. Awareness is key. It was a great lesson to understand I wasn't angry at all — just extremely sad about the situation, as I never expected to get a divorce when we first met in college over three decades ago.

Loneliness

My sons are in college and focused on some of the most exciting parts of their lives, so they are rightly focused on their own lives. I engage with my friends as often as possible, but they also have priorities. I'm thrilled when I connect in person with my friends in Seattle, but I'm working from home, and my day-to-day interaction is all about taking Suki, my cute chocolate Labrador Retriever, for excellent walks. Sometimes I feel lonely, but I can look at the bigger picture and understand what my future life might look like. Instead of being angry when I'm alone, I think about myself being lonely and ponder what I can do to get through that feeling.

Isolation

When the global pandemic of 2020 hit us all, I'm sure most people felt isolated. Zoom calls helped a bit but still felt "remote." I've traveled some, but those trips seem shorter than I'd prefer. My home office is great, but it feels as if I'm in this tightly controlled little space 24x7. My focus on spending time in the future with friends and family helps me get through the tough days of being isolated.

The bottom line was that there was no use in getting mad about being isolated in a small basement apartment.

Today I feel much better about what other emotions I might be experiencing when I'm angry. My first step is to simply notice that I'm angry. Then, I take a deep breath, force myself to think about *why* I'm angry, and truly dig into what else might be present for me. Once I'm more aware of the other emotion/s I'm experiencing, I can process those emotions since I understand more specifically what's happening to me.

And, to be totally transparent, if I'm not processing one or more of these emotions with my therapist in real-time, I'll pull out this list of different emotions when I'm initially feeling angry as my "cheat sheet" to figure out what I'm truly experiencing at the time — since I now understand that I'm probably going through something different than just anger.

LESSON LEARNED

First of all, it's OK to be angry. That's what is on the surface. But take a deep breath and go deeper. What's under the anger? Feel free to start with this list, add your emotions, and look at it when you are angry to understand your feelings better. Identify the fundamental emotion that's present for you, and then you can figure out how to address it. Without truly exploring the depth of your feelings, you'll never be able to deal with the emotions that are present for you effectively when all you think of is being angry - at someone or something.

COMPARTMENTALIZATION

"the division of something into sections or categories."

Can you picture those old-time manufacturing locations? The buildings that have five or six or more individual smoke stacks coming out the top? When I think about compartmentalization, that image comes to mind.

And who doesn't get stressed about everything happening in life? How do you find balance across all of these activities? For me, the easiest solution was to compartmentalize pieces that I believed were important and needed attention at that time. In doing that, I put each piece in a silo and worked through them individually. I often had an extremely challenging day at work and had to use the ten-minute drive from work to pick up one of the boys from home to take them to practice. I quickly had to compartmentalize my frustrations into my "work silo," put a smile on my face and get excited as my "coach silo."

A few years ago, I was re-reading one of my favorite Dr. Seuss Books, *Oh, the Places You'll Go*. This is one of my favorite books to give to someone graduating from high school or college. It's a quick read and offers many great phrases they might be able to apply to many life aspects.

One of the lines in the book stuck out to me at that time — *"Step with care and great tact and remember that Life's a Great Balancing Act."* It resonated with me because I was trying to do three or four different roles within my company — while also managing my other roles in life (spouse, father, friend, community member, board member for two nonprofits, etc.). I got really good at having NO balance and simply compartmentalizing everything.

278

The image I had in my head was that manufacturing plant with all of the individual and compartmentalized smokestacks except the building was a single story, and the smokestacks were a mile high and representative of each silo in my life (three or four work roles, four or five life roles, etc.).

Another week later, I shared this perspective with my professional coach, Don. I told him about the stresses at work concerning managing multiple roles and the stress it was causing me during the day. And then how that stress was magnified in the evenings and weekends when I had to operate in my other silos. There was zero balance across all of these disparate silos.

His question was so simple that I'm embarrassed that it wasn't more evident, *"What is the common theme across all of these unbalanced silos?"*. It might have only been a minute, but it felt like 15-20 minutes before I was able to come up with the answer.

Me.

No matter which silo I was operating in, I was always present in that silo. It was a transformative discussion because I realized how much baggage (or smoke) I was bringing from smokestack to smokestack without knowing I was doing it. In reality, the building was one hundred stories tall (me across the whole thing), and the silos were simply one-story tall little nubs on top.

Certainly, there is some value in compartmentalizing a very complex situation or task. But it is *not* at all useful to do it across everything happening in your life. STOP IT! Your confusion or challenges or heartaches or smoke in one silo will follow you to the next one - no matter how well you think you compartmentalize (you aren't able to do it)!!!.

I've heard the phrase "Work-Life XYZ," where the "XYZ" could be Balance, Integration, Wobble, or any other easy metaphor. But the reality is that the balance comes from within. The fact that YOU are present in life, work, and everything else is the key to truly understanding how to "de-compartmentalize" those smokestacks across your life. Don't be surprised if it takes an expert to point it out for you and help you to deal with it.

LESSON LEARNED

The best way to think about compartmentalization is to look at it externally and internally. On the outside, you will have multiple roles: friend, child, parent, partner, community member, neighbor, and potentially several others at work. These external roles have different accountabilities and require varying amounts of time dedicated to each. However, no matter which role/silo/smokestack you happen to be operating in at the time, YOU are always present.

Internally — you are your emotions, thoughts, ideas, passions, behaviors, habits, interests, desires, etc. YOU are that "something" you've attempted to break into smaller components.

STOP IT!

Life is more about understanding yourself and your ability to be present as you across any/all of these roles all of the time versus attempting to compartmentalize them into smaller components. Each and every one of those internal *and* external aspects of your life are present across *all* of the silos or compartments you naively think are separate.

CONTEXT

"the circumstances that form the setting for an event, statement, or idea, and in terms of which it can be fully understood and assessed."

"Ladies and gentlemen, let me tell you why we are here today." That's a line you'll often hear at the beginning of a meeting or a conference. Setting the context for the afternoon or day.

Full disclosure — I'm a huge fan of elephants. For whatever reason, I grew up totally enjoying the fact they were the largest mammals on the planet. Yet, they were vegetarians with no natural predators (other than humans — but don't get me started there). So, during my trips to Kenya, I was fascinated by getting as close to these amazing creatures as possible — even if our little van with six–seven people was barely as big as a single elephant.

When I first thought about the idea of context, the parable about the blind men and the elephant immediately came to mind. For those of you unfamiliar with this parable, it's a story about a group of blind men who encounter an elephant — a creature none of them have previously encountered. Each blind person feels a different part of the body and believes the tusk is simply a spear or the leg is the base of a tree. Sadly, everyone disagrees about what they are experiencing as each individual tends to focus only on their partial experience. As a result, they can't agree that they are each experiencing a part of the elephant.

Whether in a group or as an individual, it's important to clearly understand the "whole" context versus the individual parts. It's complicated and doesn't reveal the full story if you only share part of the story versus the whole thing. You need to fully understand an event's circumstances to understand the context entirely.

Context, in the sense of something physical, is reasonably easy to understand. Context in the sense of an idea or event is a bit more challenging.

My eighth-grade science fair project with Jeff Fox came to mind when thinking about more ambiguous forms of context. We went to our first science fair with a poster board of our experiment of flipping coins and mapping out whether the result was heads or tails. Our goal was to explain the idea of genetics as our science fair project in terms of how random flips of a coin (heads versus tails) was a simple metaphor for how the random selection of dominant versus recessive genes played a role in the evolution of specific characteristics. We thought we had a great story pulled together for the science fair — including my huge smile when I got to describe some of the historical contexts, given that Watson and Crick are most notably associated with many significant advancements in the world of genetics.

The first judge asked us, "Why did you select this coin-flipping experiment?". It was a simple question we answered innocently enough before fully adjusting our thinking and future response. For us, assigning heads to the X-gene and tails to the Y-gene seemed to be a simple explanation.

A quick break from the story, and more context here, how many of you grew up in the Midwest or another part of the world where it can get frigid at night? There were times in the winter when water would freeze in our garage. And can you guess what else might also freeze in a garage with temperatures close to the outside temperature? Fruit flies.

Our *first* experiment was about understanding fruit flies' dominant and recessive genes. So we were looking at our fruit flies' eye colors, matching the male and females with different eye colors, and understanding what their babies looked like. And what parents would want their children to breed fruit flies in the house when a single female can lay over 2,000 eggs and have fully "grown" fruit fly children in less than three days?

Needless to say, we ended up doing our experiment in my garage. Knowing that our science fair was in the early spring, we conducted our experiments in late winter. We had a few sets of fruit flies identified and ready to reproduce. Just a few days later, we were excited to evaluate our results.

Spoiler alert — all of our fruit flies had died in temperatures dipping into the single digits in our garage. So what eighth grader is thinking about heating your garage to support a science fair project?

We only had a week or two before our science fair project needed to be completed, and we had nothing. So we quickly came up with the idea to flip coins and show the concept of genetics that way.

The next time we were asked the same question by a different evaluator, "Why did you select this coin-flipping experiment?" We described our fuller story and the circumstances under which we ended up doing that version of the experiment. This time, the person evaluating our project *loved* the story. The evaluator suggested that our science project for next year was the follow-up of an experiment with the fruit flies ready for our *next* project. Wow — how our science fair project just kept getting better. All by giving a fuller context to the situation.

Reflecting on my eighth-grade lesson learned, I'm still learning how to provide the right amount of context at the correct time. There's always a balance as well. Sometimes my stories are *too* full of context, and other times, I need more. It's a process I'll keep improving for the rest of my life with a lot of input and perspective from others, but I have learned that more context is often better than less. So, my apologies if you found *this* story about context too long!

SELF-ACTUALIZATION

"the realization or fulfillment of one's talents and potentialities, especially considered as a drive or need present in everyone."

The idea of self-actualization is best (in my opinion) represented in a pyramid called *"Maslow's Hierarchy of Needs."* When I diligently dug into the pyramid and attempted to understand each level, I finally realized what self-actualization was really about.

Part of my journey in providing lessons learned for my sons must include a self-assessment on multiple levels. Maslow's Hierarchy of Needs is an excellent means of understanding where we are in our growth. And while I love the idea of SELF actualization, it is super helpful to have others provide guidance and support on your deeper understanding of self actualization.

Before I was formally responsible for coaching and mentoring others, I only had a basic understanding of Maslow's Hierarchy of Needs. As a result, I spent three to four hours on each of the five levels to more deeply understand what each level meant — beyond the basic definition. If I didn't truly understand each level and how I did (or didn't) evolve through them, I could never have helped others understand their journey.

My goal here is to provide some advice for you, the reader, about how to traverse the path from Basic Needs to Psychological Needs to Self-Fulfillment needs through your journeys. And to be clear, this is *not* a linear journey. There will always be circumstances and situations in our lives that cause us to traverse back and forth across the different levels. I hope to share my own experiences, as well as the reflections of others, with you as an aid to understand and shift through each level:

Physiological Needs
Food, Water, Warmth, Rest

Fortunately, my ex-wife and I have provided much of my sons' needs regarding food, water, warmth, and rest. Through some amazing nonprofit organizations, the boys have had a chance to see what the rest of the world might struggle with and enlighten them with an understanding about how other people around the world live.

For example, when my oldest son was just in the third grade, he had the opportunity to travel to Kenya and live in a Maasai village through a local nonprofit called maasai-association.org. He had a chance to learn how the village established programs to support and improve sustainable traditional livestock practices to ensure food security.

Looking at the importance of physiological needs through the lens of others helps my sons appreciate what they have and need to provide for their own families.

Overall, be aware of the importance of each of these. For example, there are significant shortages of water around the world. Supply chain disruptions impact the delivery of food to specific locations. Warmth is on the list, but safety from extreme cold *and* heat might be more appropriate. And rest is always important — even with social media and a million other distractions for our time. I assume most of this book's readers are well set here, but you should be aware of what others worldwide might be suffering through themselves.

Safety Needs
Security, Safety

The other basic need is that of security and safety. Yet again, another great nonprofit organization, kidstown.org, helped my sons to understand how important it is to be safe and secure. This organization has saved hundreds of orphans from dire situations and provided a safe and secure environment for them to grow up in.

Of course, security and safety can also be viewed through a lens of mental safety and security. This is also a meaningful way to view some of our most basic needs — though this starts our progressions from basic to psychological needs.

Security can also include cyber security and even the security of those basic needs (food, water, etc.). And safety should be viewed through a very personalized lens. An environment or situation that seems safe to one person might be perceived as dangerous or threatening to another. In any case, ensure you are comfortable with both safety and security.

My wish and hope for you is that you are secure and safe and have an awareness and appreciation that others might not enjoy the same levels of safety and security.

Belongingness & Love Needs
Intimate Relationships, Friends

About 13 years ago, I suffered from a viral infection in my brain and spine. As the doctors tried to figure out how this acute inflammation was attacking my brain tissues, they suggested that I might not survive.

I discovered a book called *Chasing Daylight* by Eugene O'Kelley through this process. The message from the author's book was how everyone should embrace their relationships — your immediate family (spouse, children), extended family, lifelong friends, close business associates, and anyone else who impacted his journey through life via shared experiences. It enabled me to examine my relationships with fresh eyes — trying to understand what I appreciated about so many people who touched my life. It makes complete sense how intertwined other concepts like love and belonging are with people and the intimate relationships we form with others.

As my boys establish their relationships today, I help them understand how I've maintained relationships with people I've known since fourth grade or first met in middle school or high school — and reinforce what I've done to stay close with these people for more than forty years in many cases. We also discuss establishing brand new relationships that may become another 30+ year relationship over time. I'm strongly encouraged as my younger son is still friends with a neighbor he's known since they were two years old (they are 20 now). Another example: My older son was roommates in college with a high school buddy he'd known since elementary school.

No matter how introverted or extroverted you might be, we are all social beings. Intimate relationships, love, kindness, belonging, and empathy are critical to our survival. You first must understand precisely what you need in terms of relationships. Then work your ass off to build out these relationships for the entirety of your life on this amazing planet.

285

About one-third of the people I work with are "stuck" in this Maslow's hierarchy section. And it is usually some combination of both love and belonging. As I shared in the story about **Love**, I didn't fully understand love until I learned to love myself and felt I belonged anywhere at any time.

Esteem Needs
Prestige & Feeling of Accomplishment

Prestige and a feeling of accomplishment are critical to view through the lens that's most relevant to yourself. One of the hardest challenges here is to understand the balance between the expectations of others (prestige — see below) and your own expectations — being self-aware about what is and isn't important to you. Some people will feel a sense of accomplishment through success in sports, while others might find success through the lens of art, music, or achievements at work. Learning as much as possible about yourself and understanding your passions and desires is important.

The feeling of accomplishment can be as simple as checking something off a daily to-do list to something as difficult as qualifying for the Olympics or starting your nonprofit organization. And your feeling of accomplishment will definitely change throughout your lifetime. For example, what seemed necessary as a high school student differs significantly from what's important to accomplish as a father or executive in a company.

I feel as if prestige might get in our way at times. The definition of prestige states it is "widespread respect and admiration felt for someone or something based on a perception of their achievements or quality." Be aware that viewing accomplishments or achievements through the eyes of others might taint your own needs of self-esteem. And this goes both ways.

You might be disappointed by an artistic rendering you've created, while someone with zero artistic talent might hold you in very high regard. The opposite is also true —— don't be distracted when you did your best and made nine out of ten free throws by the person who criticizes you for not making all ten.

Focus on your sense of accomplishment more than any other person thinks about your achievements. Over 50% of the people I've worked with over the years spend much time in this section. Both prestige and a feeling of accomplishment can feel like a constantly moving target depending upon whose point of view you are accepting.

My personal experience is that you need to clearly establish your OWN definition of prestige and accomplishment and not get caught up with what others expect. Granted, that can be challenging in a long-term relationship or a career where you must keep others in an organization happy. Anything you can do to simply be yourself instead of attempting to be someone else that others want or need you to be will help solidify your sense of prestige and accomplishment.

Self-Actualization
Achieving One's Full Potential, Including Creative Activities

When I consider the concept of self-actualization, I always return to the word "journey." There are many well-known quotes about the journey, this quote from Arthur Ashe is a great one:

"Success is a journey, not a destination. The doing is often more important than the outcome."

To me, self-actualization is not a destination or an outcome but a journey or process that will never end. Only you can decide when you've reached your full potential.

When I start to do something very well, I do everything I can to improve upon it. What's next? You can teach others about your journey and help them along their path of self-fulfillment. Or you can discover something new and attempt to reach your full potential in that endeavor.

Maslow himself spoke about self-actualization as a desire to reach self-fulfillment.

Self-fulfillment might be based on your goals of becoming more emotionally aware or spiritually enlightened. It can be in pursuing something. Whether it be knowledge, artistic, or athletic achievement.

As a Seattle resident, I'm continually inspired by the Bill and Melinda Gates Foundation and their desire to take on some of the most difficult challenges worldwide and positively transform society for good. For example, one major goal was eradicating malaria from the earth. But even Bill and Melinda consider this a step in their overall journey to achieving the full potential for the Foundation.

Lastly, while focusing on the journey is important, remember to enjoy each day. As Master Oogway shares with Po in Kung Fu Panda: *"Yesterday is history, tomorrow is a mystery, and today is a gift... that's why they call it the present."* Live in the moment as much as possible.

Only about one in ten folks I'm working with have thoroughly covered all other levels and embraced their exploration within self-actualization. I don't fully embrace the idea of "full potential" as I prefer to think about life infinitely. We can all continue to grow, develop, learn, mature, progress, evolve, shift, and build new habits and behaviors until our last breath. Self-actualization is an ongoing process — even if you find yourself slipping back into a previous phase due to specific circumstances. Get through those challenges and continually dive into self-actualization.

LESSON LEARNED

Take time to figure out where you are on your journey to self-actualization. You will realize you might be there with a few aspects of your life but not others. That's totally OK.

The bigger point is to make yourself aware of what's important in the journey and how to get there. If you view self-actualization through the lens of an infinite and never-ending journey, you will continue to grow until your last days on this beautiful planet.

LIFE

"the condition that distinguishes animals and plants from inorganic matter, including the capacity for growth, reproduction, functional activity, and continual change preceding death."

Who do you want to say "Thanks" to for everything you have in your life?

During one of my visits to Chicago, I walked around downtown and ended up at the hotel where many of us gathered to celebrate the extraordinary life of my friend Nick. I spent a few hours at the Irish Pub in the hotel, where our college friends shared great stories about Nick during the celebration of Nick's life. While I was there, we had a fun little text string across our same group, "raising a glass" to Nick.

Later, during the same visit to Chicago, I connected with the mother of another friend, Natalie, who passed away a year after we graduated from college.

Up to this point, I was usually reflective about life and the times I had spent with Nick or Natalie and how much fun we had together over the years. Most of my contemplation was about fun adventures, wonderful experiences and/or joyful times with them.

But I never really thought about how to enjoy life going forward until I decided to share my thoughts about life, reflecting backward *and* going forward, with my mom and dad — sadly, only a year before my dad passed away.

My overall thinking about a life transformed from only thinking about it in the past tense when someone dear to me passed away to explicitly sharing past and future stories with those I love in the present.

Here's how I celebrated life for my mom and dad when I visited with them during that same Chicago visit:

Friends

My parents were only children, so my family growing up comprised of Mom, Dad, my brother, and Grandma. My parents always encouraged me to build new and deeper friendships. They enabled me to have last-minute dinner guests and sleepovers with my friends. They allowed me to take off on my bike at 8 A.M. on a Saturday and not come home until well after dark. And when I could drive, I could explore a much larger area than Sleepy Hollow and Dundee, IL, with my friends. I'm grateful they helped me build my "relationship muscle" and celebrate life with good friends - a "muscle" I still use frequently today.

Sports

I was very active in many sports. Somehow, my parents facilitated my getting to baseball, basketball, track, cross country, and golf across countless practices, games, and tournaments every month. We created baseball fields on open lots and football fields in our yards and installed more than one basketball hoop in our garage to create the ultimate driveway basketball court. As a result, I learned how to compete individually and as a team. I discovered the balance of how to enjoy any game fully, what it means to be a gracious winner, and how to suffer through defeat and learn lessons even while losing. Confidence, fairness, relationships, and fun are just a few of the values I derived from my many athletic endeavors growing up and I let my mom and dad know how they contributed to building the baseline of many of my values, providing an excellent foundation for my life going forward.

Music and More

With so much effort with friends and in sports, how could there be any time for something else? Fortunately, my parents encouraged me to explore other activities as well. As a result, I learned how to play the piano, sang in the choir, joined the jazz club, and even attempted acting in our eighth-grade rendition of *Willy Wonka*. One of my favorite memories was playing The Pink Panther (see the story **Nervous**) with two of my best buddies as sixth graders in front of the entire middle school. I'm grateful to my parents for encouraging me to explore fun outside of sports, and I'm *thrilled* that none of those performances are on YouTube! Life is more fulfilling with music, art, science, and more!

Career Focus

Growing up, we always discussed what's important today for your fuller career. Do you get a job out of school? What about an MBA? Any interest in a law degree? How do you navigate these multiple, complex decision trees? I'm still growing and expanding my thinking about career development. However, my parents instilled in me a great sense of responsibility for making choices today that have the potential to impact my future. I went into engineering knowing that I could apply those general lessons (problem-solving, systems thinking, complex structures, learning how to learn, etc.) to almost anything I wanted to do in life. And my first job out of college with IBM was practically a "mini-MBA" in learning the importance of being with an organization genuinely focused on career development.

Thanks, Mom and Dad, for guiding me to execute my plan and be prepared for the various ups and downs along my career journey.

Travel

We didn't have the classic Griswold Family Roadster growing up. Still, we did drive around the Midwest and Canada a bunch and even flew to Mexico, California, and several other places across North America. We learned to appreciate the outdoors and what living in other parts of the country would be like. We met locals and listened to their views of the U.S., the world, and more. My parents even facilitated our version of an exchange program — enabling me to live in Spain for a summer to explore what it's like to live in a totally different culture. I've taken those lessons learned about travel and applied them to my own travel experiences for my sons to allow them to see as much of the world as possible. Yes, if you haven't read it, there's a story called **Travel**.

Life is truly a journey, and travel is an essential component.

Core Foundations

My mom was a Math teacher. My dad has a background in chemistry and even learned German to read his chemistry books. They both instilled the importance of establishing the core foundations of math, science, arts, English, other languages, and more as a basis for lifetime learning.

How many times, growing up, did you ever ask, "When will I ever use this information again?". I'm not sure I truly appreciated the importance of building upon these core foundations until I had my kids. Seeing my sons leverage similar foundations is a tremendous validation of what my parents gave me.

Thanks, Mom and Dad, for teaching me, in advance, how to be a good parent myself and share some of the core foundations of life lessons with my sons.

Love

One of my biggest regrets is that I didn't say "I love you" to my mom and dad often enough when I was growing up. My parents did everything out of love for my brother and me. I knew they loved each other and loved us as well. This story is one attempt to share that message now. And, for the record, now that I realize the importance of saying "I love you" as an adult, I let my mom and dad know that I love them every time we speak and see each other.

Take time to develop your list of what you'd like to celebrate with someone else. It will grow exponentially as you'll discover that what you'd like to share with one person is different from what you'd like to share with someone else. Think about the list as endless as you celebrate life with so many others. And, if you are a patient reader, one of my last stories is called **Love**.

ADAPTABILITY

"the quality of being able to adjust to new conditions."

Where do you wish you could master adaptability to make you more effective in your life?

VUCA stands for Volatility, Uncertainty, Complexity, and Ambiguity. It's hard enough to respond to one of those, but you need to have a high tolerance for adaptability to handle more than one or *all* of them.

When I think about adaptability as a noun, my eCash Technologies employment comes to mind. It was my first time working with a startup company. The founders had acquired some patented technology called "blind signature encryption" from a company with a few existing customers in Europe. They asked me to be the first U.S. employee as they tried to convince two other individuals in Europe to come to the U.S. and join our little startup. I had done *none* of this previously and had to adapt to a whole new set of circumstances quickly. More on this in a minute.

My years at IBM taught me a lot about structure and processes, problem-solving, and more. The training was exceptional, the people were extremely helpful and impressive, and my learning opportunities were tremendous. My subsequent two job experiences after my days with IBM were also extremely educational and closely "connected."

My days at COMSI revolved around selling the same IBM hardware I learned about at IBM, and taught me a bit more about the importance of offerings like software and professional services, both offered by COMSI.

That experience made it easy for me to shift to InterTrans Logistics which was also a mix of selling software (still running on IBM hardware) and professional services.

So there was always some "content connectivity" across my career moves until I joined eCash Technologies where VUCA hit me hard.

Up to this point in my career, my focus was almost exclusively on the sales aspect of the business. I learned how to engage with existing customers, build new relationships with interesting prospects and discover how to engage with key business partners most effectively. Learning about new industries, exploring different geographies, and managing many personality types would be fun.

But very little of this helped me in the early days of eCash Technologies.

How do you find the optimal location for the office? Much less find the optimal office space itself? What's the best way to hire someone? And in what order? Who takes the manager role when no one reports to anyone? The board was the boss, but I was the first employee and drove much of the activity. Was I the de facto boss?

And I knew nothing about banks or financial services — even though I could leverage some of my sales experience, these were very different industries for me to learn.

I didn't realize it then, but I learned a ton about various aspects of adaptability. Of course, my lessons learned didn't come from the lens of **VUCA**, but I can use that acronym to share those lessons anyway.

V — Volatility

Volatility is when something has the "liability to change rapidly and unpredictably, especially for the worse."

We discovered someone was stealing from the company and had to walk them out the door and fire them immediately.

The first president drove us in the wrong direction, and we needed to replace him. Worst of all, we didn't know at the time that we were in the middle of the Internet crash of 2001.

My adaptability muscles started to grow when I accepted that something would change rapidly and unpredictably and was confident enough to know that I could handle it. I learned from each volatile situation and was more prepared for the next, even more volatile, situation. I made a few missteps, like assuming the Internet crash was just a small "blip" in the rapid growth of the Internet at the time, but I recovered from each quickly.

U — Uncertainty

Uncertainty is the "state of being unable to be relied on; not known or definite."

We needed customers to drive revenues. However, it was completely uncertain where we would get customers to pay us for our software. We had some ideas about what our software might eventually be used for, but how do you build a customer base with nothing definitive to sell them?

That was my job. And I had a blast doing it. What I learned about adaptability was to take the process step-by-step. First, I'd engage with potential prospects and learn what's important to them. Then, we'd discuss whether this unique technology could help them solve their fundamental business problems. Over time, I slowly identified what we could rely upon, what we'd know more about, and how much more we could define in terms of our core software offerings. It was still very uncertain, but I slowly eliminated the unknown until we had more clarity.

C — Complexity

Complexity is "the state or quality of being intricate."

The Internet space was incredibly intricate at the time — partially because it was so new to almost everyone and not as ubiquitous as it is today. No one had an idea of what it could be. Many companies carved out their niches early and created many opportunities for others to follow suit. And many others failed miserably. It was a bit chaotic.

Within eCash, we changed our focus multiple times. Initially, we thought we could create our own brand of currency. We had a cool marketing strategy planned and wanted to compete with the largest credit card companies around. That didn't work.

We also tried electronic gift cards, long before they became a "thing" we all know about today. This was another tough market that we didn't know anything about. We were able to establish some early customer relationships, but this approach eventually failed as well. Consumers were not ready in 2001 to give up their physical gift cards for an electronic link.

Instead of messing around with complex business models, we discovered that we needed to simplify everything. So we eventually focused on being a technology company delivering specific capabilities — electronic value only for gift cards and peer-to-peer payments. Taking something complex and driving it towards simplicity is another way to adapt to your challenging and chaotic environment.

A — Ambiguity

Ambiguity is "the quality of being open to more than one interpretation; inexactness.".

To me, this became a people challenge. We had a diverse set of employees with a vast expanse of experience. Combined with the challenges across the Internet space, there were multiple interpretations about how to proceed.

Should we build our own brand or be a technology company only? Should we focus on financial services or, more broadly, across many industries? Which of the many other startups should we attempt to partner with?

This is one of the "easiest" areas to adapt to. I love the idea of having something with multiple interpretations because it forces you to consider many other options. You can compare and contrast different aspects and determine what's best. You can force yourself to come up with more interpretations to challenge yourself.

Adaptability in response to ambiguous situations is a great way of developing a strong solution. Fortunately, I had a lot of smart people I could seek support from as I developed my own methods for dealing with VUCA via adaptability.

DEVISE

"plan or invent (a complex procedure, system, or mechanism) by careful thought."

What would you invent if you had unlimited resources (time, money, ideas, assistance, etc.)?

Here's a pretty good sample list of some of the best inventions in the history of humankind:

- Wheel
- Nail
- Compass
- Printing press
- Internal combustion engine
- Telephone
- Light Bulb
- Penicillin
- Contraceptives
- Internet

How cool would it be to devise something on that list? Something new came from your thinking. I can't claim to have developed anything as concrete or valuable on that list, but I was surprised by how much careful thought it took to devise a plan for my sabbatical.

Most of my peers who had gone on sabbatical could transition their roles and responsibilities to others during their time off as a temporary situation. In most cases, these individuals were returning to their same role and they were working with the same individuals in their office.

As I was planning for my sabbatical, there were several additional "moving parts" for me to consider:

- Upon my return, I was asked to take on a new role within the organization.
- We had just hired a few new leadership team members.
- The new role wasn't even based in the Seattle office.

Instead, I would be working with a team based in Dallas while working from Seattle, which seemed more challenging pre-pandemic.

In any case, I needed to devise a plan to handle things while I was away and transition roles and responsibilities to others — most of those transitions were permanent. Though I didn't do something as impressive as creating the Internet or the next iPhone (yes, I was surprised that wasn't on the list when I Googled "Top Inventions in history"), I still learned some great lessons from devising a procedure for my being away for a month.

Iterate. Again. And Again. And Again.

There was no way the first version of my plan would be "right." I put a lot of careful thought into what I was creating. But I didn't pressure myself to have the perfect plan with my first iteration. Instead, I pulled together the first iteration and challenged myself by putting myself into the shoes of others. Over and over again and getting feedback from many others each time.

Thomas Edison iterated thousands of times with the light bulb.

Learn From Others

Though my situation differed significantly from others' sabbaticals, I still asked for their plans. I connected with others to learn what worked for them and what didn't, and I inquired about those who owned the responsibilities from those who had left. Learning some lessons from others informed some components of what I was ultimately devising.

The telegraph existed before the telephone, and there were many opportunities to learn from others who wanted more than a telegraph.

Ask for Perspective

I also worked with several folks with whom I was transitioning many of my roles and responsibilities. What did they need? How much or how little support or coaching did they need? Who else would we need to involve to help with this transition? One of the transitions included shifting the leadership role of our largest account to one of my peers. Darin was great about sharing what he needed to take this role full-time with me. Though I was responsible for devising the plan, I wanted to ensure I included others' perspectives especially since the plan impacted them. Darin shared a lot with me about what was needed for this specific role, and I also applied those ideas to some other transitions.

The Internet served many purposes and included many different perspectives and reasons for someone to leverage the power of the Internet.

Time

There are several elements of time management to address. First of all, give yourself enough time to devise the plan in the first place. Second, include extra time to test, experiment, and ensure the plan is feasible. Then provide enough time for others to understand how to leverage the plan. Working with many other people helped me understand time through a variety of perspectives - lead time, duration, focused time, etc.

There are many moving parts in the internal combustion engine that took a lot of time to bring together. Some elements were quick to build and required little lead time, while others took a lot of time as the inventor was creating something entirely new that had many intricacies.

Breadth Versus Depth

There's a spectrum of providing too much or too little information about this new invention. Since this is something that's totally new and different, you must ensure you provide both the breadth of awareness across the full spectrum of the plan/invention and the depth needed in specific areas. As you engage with different people along the way, you quickly realize everyone needs a slightly different formula for breadth versus depth.

For example, the wheel was a lot more about the breadth of use cases and didn't require as much depth to devise as the thousands of moving components in the printing press.

If you were to Google "Top One Million Plans," the transition and sabbatical plan I devised wouldn't appear on the list. But learning just a sliver of what so many others have done to devise amazing inventions throughout history was a great process.

LESSON LEARNED

Not everyone has the "invention gene." But we all can devise something new no matter how large or small. Start by developing something simple and get more and more complex over time. And, to be clear, you can devise something that is NOT entirely new as well. Taking many different component parts and pulling them together in a totally new and different way is another way to devise something.

Chapter 9

Get as much help as you can

Several aspects of my life fall into this category because they can be challenging and have unlimited potential. Love. Joy. Fulfillment. Equanimity. Perseverance.

Why would you ever stop trying to learn more and more lessons about these?

This book won't cover my journey with vulnerability. But it is a long and winding road and continues to this day. I started with my research, but I quickly realized that I needed help from others. I worked on vulnerability with my therapist, a couples therapist, and my professional coach. I shared my growth with my mentor and sought feedback from many folks around me. I'll continue seeking as much help as I need to grow this infinitesimal muscle.

Bottom line - whether some of these stories in Chapter Nine "belong here" for you or they don't, please get as much help as you can for those topics that are extremely important and/or difficult for you to handle on your own or even with support from friends. Some aspects of ALL of our lives need more support than we can ever imagine.

More than anything, these topics feel like the "deepest" to me in terms of what makes me ponder my life across many different aspects.

VALUES

"a person's principles or standards of behavior; one's judgment of what is important in life."

That definition seems pretty easy... or so I thought.

One day during a mentoring session, my mentor asked me what values were important to me. Dumbfounded that I didn't have a quick answer, I asked, "What do you mean by values?". Looking at the definition was helpful. But the idea intrigued me because I had yet to think about values in terms of priorities or importance to my growth or my life. So I started by asking my mentor what her values were and how they were important to her.

My discovery process continued the same way most people look for information today — a visit to our friend Google. I found four sites, each claiming, "These are the top five values for an individual." So I created a list of 17 distinct values across those four sites. No one, it seemed, had the "answer." So I kept searching Google to find more values.

120+

Ultimately, I constructed a list of over 120 values. I visited dozens of websites and used varying questions to inquire about values. In addition, I read a few articles and many blog posts. It was a fascinating trip to come up with a list of values. Some of the values were very similar, and others didn't make sense to me as a value. For example, family and relatives were similar, while kids didn't make sense to me as a value by themselves.

93

I consolidated that list of 120 values down to a list of 93 values by using another "technology friend," an Excel spreadsheet. Some of the words were closely related and others were simply redundant. Then, I read each of the 93 values and came up with a definition for each. Family, for example, was more focused on my kids than my mom and dad (and brother — sorry, Michael!). My good friends at Oxford Dictionary have great definitions... but you need to define each value in your own terms to truly understand them.

17

My next step was to prioritize what values were most important to me. I whittled the list of 93 values down to 17 values that felt aligned with where I was in my life at that time. And where I wanted to go in the next phase of my life. In some cases, I combined several values into one. For example, relationships and friendships were so closely aligned that I combined them under "Friendships."

7

The next step was more challenging — getting to a list in the single digits. I looked up the definition of each value (Oxford Dictionary and not Wikipedia) yet again to ensure I understood the meaning. I merged a few others and modified the definition of others to make more sense to me, and I kept asking myself the hard questions about what was MOST important to me right now. I ended up with a list of seven values. But that was still too many values for me.

5

Maybe because it is half of the famous "Top Ten" lists out there. Or I wanted just five to write one on each finger or toe. Bottom line, I used a Bubble Sorting algorithm to reach my Top Five. For my non-geeky friends, this is simply "playing everyone against each other one-on-one at a time". For example, I played my Confidence value versus my Friendship value, and Friendship was the winner. Friendships got one point. You "play" each value against each other, tally the total points and set your priorities.

My results were as follows:

#1 Friendships

This was interesting, especially since it landed in my number one slot. My grandmother was the only family member I knew outside my mom, dad, and brother. My parents were only children — so I don't have a bevy of aunts, uncles, cousins, etc., like many others. For me, friendships are all wrapped together by relationships, family, friends, children, etc. It means being authentic to others in my life and being vulnerable. Letting others know who the "true me" is also falls into this value. Overall, this is about one-on-one connections I can make with others — regardless of where it initiates.

#2a Fairness

At the core of this value is being rule-bound and having no shades of gray. Growing up, sports were my true measure of this value. I was highly competitive (see **Competitive**, **Fairness** and **Competition**) and wanted

302

to play sports with/against kids older than me. My feeling was that I wanted to compete when it wasn't fair to me and forced me to get better. But when I played against kids younger than me or less skilled in that sport, I would intentionally modify the rules to make it fair for others to compete. For these reasons, golf is my favorite sport — you use handicaps to make the match fair against each other, and you don't truly compete with anyone other than yourself since you aren't playing defense against each other. Fairness applies to rules, morals, sports, competitions, work, community service, and much more throughout my life.

#2b Optimism

Fairness, Optimism, and Perseverance finished in a three-way tie for second. For me, optimism is about choosing hope. It's seeing the proverbial "glass is half-full". It's taken me some time to understand that life is choice-based. As a result, I tend to always have a positive lens or filter on most situations in my life while balanced against a solid dose of reality. While some of my ongoing growth is in understanding the potential impacts of risks or downsides to specific situations, I'll still choose optimism as my first lens to any situation.

#2c Perseverance

Not surprisingly, my perseverance seems closely tied to optimism. It's all about holding a clear intent while pushing your limits as far as possible. You need to deal with situations in the short term while having a vision for the big picture in terms of long-term growth. This includes some of a growth/development impulse — both as an individual as well as for helping others make themselves the best they can be. Or, since I'm a big fan of dogs now, I'm like a dog persevering with a bone — especially one that's tasty!

#5 Confidence

Frankly, I was pretty surprised this only ended up as number five on my list. Being vulnerable for my audience here, I'm actually *very* confident in several aspects of my life, but I'm not as confident in other aspects. Maybe that's why confidence "lost" in most head-to-head comparisons during my bubble sorting process. As I shared this perspective with others, they remarked on my confluence of confidence and competitiveness across many aspects of my life as they knew me. Again, this is about self-efficacy and optimism about the capacity to get major goals accomplished.

My goal was to develop a Top Five list, and there it is. But I wanted to share my #6 as well — Fun. I hope everyone has this one on their list somewhere. For me, fun is interwoven into all of my values.

Most importantly, I divulged my values to my mentor and related stories about my work and personal efforts that demonstrated a congruence between my values and actions. I continued to reveal my values to others until it became a very natural conversation in conjunction with the decisions I was making or paths I was choosing to follow. My values became my "North Star" regarding career choices, personal decisions, and life's journey overall.

LESSON LEARNED

My hope for you all is to understand what your values are — and much sooner in your life than I did. More importantly, I hope you find ways to seamlessly embed your values into your work, family, home, and all aspects of your life. Not having a clear understanding of your values is like not having any steering for your car. Whether my process is helpful or you develop your own, I highly recommend learning what's important to you. More importantly, revealing your values is a great way to share with others more about yourself. Lastly, don't hesitate to contact me if my list of 93 values is useful as a starting point for your value discovery process. Whatever it takes, figure out your own values as soon as possible. The rewards are immeasurable.

JOY

"a feeling of great pleasure and happiness"

Wonder. Awe. Happiness. Delight. Jubilation. Exuberance. Elation. Joy. Just try *not* to smile when you read these words!

Growing up in the Midwest, sports fell into three seasons: fall, winter, and spring. My winter sport was always basketball, and my spring sport was always baseball. As a first- and second-year student, my fall sport was cross country. I planned to run with the team all fall and get in shape for the winter basketball season.

304

But leading into my junior year, one of my friends convinced me to try out for the golf team in the fall — instead of running cross country again. I used a beat-up set of used golf clubs my dad had found for me, but I still managed to make the junior varsity team. I learned a lot and had fun along the way. Eventually, I bought a new set of clubs and continued to upgrade my playing skills.

As a senior, my golf game improved enough that I made the varsity team. Usually, seven players were on a team, and I was number seven. It was a blast for me to travel with the varsity team and play courses I'd never played before along the way. My buddy even gave me a hot dog putter I occasionally pulled out for fun during a match. We had fun my senior year, and our team was great. We did well in our conference season and were poised to do well in the state playoffs. Sadly, for me, the playoff team only consisted of the top SIX players. I was continually improving and playing well, but my game needed to break out of that seventh position. And it never did. #7 didn't get to play in the playoffs.

The coach was so appreciative of my energy and light-heartedness that he allowed me to travel with the team and watch the playoff match from the "inside" — like being another coach versus observing only as a fan. It was great to see our team perform well during those playoff matches and make it to the next level of the playoffs. We had four solid players, but the fifth and sixth golfers struggled a lot in that round.

The next challenge for our coach was selecting a team of FIVE for the next round of the playoffs. The top four were obvious. But the fifth and sixth were scheduled to play a practice round with the head coach the next day. So, again, I was grateful for the coach to let me practice one more day with my friends and the team. I was there to have fun with the team before basketball season started in a few weeks.

I played in the foursome behind the coach and my fifth and sixth teammates. Frankly, I wasn't paying attention to them; I was just having fun with my other teammates and actually shot one of the best rounds of my life to that point. It was a great time. As I walked off the last green, I walked over to the head coach to say "Thanks"...and to return the driver he had let me borrow for the previous few weeks of the regular season.

As I handed him the driver, he asked, "How did you play today?". I told him I was having fun and posted one of my best scores. I'm not sure how long he

305

paused, but he handed me the driver back and said simply, "You'll need this for the weekend."

WHAT JUST HAPPENED?!?!?!?! I am trying to remember the details, but fifth and sixth could have played better in a stressful situation. So my coach decided to make me the fifth player on the team. I was thrilled. *Pure. Unadulterated. Joy.*

"Great pleasure and happiness" doesn't begin to explain that feeling of joy. I couldn't believe what had just happened to me. It was awesome, and I felt amazing throughout my entire body. Thinking back to that situation now makes me smile and warms my heart. Very cool feeling the first time you feel true joy.

As I think about joy throughout my life, here are some thoughts about how to view joy:

Spiritual Connections

While some people view spirituality through a religious lens, I prefer the definitions related to affecting the human spirit, like common beliefs, reflections, or celebration of awe. How do you connect with others if you remove the material and superficial things in your life? I had the biggest smile of any golfer at that playoff match the following weekend. Being connected to my teammates during an important event was so much fun. I even played well for the team and better than a couple of my four other teammates that weekend — though not as well as the excellent golfers headed to the state playoffs.

Pleasure

We can all discover a good experience or find something we can enjoy. I hit a few bad shots, but it was easy to find pleasure in many other good shots I made that day. AND simply the fact I was playing at all. If you take five minutes from your busy life and look around, you can easily find something pleasurable. And it doesn't have to be recent. As stated above, I still smile while thinking about a joy-filled experience on a golf course I didn't even remember until writing this story.

Appreciation

It may be an age thing for me, but I greatly appreciate life more and more right now. I'm grateful for the people I spend time with, the experiences I get to partake in, and the places I've been fortunate enough to visit over the years. And again, *sharing* that appreciation with others is extremely empowering and fun. Even during the round, I could tell our head coach how much I appreciated the opportunity to play one more round with my teammates during such a critical match.

For the reader, I'm a bit surprised Joy landed in this chapter. Though I happened to find joy early in my life and keep it fairly present, I've discovered that many others struggle to find joy more often than not. Partially because I view joy as being such an important aspect of your life and partially because I know it can be difficult for many to discover joy, I've included it in this section.

LESSON LEARNED

Joy can be unexpected, happen to you immediately, and be quick to experience and land very intensely, and the good news is that you can also *create* joy any time you want. Look outside. Close your eyes and think of a fun experience. Check out a photo and smile at the memories. Remember what last caused you to laugh uncontrollably. Lastly, consider how to spread joy to others as well. Not only will you experience joy yourself, but it will feel twice as great when you experience it through others.

PERSEVERANCE

"persistence in doing something despite difficulty or delay in achieving success."

The Cubs lose. But can you win after a long delay by losing first?

After watching the Cubs win the World Series in the fall of 2016, it was disappointing to watch them lose in the playoffs in October of the following year. But it got me thinking about losing and failure in my life and career.

Most of my life successes were based on lessons from an earlier failure. Even though everyone was focused on the fact that it took 108 years for the Cubs to win the World Series in 2016, they learned more by losing to the New York Mets in 2015 than at any other point through those 108 long years. Each of those players learned their version of perseverance.

My first role with IBM gave me my first lesson in perseverance.

In the IBM Peoria office, about 75% of the team was focused on working with our single largest account — Caterpillar. The next group worked on smaller yet significant accounts that generated solid revenues for the IBM office. The third set of IBMers focused on developing new relationships with potential customers. My start was in the middle group.

I was fortunate to be paired up with one of the most successful IBMers in the office — Keith Liszewski. He had successfully engaged with many of the most prominent clients IBM Peoria supported besides Caterpillar. So, while many of my peers just out of college started in little niche areas of working with Caterpillar, I had the unique opportunity to work with a senior IBMer and help manage his two existing clients - some of the largest in the office other than Caterpillar. The idea, over time, was for me to be next to the lead person for one or both of those accounts.

However, what was initially "over time" became "very quickly." The good news for me was that Keith was promoted to a Manager role within my first year. The bad news for me is that Keith was promoted to a Manager role — meaning he now had to support everyone on the team and had fewer cycles to help me out.

Needless to say, I could have been more successful. I had no idea what it took to nurture a long-standing relationship. I didn't know what I didn't know — meaning I didn't even know what questions to ask. Or when to ask for help. I needed direction and coaching, and Keith only had time for support and mostly delegation. Not his fault at all. It was just the situation we were in.

Keith pulled me off those accounts — and rightfully so. It felt like I had gotten fired, and maybe I would have been if IBM wasn't such an amazing employer. Keith needed to bring a more senior person in to lead those accounts, and I moved into a different role with another Manager, Deb Taufen, calling on the new business customers in that third category I referenced above.

I persevered and eventually sold my first of several new deals. And I persevered and experienced many more successes within the world of IBM for several years beyond that.

Over the years, I've experienced several different takes on perseverance. Here are a few different takes from my life, coupled with famous quotes that touch upon perseverance, that are worth sharing here regarding how I persevered in challenging situations.

Set an Even Bigger Goal the Next Time

"Only those who dare to fail greatly can ever achieve greatly."
— Robert F. Kennedy

Many times in my life, I set a goal but didn't fully accomplish it. Instead, I focused on the steps it took to (almost) reach the goal. After understanding the steps along the way and identifying where I could improve, I would set an even bigger goal the next time. I found that making my original goal just a new step in the process made it easier for me to "dare to fail greatly."

Growing up, I used to see how many free throws I could make in a row. I might set an objective to hit 15 and only get to 13. Then I'd set a goal to make 20 in a row and only hit 17. But I blew through my original goal of 15 by stretching even further.

Try it yourself — you might be surprised how much easier it is to stretch your goals.

In the case of my IBM experience, the revenue goals were significantly smaller. But the goal was bigger because I had to sell to brand new clients without being able to leverage a long-standing relationship with IBM. My failures with existing clients taught me how to succeed with a different set of potential new clients.

Persistence

"I have not failed. I've just found 10,000 ways that won't work."
— Thomas A. Edison

When I hear the word failure, this quote by Thomas Edison always resonates with me. The critical part of the quote above is to realize that he didn't attempt to keep doing the same thing over and over (see Einstein's quote below). He deliberately tried 10,000 *different* ways to get the light bulb to work. It's important to try *"different* ways" to avoid being entrapped by another funny quote from Einstein that I also love: "Insanity = doing the same thing over and over again and expecting different results."

Persistence is all about finding a (slightly or totally) different way to figure out how to make something work. I can't tell you how many times I tried a slight variation in a recipe until I figured out how it was MOST tasty. Be persistent. Keep trying different ways to discover something new.

With IBM, persistence was the name of the game. I had to make dozens of phone calls and get a lot of "No Thank You" messages back. Fortunately, I didn't need to make 10,000 phone calls to finish that first deal!

Stay Enthusiastic

"Success is stumbling from failure to failure with no loss of enthusiasm."
— Winston Churchill

It takes a lot of work to keep going across multiple failures. There are many different ways to stay positive along this journey. Many people think about their past successes. It reminds you that you've persevered in the past and can do so again. Other people also focus on the steps to reach your ultimate goal. When my sons were younger, we used to go on long bike rides that seemed insurmountable to them. They would get tired along the way — especially when going up big hills. I asked them to focus on a short goal, "Just bike to that red car" or "Let's push ourselves until we get to that green mailbox." They were able to stay positive along the way. And no one thought about stumbling across our other failures through the bike ride.

IBM Management was very encouraging to someone like me who was learning how to succeed in the world of technology. As a result, I stayed enthusiastic through such a dramatic change.

Learning by Losing

"You learn more from losing than winning. You learn how to keep going."
— Morgan Wootten

When I think about this quote, it reminds me of my first attempt at becoming a Sales Manager. I was a very successful sales rep and was asked to be a Sales Manager. Unfortunately, not only did I miss making my sales quota, but I missed it by more than I had ever missed a quota in my life. In addition to missing my quota, I failed to manage several people who worked for me effectively, needed to learn how to prioritize across ten different people, and basically sold a deal for one of my people instead of teaching him how to do it.

I still think about the lessons learned from that experience today and have applied those lessons to many other situations throughout my career. Lessons Learned can also be used when you experience success. Development teams ask great questions during a retrospective — two directly apply here. "What did we do well that we should continue doing?" and "What didn't go well that we should do differently?" are great questions to understand your lessons learned for almost anything.

At IBM, "losing" an opportunity to work with an existing client prepared me better to support my next client in my new role. And I learned how to help existing clients more effectively in future roles after my days at IBM.

Keep a Positive Attitude

"Words can never adequately convey the incredible impact of our attitudes toward life. The longer I live, the more convinced I become that life is 10 percent what happens to us and 90 percent how we respond to it."
— Charles R. Swindoll

This quote was a perfect way to close out. It captures many words and ideas above about persistence, learning lessons, staying positive, or setting even bigger goals. There are so many different ways to deal with loss or failure.

When I think about my life on earth, does it matter that I only hit 17 free throws in a row or failed in my first opportunity as a Sales Manager? At the time, it was tough to handle. But, I did everything I could to keep a positive attitude and keep moving forward.

At IBM, I needed support from my peers and guidance from Keith and Deb, but I stayed positive.

EXISTENCE

"the fact or state of living or having objective reality."

Savor every moment.

Paul Allen passed away a few years ago. At the time, my company hosted an event at one of his legacy businesses — The Living Computer Museum — just a few days after his passing. It was an incredible reminder of how much good Paul Allen contributed to the world — well beyond his initial starting point with Microsoft and his friend Bill Gates.

Paul Allen left Microsoft because he felt he could "make the world a better place" outside his day-to-day work at Microsoft. One of the companies he founded, Allen Institute for Brain Science, is just one of his many philanthropic efforts, for which he has donated over $2.6B of his wealth.

After visiting Paul Allen's museum, I thought a lot about my friends and family who passed away over the years and how that impacted my life. So, while I hope to create my legacy in making the world a much better place, I'm starting by inspecting my feelings about three people who passed away in my lifetime and how I can take what I learned about their existence and share it with others.

The first person was a woman I went to high school and college with — Natalie. She passed away only a few years after we graduated from college. I was only 22 years old then, and I was shocked, confused, sad, and many other emotions I didn't know how to experience or feel at the time.

312

Spending time with my friends from high school and college at her wake and funeral made me think about how much I had taken my brief time on this planet for granted. My friend wouldn't get married, have children, and establish her legacy over time. She was an amazing person who always seemed to know how to live in the moment. My relationship with her was very different from her public-facing personality. She taught me to be vulnerable, open, transparent, and real. She helped me understand the pressure of being "who everyone expects you to be" versus simply being the person you want to be. I do my best to keep up with her mother during the anniversary of her passing and her birthday. I wish I could have said "I love you" to her for our deep friendship as I transitioned from an awkward teenager to a slightly less-than-awkward college student. I'm fortunate to stay closely connected with half a dozen of my high school friends — and we usually spend some of our time together remembering the best of our friend Natalie. I miss her.

Less than two years later, my grandmother passed away. Of course, it's always tough for most people when a grandparent dies. However, it was a little different for me because my grandmother was the *only* grandparent I truly knew. And with my parents being only children, my grandmother was the only family member I ever knew beyond my brother, my mom, and my dad.

We lived in the Chicago area then, but my grandmother had lived most of her life in Cincinnati. My mother asked me to do the eulogies in Chicago and Cincinnati. While teenagers in high school and college primarily focus on becoming their own person and rarely spend time with anyone outside their friend cohort, I partially broke away from this pattern to take my grandmother to many lunches over the years. It was awesome to learn so much about my grandmother from her directly. I was amazed by so many of her stories. As her eldest grandchild, I grew up knowing her simply as Grandma. But, as a young adult, our lunches were an amazing opportunity to better learn about the journey through my grandmother's life. Who would have guessed she was a teenager, mother, and other personas beyond just being my grandma?

I tried to get my thoughts written down for both eulogies, but I'm not the type of speaker who reads speeches very well. This was fortunate because I spoke with many of my grandmother's friends before the eulogy and quickly assimilated those stories into my talk about my grandmother. My favorite story — sharing how my grandmother taught me so many card games ranging from solitaire to poker. It was a blast sharing how much I enjoy playing cards with my friends and learning how much fun my grandmother had playing cards with her friends over the years. Fun stuff.

Lastly, I'll use card playing as my segue to my final story.

My college roommate Nick passed away when we were just 47 years old. Among other things, he taught me how to make the "bridge" to shuffle cards and how to actually play the card game called Bridge. Of course, we all did our fair share of studying in college, but we also played many games of cards. That's just one of my many fond memories of my college roommate.

My friend's passing several years ago impacted me in so many ways. I flew from Seattle to visit him in Chicago only a few days before he passed away. I'm not sure he knew I was even there, but spending time with him, his wife, and his mother was incredibly emotional. I couldn't stop crying as I talked with his wife and mother — my post-college "mother" for years when I lived in Peoria, IL. My buddy was from Peoria, and we had a chance to spend many years together, post-college, between Peoria and Champaign.

Maybe it was because I was nearing 50. Or perhaps it was because I couldn't imagine leaving a wife and two children behind. Or maybe because so many friends from college were around — sharing great stories about our life and times with him. I'm unsure why, but his passing impacted me more deeply than anything I've ever experienced. It may have been the first time I felt my mortality and was fully aware of my existence.

LESSON LEARNED

Our existence on earth is short-lived. Objective reality — get to know people now while you can. Ask questions and be inquisitive. Listen with your ears as well as your heart. Be yourself no matter what "role" you think you are operating in. Be vulnerable and genuine — all of the time. Existence is about fully embracing your time on this planet.

Please don't wait for someone important in your life to pass away before appreciating what existence means — to you, them, and everyone else on this planet with us. I highly recommend exploring your existence with others; elders in your life, someone who shares your religious beliefs, or even friends/family who may have recently lost someone close to them. It can be super scary to acknowledge your mortality, but you'll cherish your existence once you embrace this reality.

FULLFILLMENT

"the achievement of something desired, promised, or predicted."

What do you call "a soft, white, chewy confection made with sugar and gelatin"?

This story starts off talking about marshmallows. I've always enjoyed learning more and more about the famous "Marshmallow Test." If you want a quick laugh, do a quick search for "The Marshmallow Test" and watch a couple of the videos. For those unfamiliar with this test, the premise is as follows. It started with a study across a group of third-graders. You put one child in a room with one marshmallow, tell them *not* to eat the marshmallow in front of them, then you let them know that if they can wait until the examiner returns, they can eat TWO marshmallows. Most kids didn't wait very long until eating the one marshmallow.

The bigger story is about delayed gratification. The idea is to demonstrate that delaying your gratification for one marshmallow will result in a much grander achievement — getting to eat two marshmallows instead. The focus should be on "something promised" in the future. But for a third-grader with a tasty, chewy confection in front of them, ten minutes seems like a lifetime! It's tough to delay your fulfillment.

The idea of delayed gratification got me thinking about what in my life was delayed, and then I was finally fulfilled.

Driving a car.

In some cases, I couldn't drive a car for nearly a year after many of my friends started driving. That feels like something "promised" and delayed significantly in my life. And not being able to drive for one year for a fifteen-year-old probably felt like not being able to eat that marshmallow and waiting for the researcher for at least ten minutes to return for those third-graders!

My parents put me into kindergarten early — starting me out when I was still four years old since I was due to turn five in October. Growing up, I missed many age-related cutoffs and effectively played at levels one lower than I should have simply because I had an October birthday. I was always among the youngest in my classes, including my driver's education class!

To make matters worse, and my desires seemingly more unreachable, the school put me into driver's education class a year sooner than they should have. They probably looked at my birthday and overlooked the *year*, so I had to take a whole semester of a class that wouldn't be helpful for another year. Bummer. Not only did the class further fuel my desire to be driving, but it also drove me *crazy* to be so close to something but unable to achieve it or gain a sense of fulfillment.

My friends were great — letting me drive their cars for short periods to practice. I learned how to drive a stick, what's needed to drive big cars, how to fit into small cars, and much more. And my parents practiced with me in parking lots and local neighborhoods.

The worst part of this delay in driving was school dances and dating overall. I had many friends that I double-dated partially because I couldn't drive anyway. Even my girlfriends at the time could drive and pick me up — frustrating for a clueless young boy in high school without his driver's license.

Until this point in my life, most of my achievements were within my control — how fast I ran in a race versus how well I played baseball or the piano or how much I studied and got good grades. But this was the first time my potential gratification was delayed because it was 100% out of my control

— there was no way to drive until I turned 16, and I wasn't going to speed up the aging process. Fulfillment with driving seemed so far away.

How did I get through nearly a year of *not* being able to drive like most of my friends? As I thought about that tortuous year or more of delayed fulfillment, here's what occurred to me.

Patience

Easier said than done, for sure, but I had no choice. Whether it was desired, promised, or predicted, I wasn't driving on my own until October 19th, 1983. It was my version of having to wait patiently for Christmas Day to open up those presents that had been under the tree for weeks.

Creative Options

I had to get creative to get my friends to pick me up and take me places. Buying something to eat or drink was a frequent "Thank You" for going four or five miles out of their way to pick me up. Other times, I'd offer to ride my bike to their house so that I could drive with them the rest of the way. I also paid for many movies and fun dinners to get dates to pick me up.

Future

It was also helpful for me to think about the future — when I can drive and have my car. In some cases, the visualization helped me. In other cases, the future involved payback for me picking up my friends or dates to compensate for the many times they gave me rides. Focusing on the present wasn't going to reach fulfillment behind the wheel of a car.

Good Thoughts

Though getting a driver's license was 100% out of my control regarding the specific timing, it was still helpful to think about past situations where I was fulfilled. Some of those situations were more in my control. But it's still beneficial to channel the good thoughts about being fulfilled by something else while you wait for the current desire. I often thought about picking up a date as a motivation to get through this delayed fulfillment.

Go back to the story of the third-graders and fulfillment. Wouldn't you be more fulfilled if you waited for *two* marshmallows instead of one? Delayed gratification to chase some sense of satisfaction is well worth the wait!

LESSON LEARNED

The starting point is to understand what is and isn't within your span of control. For example, no one was going to change my birthday. In other cases, you can partially satiate your desire, reset expectations against a specific promise, or gather more data to increase your odds of making a prediction. Focusing on the positive aspects of the ultimate achievement (versus the delayed gratification of not being fulfilled) is the best way to be patient on your path to fulfillment, and you will enjoy your achievement that much more.

I intentionally share a story about fulfillment that's relatively straightforward. The suggestions in the story — patience, creative options, future and good thoughts — are suggestions from my coaches and therapists over the years to reach my levels of fulfillment across much more complex topics like self-compassion, tranquility, and self-awareness. I'm still working on those areas of my life, and I have a lot of direct help from others on my journey.

INTROSPECTION

"the examination or observation of one's own mental and emotional processes"

How often do you look at yourself in a mirror? Or while taking a selfie? Introspection is like that, except it is all about looking at your insides (mental, emotional, physiological, etc.).

One of my employers was adamant about making sure you objectively evaluate yourself annually. There was a very prescriptive guide for completing an annual self-assessment that forced each of us to be thoroughly introspective. I've done self-assessments at other times in my life, but this process was genuinely transformative regarding how deep and thorough an introspection I went through. Before this self-assessment process, I worked hard to justify everything I did that was "good," "right," or "positive." I wasn't willing to dig deep enough to understand what might be under the covers of a more thorough assessment of myself.

Galileo stated, "You cannot teach a man anything; you can only help him find it within himself." Here are eight different sources I leveraged to "find it within" myself and construct an introspective self-assessment. Which ones resonate with you?

Personal Values

Earlier in this chapter, I spoke about understanding and weaving my values into daily life (see **Values**). The role of introspection with your values is validating that those values are still important guardrails for your journey. As I think about my values, my inner emotions are deeply tapped.

Leadership Styles — for Others AND Myself

The Situational Leadership model walks through four different leadership styles based on the needs of the individual. Learning when to Direct, Coach, Support, or Delegate is the idea. The model is a great way to balance supporting and directing behaviors as you engage with your team and your leadership chain. More importantly, it is a model I leverage to validate that I'm using effective communication and processes when coaching new managers and leaders and communicating to my leadership how I'd like to be led based on the situation. Even better is when your team can use the model to tell *you* how *they* want to be led.

Vulnerability

Since investing time in reading books by Brené Brown about vulnerability, I've been a massive fan of learning how to weave the idea of vulnerability into both my work and personal life. The four pillars she puts forth are: Being Vulnerable, Maintaining your Values (see a theme here?), Trusting Others (and Yourself), and Persistence. More importantly, I've invested much time and effort growing my "vulnerability" muscle — definitely *not* something I'd see in a mirror. Delving into my vulnerabilities helps me to be more introspective across other areas of my life.

Strengths

A book called *StrengthsFinder* includes a guide by which you understand your Top Five strengths based on their overall list of 34 strengths. The book guides how to lead people based on *their* strengths and how you can leverage your strengths as an individual leader. There are four major themes, and my strengths fall into three of them: Executing (my two strengths in this theme — Achiever and Responsibility), Influencing (Activator), and Strategic Themes (Learner and Analytical). I've been working on how to best leverage these strengths depending on my specific situation and the individuals or groups I'm engaged with so I could "feel" these strengths sometimes and understand when I'm using them appropriately or not. I check in with my head, heart, and gut to validate that these strengths are still important and present for me.

Invest in Your Coach or Advisor, or Therapist — Or ALL of the Above

The advice I've garnered from my therapist or coaches has been excellent. While trained to "help me," they are unafraid of asking hard questions and challenging my thinking and feeling. They often "extract" something I'm entirely unaware of deep inside. In my role, I can definitely help others find what's inside of them, but it is crazy that we can't be truly introspective without some help from the outside.

Trust

There are many different frameworks for trust. One that I like emanated from a Harvard Business School professor who took a job at Uber to help them re-establish trust with their customers. She shared her framework for striking the right balance among three pillars — Empathy, Logic, and Authenticity. Empathy, logic, and authenticity are internal "feelings" that can easily be shared with others externally. But you need to be intentional about how you display each to earn the trust of others and be truly introspective about how others truly feel about what you are displaying.

Making Hard Decisions

The Cynefin Framework "allows executives to see things from new viewpoints, assimilate complex concepts, and address real-world problems and opportunities." The framework breaks down complex decision-making into four quadrants. First, with a Simple decision, you learn to sense, categorize, and respond. The next is a Complicated decision where you learn to sense, analyze, and respond. The third quadrant is a Complex decision — where you first learn to probe and then feel and respond. Last is the Chaotic decision, requiring you to act first, then sense and respond. One of my areas of growth one year was to reduce my proclivity to "act first" in almost all situations. I realized I was incorrectly categorizing too many of the decisions in front of me as Chaotic. Instead of consistently assuming all decisions were "hard," this framework helped me to reevaluate my decision-making process and improve upon it.

Applying Neuroscience

The Whole Brain model has been around since the mid-1970s and breaks down four distinct and specialized structures in your brain: the first one answers the "Why?" — The Experimental Thinking part of your brain; the second one answers "What?" — the Analytical Thinking component; the third addresses both the "How & When?" questions — the Practical Thinking part of your noodle; the last one is "Who?" — and appeals to your Relational Thinking. This model helps me understand my thinking and mindset preferences and how to engage with others based on my interpretation of *their* thinking and mindset preferences. As I coach others today, we often begin with understanding thinking and mindset preferences as a platform for growth and development and building new habits.

My mentor's feedback was that this was the best self-review he'd seen in a long time because it was honest, open, and genuine. It also helped me become a better leader, coach, and executive because I could help others get to their true self-reflection.

However, you are also discovering one of my "weak" points: wanting to help others so much that I give too much information and confuse them. Each one of these eight suggestions could be a story by itself (and at least one is). Several lean into an existing framework and require a deeper introspection by itself…or with help from others!

I told you this chapter was a tough one!

LESSON LEARNED

Introspection can be challenging. You can look at the positive or the negative, but at the end of the day, you are just looking at yourself, so be as objective as possible. You can be objective and still be emotional — evaluate yourself and find ways to grow. If you don't know where you truly are, how do you know where to begin? There are many other "lenses" through which to view yourself. The eight perspectives I shared above are a small subset of what you can leverage to be entirely introspective. Again, this is a great example of where one or several professionals can provide an objective lens to support your journey toward introspection.

SELF-COMPASSION

"sympathetic consciousness of your own distress together with a desire to alleviate it."

I used to tell people not to "beat themselves up" over something that happened to them. Now, I'm more focused on encouraging others to practice self-compassion.

The phrase "Don't beat yourself up" is in my head because I often have to use that phrase on myself. My most frequent challenge is weight loss. How many different types of diets have I tried? It was awesome to lose weight on a specific diet and then sucked to gain it back in only a few weeks or months at the end of the diet.

Something had to change. At my age, it is not only about weight loss now. Many other health factors in play are important as well. I needed to find a way to alleviate the challenges I've encountered with eating.

Instead of applying the specifics of yet another diet, I focused on a "best of breed" approach that aligned with my desire to make permanent changes. I stopped focusing solely on weight loss but also on the overall journey of getting healthier — including eating better (and less) overall, being healthier to myself (avoiding bad choices like buying pounds of cheese), being more aware, learning from how I feel (I love red meat, but I no longer love how I feel in the morning after eating it for dinner the night before), and, most importantly, being kind to myself.

Through this whole process, I learned to appreciate self-compassion in a very different way. And here are a few other examples of how I'm applying it to other areas of my life.

Goal Setting

I used to focus on reaching (and exceeding) goals all the time — and then beating myself up when I didn't reach them. Now I ask questions like "Was it the right goal?" (exercising too often and hurting my knee); "How do I truly feel about missing the goal?" (losing 15 pounds on another diet was awesome, but my goal was 20 pounds); or, "Am I happy about the journey?" (setting an impossible goal enables me to focus on the journey and small successes along the way). For example, if my goal was to lose 30 pounds, I only lost 29. I won't be too upset about missing my goal and will apply self-compassion.

To-Do Lists

This one might seem silly to some folks, but I *love* to check everything off on my to-do list for the week or weekend. It used to drive me crazy when I didn't finish the list at the end of the day or weekend. I usually overestimate how much I can get done in a day or weekend and underestimate what I can accomplish in a year or longer. My to-do lists are still long, but now I better prioritize what *must* be done versus what *should* or *could* be done (and be OK with what *won't* be done). Then, I grant myself some self-compassion and add those items to my list for next week!

Connecting With Others (and Myself)

This is the first time in my life I've lived alone. Connecting more deeply (versus broadly) with family or friends or my dog Suki is usually top of mind for me, and it frustrates me when I don't invest enough of my time in being with others. But as I've practiced meditation more frequently, I've learned that I'm much happier and more relaxed if I take a little time for myself. So while connecting with others is important to me, I've also learned to value some time alone, my version of self-compassion.

Productivity

I used to get totally frustrated if I didn't find myself "in the zone" most of the time. I like to be active and operate in a "get s**t done" mode. In this case, self-compassion helps me to remember that if I was highly efficient for a large percentage of the day AND I got a lot done effectively, but I'm taking a break right now, that's OK.

Imagination

This is all about what's possible in the future. I love to think big and set up crazy, impossible goals in the sense of something I'd love to do in the future. I used to get frustrated if something I envisioned didn't come to fruition. However, over time and with lots of self-compassion, I've realized that often one vision leads to a slightly altered version of the vision I chase, grab, and execute.

I work, coach, and spend time with high achievers who accomplish incredible goals. Unfortunately, many of these individuals will spend way too much time criticizing themselves or focusing only on "What could I have done better?". My guidance is to celebrate what they did achieve and work on those gaps where they can improve further. We can all use more self-compassion!

LESSON LEARNED

I always love the idea of treating others as you wish to be treated. For that reason alone, self-compassion should be at the top of your list. Forgiving yourself first is a great way to learn how to forgive others and how to model for others how they might forgive themselves and celebrate the unique gifts they can offer the world. But, truly understanding, embracing, and consistently practicing self-compassion is mentally strenuous. I'd suggest finding someone who can support your quest for self-compassion.

EQUANIMITY

"mental calmness, composure, and evenness of temper, especially in a difficult situation"

My vision here goes to the "eye of the storm," where there is complete stillness and calm in the middle of a violent thunderstorm or tornado.

Buddhists "hold hope lightly," meaning hope is often based upon what you'd like the world to be instead of how it is today. More than ever, the world is in a state of VUCA — volatility, uncertainty, complexity, and ambiguity. Equanimity is a much better state than counting on hope to overcome any aspects of VUCA.

Here are several examples across all aspects of my life from 2021 which review the before (VUCA — Volatility, Uncertainty, Complexity, and Ambiguity) and the after (equanimity):

Divorce

Before: It had been years coming and the pandemic only lengthened the process. I was hoping it would be finalized sooner and be crystal clear in terms of how we needed to operate going forward as co-parents, but there were multiple areas of the separation agreement that were still ambiguous.

After: Eventually, I just realized I needed to be calm and let the process happen as it needed to. With just a few days left in 2021, we finalized the agreement. Calmness with a lot of help from experts in the divorce process like lawyers, former judges, and several therapists.

Pandemic

Before: Like many people, I constantly wished it would just end. I'm grateful for the medical professionals who gave up so much to help everyone else through the pandemic. But, unfortunately, we all learned there are more variants of COVID, and it might just be something present with us forever — our respiratory system sickness version of the common cold.

After: I couldn't control the pandemic — just how I reacted to it. So I'll be cautious where warranted and do what I need to be safe (vaccinations, masks, social distancing, etc.). Acceptance with guidance from several doctors and nurses dealing with the pandemic on a daily, and even hourly, basis.

Health

Before: In college, we discussed gaining weight freshman year — the "freshman 15". During COVID-19, many folks talked about over-eating and drinking and gaining *the* "COVID-19". I felt like I added two times the 19 pounds leading into 2021!

After: I can actually "feel" why I'm hungry now. I realized that I was eating and drinking more than needed due to my stress from the pandemic. When I put my health first, I started to eat better, less frequently, and healthier. 2021 was a great platform to build healthy, long-lasting habits. Peaceful after working closely with a dietician and my doctor.

Suki

Before: Though I've had dogs, I have never raised a puppy alone, and I've only had black Labrador females. Some friends warned me that "chocolate labs can be a bit crazy," but, of course, the puppy I fell in love with during my visit to the breeder was a cute little chocolate lab I named Suki. If you've ever had a puppy or kitten, you know the definition of volatility and a little crazy!

After: Suki, like most dogs, is a pseudo-barometer for the owner's temperament. Now, I exude being the "calm, cool, and collected" owner and Suki reacts the same. She's my little mirror in case I get frustrated or upset with something.

ThinqShift

Before: While excited and energized to start with ThinqShift, I quickly realized I was over my head on multiple fronts. I've been coaching and mentoring for over a decade, but I was never paid independently for this work as it was part of my accountability. Coaching and mentoring in a paid position can be entirely different. We talk about what we do as Leadership Services. I've been in the technology space for three decades; this Leadership Services stuff is something I've done in the context of my executive roles with other organizations but not as my full-time job! Lastly, as the person who relies extensively on his network, I had zero networks in this line of business. Talk about VUCA!

After: I realized I wanted everything right away, even though the founders of ThinqShift told me the process would take 18–24 months. I started to work with one person. Then two. Then several companies and their leadership teams. As my mental calmness kicked into gear, my discussions with new people became easy and fun — tranquility with amazing support and understanding from the two co-founders of ThinqShift and a professional coach.

Why did I share many little examples with a before/after? To start, it is helpful to understand your state of mind or feelings you are experiencing before you can even imagine the potential destination to be much more composed. Part of my growth into equanimity was understanding that I didn't need to accomplish everything at once. Instead, I slowly built new habits and mindsets and let myself shift over time. So instead of telling one long story, several smaller stories with an explicit before/after perspective might be more effective in discussing equanimity.

LESSON LEARNED

"Hope is not a strategy" is a phrase I've often heard. We can consider how we'd like to see the world but still need to be grounded in how it is today. We can always leverage our lessons learned and wisdom more in the context of the now. Discover your own smaller areas of your life where you can establish equanimity and build upon those. The lessons you learn can be applied, over time, to all areas of your life. Don't be afraid to ask for a lot of help and support along with this more profound understanding and application of equanimity in your own life.

STRENGTH

"the quality or state of being physically strong." But for this book, I'm going with definition number two: "the capacity of an object or substance to withstand great force or pressure."

The first image that comes to mind when I think about strength is someone lifting weights. You know that image where someone is holding up a heavy weight over their head with the bar bending and huge weights connected on either side?

That's not the strength I'm talking about.

The second definition is what I'd like to chat about using myself as the "object or substance" and a complex situation as the "great force or pressure." In my days at U of I, I learned about various aspects of definition number two of strength. Until then, strength was usually that image of lifting weights or carrying bags of wet leaves in the fall.

During my first few days at U of I, I reconnected with many friends from high school who also decided that U of I was for them. While I had a great time with existing friends, I was determined to develop new friendships. I met people on the basketball courts, there were interesting people in my classes and my dorms, I got invited to fraternity and other parties to meet people. While some of my high school friends continued to get together amongst themselves and (gently and nicely) pressured me to join them, I frequently declined with a focus on developing new friendships.

In this case, my desire to learn how to build new relationships/friendships as an expansion to nurturing existing **relationships** was my strength.

I was accepted as a potential Computer Science major at U of I in the College of Engineering. However, as I'll share a different story, I quickly learned that I didn't enjoy computer programming. I wanted to stay in engineering and felt much pressure to just swap into General Engineering. My counselor and multiple friends pressured me to go down this path instead of something more specific that I might not enjoy, but I decided to major in a more challenging degree — Ceramic Engineering.

Confidence was my strength during that decision process.

There were not too many ceramic engineers across campus. There were only about 30 to 35 students in each grade, meaning the whole group was only about 130 students — out of roughly thirty five-thousand students across campus. Fortunately, I had a connection with someone who was two years ahead of me. She gave me a wealth of information through her notes and study guides about upcoming classes. Some people suggested that I take advantage of that information to improve my chances of getting better grades than my peers. My perspective was to share these study assets with one of my friends and fellow ceramic engineers, Kurt. We quickly decided it would make even more sense to share this information with all of our classmates.

Fairness was my strength.

Another downside of Ceramic Engineering was the discipline required the second-highest number of credits needed to graduate across ALL majors at U of I. This meant I needed 16–18 credits per quarter when my peers might have only needed 12–14 per quarter. That extra class each semester meant 3–4 class hours and 10–12 additional homework/study hours than others. Kurt and I spent many hours together studying for quizzes and final exams over the years. Again, there was pressure to change to other majors, but I refused to make a change.

I leaned into another strength called **perseverance.**

As I neared the end of my senior year, most of my friends had dozens of companies to choose from regarding interview options. There were several job fairs, but NONE of them included any firms in the world of ceramic engineering. So I had to research and reach out to firms where I might discover my first job. I felt a ton of pressure to take the job where my (previous) summer internship was — a company in the Chicago suburbs offering me a job after a summer where I learned what it meant to be a Ceramic Engineer in the real world — but I didn't want to "be" a Ceramic Engineer. Hmmm, maybe those friends were right about General Engineering. Kurt and I were the only ones NOT planning to be ceramic engineers after college. I stayed positive and kept interviewing with various companies until I happened to join a friend interviewing with IBM. After a great interview, IBM made me an offer to join them out of their Peoria office — done deal.

My never-ending sense of *optimism* was my strength.

Bottom line — strength manifests itself in an unlimited number of ways. Whether that pressure is external or entirely in your head, it's important to learn some skills to deal with the pressure you are feeling. The examples I shared above demonstrate different versions of strengths through several of my top *values*. And I had a lot of *fun* writing this story!

LESSON LEARNED

You need a strong heart to exercise. A strong stomach to avoid throwing up when something smells horrible. A strong head to problem solve — and strong bones and muscles to maintain a high level of physical fitness. Strength comes in many ways and different forms — physical, emotional, psychological, physiological, and more. And it is definitely something you can quickly build upon over time. But it takes hard work and concentrated focus. So all iterations of strength are worth building over time. My suggestion is to start with the physical strengths, like the image of the weightlifter. The hard work comes as you traverse from your head, to your heart, to your gut and develop your emotional, psychological, and physiological strengths.

PURPOSE

"the reason for which something is done or created or for which something exists."

It sucks that death was my impetus for discovering my purpose. I wish I had considered my purpose long before I lost people important to me. Not that you need the definition of death, but here you go — "*the destruction or permanent end of something.*"

Over about nine months in 2020, I experienced many different versions of death based on the definition above. First, my father passed away; second, the pandemic was exploding and literally killing millions of people; third, my job focus changed several times as I shifted focus to selling the small software business I was leading — resulting in the end of my employment with that organization; finally, as part of my divorce process, I moved from the home where my kids grew up.

Since the pandemic essentially "forced" us all to be quarantined, I had a lot of time on my hands being alone and pondering my future. Though I asked the rhetorical question, "Why?" When friends like Natalie and Nick passed away earlier in my life, this was the first time I truly wanted to understand my purpose.

So why did I exist?

I've always had a passion for helping others. Growing up, I was fortunate enough to get reasonably good grades and do well in sports. As a result, I was always willing to help others, especially those younger than me, to learn anything I could share with them.

I had some early successes in my career and happily assisted others when they had questions about what it took to be successful. I also suffered many setbacks — often sharing my stories with others so they might learn from my mistakes.

It was important for me to be super involved with my sons. I almost always coached or assistant coached their teams and taught my sons and their friends how to hit, throw, and catch a baseball, pass the ball in soccer, shoot and rebound the basketball, and play good defense with excellent spacing on the lacrosse field.

In my community, I helped multiple nonprofits with fundraising, joined (and ran) multiple boards, and provided helping hands to nonprofit events and happenings.

When I called my friend Vips to ask him for advice about my next career pivot, he kindly suggested that I might be a fit at his company, ThinqShift. After some discussions with other ThinqShift employees and friends across my career journey, I decided it would be a great shift in my career development. Our mission at ThinqShift is about "Crafting Fabulous Leaders *to succeed and reinvent the world*." Helping others succeed, Vips knew what my passion and purpose were for this stage of my life before I did.

Today, I'm fortunate to work in a role where I get to embody my purpose daily. I get to help individuals, teams, and organizations reach their potential, build new strengths where gaps previously existed, and, here's where it gets really fun, support their alignment with their work and personal lives in parallel with their purpose.

Vanaprastha is a Sanskrit word that suggests there is a stage in life to pull back and become more devoted to spirituality, deep wisdom, crystallized intelligence, teaching, and faith. This is a much deeper sense of purpose than simply understanding why we all exist. Here's my take on the various components of vanaprastha and how they align with my purpose:

Spirituality

For some, this is about religion. For others, it is a state of being that acknowledges some higher power and purpose beyond what we experience daily. My desire to help others includes acknowledging and sharing as many lessons learned across all religions to give them a great perspective of that higher power.

Deep Wisdom

Far beyond basic knowledge, specific skills, and general understanding, deep wisdom includes all of this and more as you consider the full complement of your knowledge, skills, and understanding in the context of what you are doing on this earth. To the degree I can share some or all of this profound wisdom with others fulfills me and aligns with my purpose — more than simply acquiring my additional wisdom.

Crystallized Intelligence

Content knowledge is the "stuff" you know. Positional power is based upon your role in an organization or life overall. Personal power is how others view and engage with you — NOT for the content or positional power. Crystallized Intelligence is about using this wisdom in the service of others — something I get to do daily now with ThinqShift.

Teaching

Teaching is all about communicating and transferring your knowledge, wisdom, passion, values, and more to others for their benefit and growth. Teaching feels like giving a new driver the keys to the car and transferring knowledge about driving in a practical, real-time manner. Teaching is another form of giving to others — totally aligned with my purpose.

Faith

Without clear facts or data, faith means you accept something or someone for what it is or who they are — no conditions or caveats are needed. Moving to ThinqShift, a role I've never played before in an industry I've never worked in, felt like a major leap of faith. However, it aligned so well with my purpose, I decided to join.

You do *not* need to have someone close to you pass away before considering your purpose. Most people take decades to understand and fully embrace their purpose. I'm observing that younger generations identify and live their purpose much earlier in their lives than we did. I'm happy for them. And hope you can discover yours sooner than later.

LESSON LEARNED

It is always possible to contemplate your purpose. But, sadly, we come back to death for the lesson learned — consider what you'd say on your deathbed now. Then, let that become your purpose over the following decades. You can always adjust or modify your purpose, just find the new version of your purpose as soon as possible and let your life follow that direction. I'm grateful for all the support and help Vips provided me to discover my purpose. I hope you have one or more people to help you similarly.

ADAPT

"make (something) suitable for a new use or purpose; modify."

If you like something enough, do you try it again?

I only ask the question because this is my second story about adaptability. I'm "cheating" because I also share a chapter called **Adaptability** in this book. But being able to adapt is so important. It is the second word I'm using twice — once as a noun and once as a verb!

For my entire career, I've worked for a corporation. I've been a full-time employee with salary and benefits and everything else that comes with being employed by an organization — whether a start-up, a growing company, or a stable Fortune 100 organization — until late 2021.

I was in the technology business during the first two decades of my career. I worked for large and small enterprise software companies like Oracle and IBM. Depending on the company and software I represented, I had to adapt to a new industry, technical support team, or new customers and prospects. But those were "small" adaptations.

My first experience with a larger adaptation, in terms of my career at least, was moving from the enterprise software space into the technology and management consulting world. I adapted quickly, but there were many hiccups (see the story **Conjecture**). Nevertheless, I was able to count on others and leverage some relationships to persevere and find my way through.

When I started at ThinqShift in January 2021, they hired me as a full-time W2 employee. However, as the founders of ThinqShift discussed their long-term strategy and vision for the company's growth late that summer, it made more sense to have most of the people delivering their offerings as 1099 (contract) employees. Therefore, as of October 2021, I would have to shift to a 1099 employee or search for another job if I needed to be a W2 employee.

MUST. ADAPT. IMMEDIATELY!

Not only did I need to adapt to a new type of employee experience, but I also had to adapt to an entirely different set of customers/prospects, develop a whole new set of skills (delivery and execution is 80%+ of my job now), start and learn to operate a small company and engage with a different set of offerings — Leadership Services.

I'm unsure who to quote, but I recall a phrase about adaptation: "Adapt or die." Of course, that's pretty extreme, but I felt as if I didn't adapt quickly, I'd be in serious trouble.

One of my favorite books to give as a graduation present is *Oh, the Places You'll Go*. I'm a huge fan of Dr. Seuss, and an excellent line in the middle of the book inspired me to move forward:

"You're off to Great Places! Today is your Day! Your mountain is waiting. So... get on your way!"

Like the book's character, I knew I needed to adapt quickly to my new situation while being proactive with what's important. But, then, I had to climb the mountain which meant starting a new company, building up enough business to live with zero salary, focusing on the long-term benefits of this new reality version, and surviving the potential challenges of the short-term.

I was committed. I adapted and decided to move forward. I changed a lot about how I operated at work and home. I shifted how I worked with people and adopted an abundance mindset. It was a significant change in my life. I accepted it. I had a long-term vision and was okay with a bit of struggle in the short term. The minute I accepted the struggle, I stopped struggling!

I'm still trying to understand where all of this is going. But the direction is great, and I'm in a different place than I was six months ago. So as I learn more about myself and what's important to my clients, I'm continually adapting and moving forward.

And one of the best parts about the book? It inspired the name of my LLC — Today is Your Day! Leadership Services LLC.

As I reflect on what I did to adapt, a few ideas come to mind:

Vision

I kept one eye on my long-term vision for what I wanted to accomplish. Keeping that in my head helped me overcome the short-term struggles I knew I would face consistently. However, I didn't focus on the specific areas of my life; I needed to shift rather than focus on the long-term perspective. With ThinqShift, I considered my 10 to 15 year plan toward (semi) retirement and what I'm doing at that point.

Experiences

While most of my past experiences didn't necessarily apply, there were many lessons learned that I was able to take bits and pieces from. For example, I didn't know *who* to reach out to or *what* to say to them specifically, but I did understand the concept of prioritization across my relationships and determining where to start to understand better what I was doing.

Small Successes

There were many frustrations and challenges. But I learned quickly how to celebrate small successes along the way. Not only do small victories bolster your confidence level, but they also serve as data points to learn whether your adaptations are working. For example, I'm grateful to a good friend who thought enough of my experiences to become my first engagement. It was a small success that propelled me forward.

Relationships

I needed to leverage relationships across many perspectives. I had an existing relationship with the founder of ThinqShift and quickly built new relationships with my new colleagues. Many of my personal and previous work relationships also started to view me through this new lens. And still, others were willing to connect me with *their* relationships to help me. In one situation, I had lunch with someone and started (unknowingly) to give them some beneficial advice; it was a great confidence builder and an unexpected benefit to my relationships.

Other "Use Cases"

Though this was mostly about adapting to a new world at work, I could also consider other "use cases" from different areas of my life that worked. This helped me primarily with my mental approach to dealing with volatility, uncertainty, complexity, and ambiguity. I thought through other examples of adapting and "stole" from those experiences to apply a new way to adapt to this situation. During the pandemic, it literally was time to "Adapt or die." I recalled the many changes I made during the pandemic and how I still thrived and used that confidence and experience in my work world.

Make Mistakes

I knew I would make many mistakes, and I accepted that fact. That allowed me to discover the appropriate balance between being (too) deliberate or intentionally (too) daring or risky. And I intentionally tried things out with significantly smaller opportunities. Several times I leaned into my trusted relationships and *told them explicitly* that I was trying out something new and experimenting going forward. Making calculated mistakes is part of this equation for sure.

LESSON LEARNED

Think about the long-term and set up massively audacious goals. Accept that you'll struggle along the way, knowing that adaptation is key to growth and confidence. The new use cases you'll discover are worth the challenges you'll face in this journey. I spent hours, daily in some cases, working with others who had been through similar journeys to understand how I could adapt. And I spent even more time with my professional coaches and therapist to overcome the inevitable setbacks.

LOVE

"an intense feeling of deep affection."

I love you.

Almost every connotation of love that I remember is focused on other people. Are you in love? Do you love someone else? Do they love you? It feels, with most connotations of love, there is a specific giver and a different receiver.

I remember my mom, dad, and grandma telling me they loved me when I was a little kid, but I don't remember saying it back to them until I got older. I definitely remember telling my ex-wife that I loved her — though maybe not often enough as I'm now divorced. There is no doubt I told my children that I loved them hundreds, if not thousands, of times over the years.

But I never learned how to love myself.

In my observations, very little time is spent thinking about loving yourself. It took me many years of therapy and support from books, podcasts, videos, and more to better understand what it means to love yourself. Now that I have a better perspective of what it means to love myself, I have a hundred times more capacity to love others.

I used to "beat myself up" if something went wrong., and I wonder if I inadvertently "beat up others" as well. But when I learned how to love myself and give myself grace in a difficult situation, I applied that same principle to others — loving them for who they are versus what they did (or didn't) do.

I no longer take the word love for granted, and I can see many different perspectives of love, how they apply to everyone, and how it helps me today.

Unconditional Love

There are many "flavors" of unconditional love. But for those who own pets, isn't the love you get when you return to your pet after being gone for just a few hours absolutely incredible? No matter what difficult situation I'm facing or the challenging day I've had when Suki's tail is wagging non-stop, my worries/stresses melt away, and I get a big smile on my face. I don't have a tail to wag, but now I love others without limitations or conditions.

Unrequited Love

Remember those days in middle or high school when you thought, "She will never love me." Forget the fact we probably had no clue what love meant at that time. I'm sure I'm not the only one who had multiple crushes in high school or college that never evolved into a relationship — most of you have experienced this type of love. However, I've learned to accept this without question because I don't need to be loved by others to love something or someone. I've even told some of those people, many years later, that I had some crush on them when we were much younger.

Love Thy Neighbor

I don't know most of my neighbors right now. But I tend to extrapolate this into telling my friends how much I love them and appreciate the amazing relationships we've built over the years. Now that I understand how to love myself, it's incredibly easy to let someone else important to me know how I feel about them. Even if you don't know your neighbors and can't say "I love you," consider telling them you love something about their house, yard, or specific circumstances where they are involved.

All You Need Is Love

Thank you, Paul, Ringo, John, and George! Of course, oxygen, water, and food are also nice, but love is one of the few things we ALL need some of. The Beatles are just one of the thousands of bands, poets, writers, etc., who wrote about the benefits of love. I've had a lot of struggles over the years, but love seems to persevere no matter what. Now that I understand how to love myself, I can see why The Beatles put love as their number one priority.

Love and Belonging

In the middle of Maslow's Hierarchy of Needs, the details include friendship, intimacy, family, and a sense of connection. I love ALL of these. Having a deep sense of affection for myself enables me to channel that affection toward other people, places, things, etc. When you learn how to love yourself, you can more easily share your love for others and enable a stronger sense of belonging for everyone.

Love Is Blind

Another great connotation of love means we see all of the amazing parts of the people we love and downplay/ignore the "bad stuff." Loving myself, I learned to accept that I'm imperfect and do many dumb things. I'm fully aware that I made mistakes, but I can be blind to all that in the context of fully loving myself.

Parental Love

As a father to my sons, I always wonder whether or not I shared enough warmth, affection, care, comfort, concern, nurture, support, acceptance, and more with my boys. And as a son of my mother, I wonder whether I shared the same with my parents through the years. Of course, I loved the boys when they were born and growing up. But I love them both even more now that I also appreciate what it means to love myself.

We Love Ourselves

I'll repeat a phrase I've paraphrased often from my flying experiences: "Put your oxygen mask on first before helping others." We all need to figure out how to best care for ourselves to care for others most optimally. It is not selfish at all to appreciate and love yourself first. On the contrary, it is absolutely necessary to be your best self for you and others.

LESSON LEARNED

Learn to love yourself as soon as possible. It is "easy" to say you love another human.., or a cute puppy! But it will be a challenge to truly embrace love until you learn what it means to love yourself. And once you do, you'll more fully experience many different perspectives of love — including and well beyond the list I've shared above.

Printed in the USA
CPSIA information can be obtained
at www.ICGtesting.com
JSHW080019010224
56300JS00002B/13

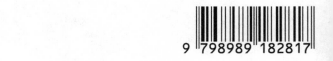